1989

University of St. Francis

SO-BHX-979

3 0301 00089076 0

Ceremonies of innocence

Ceremonies of innocence is the most comprehensive study of pastoralism in Edmund Spenser's poetry so far undertaken. It traces the evolution of Spenser's view of his own role as a poet in Elizabethan courtly society through an examination of his use and definition of pastoral. Rather than concentrating exclusively on his works in pastoral genres, it includes pastoral themes, motifs, and patterns in all of the poems. Studying the works against the background of ideas about the contemplative life, medieval allegorical readings of Vergil, and the pastoral as an established courtly mode, its specific thesis is that Spenser gradually evolves a "pastoral of contemplation" as against the sychophantic "pastoral of power" identified by some recent Spenser and Renaissance scholars.

LIBRARY
College of St. Francis
JOLIET, ILL.

Ceremonies of innocence

Pastoralism in the poetry
of Edmund Spenser

JOHN D. BERNARD

Associate Professor of Honors and English
University of Houston

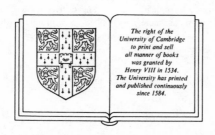

The right of the
University of Cambridge
to print and sell
all manner of books
was granted by
Henry VIII in 1534.
The University has printed
and published continuously
since 1584.

CAMBRIDGE UNIVERSITY PRESS

Cambridge

New York   New Rochelle

Melbourne   Sydney

LIBRARY
College of St. Francis
JOLIET, ILL.

Published by the Press Syndicate of the University of Cambridge
The Pitt Building, Trumpington Street, Cambridge CB2 IRP
32 East 57th Street, New York, NY 10022, USA
10 Stamford Road, Oakleigh, Melbourne 3166, Australia

© Cambridge University Press 1989

First published 1989

Printed in Great Britain by
the University Press, Cambridge

British Library cataloguing in publication data

Bernard, John D.
Ceremonies of innocence: pastoralism in
the poetry of Edmund Spenser.
1. Poetry in English. Spenser, Edmund,
1552?–1599. Critical studies
1. Title
821'.3

Library of Congress cataloguing in publication data

Bernard, John D.
Ceremonies of innocence: pastoralism in the poetry of Edmund
Spenser/by John D. Bernard.
p.   cm.
Includes index.
ISBN 0 521 36252 0
1. Spenser, Edmund, 1552?–1599 – Criticism and interpretation.
2. Spenser, Edmund, 1552?–1599 – Characters – Colin Clout.
3. Pastoral poetry, English – History and criticism.   4. Clout, Colin
(Fictitious character)   5. Self in literature.   1. Title.
PR2367.P34B4   1989
821'.3–dc 19   88–23709   CIP

ISBN 0 521 36252 0

UP

LIBRARY
College of St. Francis
JOLIET, ILL.

821.3
B517

For Artis
and for Jenny, Becca, Sylvia, Ben

133,992

Contents

Acknowledgments

Parts of this book appeared earlier as articles in other publications. I wish to thank the publishers of *ELH*, *Philological Quarterly*, *Studies in English Literature 1500–1900*, and *Spenser at Kalamazoo* for their permission to adapt them for use here. I am also grateful to the National Endowment for the Humanities for a summer grant that allowed me to do much of the research for chapter 1. The cost of typing the original manuscript and other incidental expenses were defrayed by grants-in-aid from the University of Houston through its Research Council. As for less material services, I have had an embarrassing wealth of support. To name only the living Spenserians to whom I am indebted would require more space than I can usurp here. But I would like to acknowledge collectively the many readers (and hearers) of papers in Spenser sessions of the Medieval Institute at Kalamazoo. Among these I must mention Richard Neuse, whose articles on Spenser first excited my interest in the poet, whose occasionally irascible wit has become a mark of critical conscience for me, and who provided a keen reading of the manuscript at a crucial juncture in its evolution. No one can write on Spenser or pastoral without feeling the benign influence of Paul Alpers, who was also more helpful than he can know in giving a then-anonymous critique of an earlier version of one of my chapters. To colleagues in the Honors Program and English Department at the University of Houston I owe special thanks for a continuing conversation on matters intellectual and literary. Of the former, I am pleased to name Ted Estess, the "facilitator" of the enterprise. A magnanimous and hovering presence has been Allen Mandelbaum, both "il mio autore" *and* "lo maestro di coloro che sanno." At a formative stage of my work on pastoral a colleague, Bill Matheson, and a graduate student, Adrian Frazier, produced stimulating readings of pastoral texts that were to resonate for me long after. Another former colleague and good friend, Bob Harbison, read the manuscript in its

Acknowledgments

first incarnation and was generous enough to encourage me to persevere. A current colleague, William B. Hunter, read it in its penultimate state and made invaluable suggestions for which I am deeply grateful. Special thanks are due to Lois Zamora for saving me from a particularly egregious tactical error and to Kevin Taylor and Caroline Drake at the Cambridge University Press for their care in preparing the manuscript for publication. To all these encouragers and critics, my apologies for the faults and flaws that remain. And to Artis Simonson Bernard, who is too familiar with my faults and flaws for any apologies, I can only confess that without her patience, indulgence, and understanding – not to mention her merciful *im*patience with my quirks of style – neither this nor any other academic effort of mine would have borne fruit. This book is primarily and gratefully dedicated to her.

Introduction

Current scholarship suggests the futility, if not impossibility, of reading the poetry of Spenser and his contemporaries outside its political context.[1] Even for a poet physically removed from the court during most of his mature years, that context clearly includes the circle of educated readers – statesmen, careerists, aristocrats, the Queen – who are his primary audience. Hence, one question posed by the present study is, How does Spenser view his role as a poet vis-à-vis the structure of power in Elizabethan society? Recent criticism has argued that Spenser, however protestingly, acknowledges his own fundamental lack of authority: Elizabethan poets *qua* poets are powerless; they cannot "author" their own utterances, but owe their very speech to those who may command it.[2] This view rests on a number of important assumptions that grow mainly out of the post-modernist, post-structuralist climate of the 1970s and 80s, particularly among the so-called "new historicists."[3] Contemporary readers have learned a great deal about the manipulation of utterance by political authorities; hence we are quick to recognize the propaganda potential of any discourse.

The question of the poet's authority cannot easily be divorced from the other major focus of this book, literary pastoralism. That the pastoral mode is bound up with the issue of poetry and power has been understood at least since Empson.[4] According to his thesis, the pastoral certifies a social order by imaginatively dissolving the distance between rich and poor, noble and commoner: "The effect was in some degree to combine in the reader or author the merits of the two sorts [of people]; he was made to mirror in himself...the effective elements of the society he lived in" (p. 12). Empson stresses the viability of the pastoral "trick" from the point of view of those at the top of the social hierarchy. As putative spokesman for those with wealth and privilege, the poet assures his readers that they are in effect microcosms of the social order, since they can vicariously participate in, and possess all the virtues of, its lowest ranks. On the other hand, this trick has benefits for the poet and his peers as well. For as the modest pastoral virtues are the authentic ones, there can be no reason for the spiritually surfeited to envy the mere wealth or status of their betters. They are – and must feel themselves to be – part of a plenitude. Hence for the poet the result was the sustaining illusion of personal power and freedom: "You take a limited life and pretend it's a full and normal one" (p. 110).

More recent studies of Renaissance pastoral have stressed the subservient status of courtly poets mentioned earlier. In a provocative article, Louis A. Montrose has anatomized the Elizabethan "pastoral of power," whereby poets trained in humanist schools subserve and flatter the autocratic regime to which they owe their vocation.[5] The theory of pastoral articulated by Montrose is the fullest expansion to date on the Empsonian theory. But where Empson tends to accept at face value the pastoral poet's self-identification with his social superiors, Montrose places this strategy in an ironic perspective. For him pastoral implicitly entails self-deception. For if the pastoral strategy permits the high to imagine themselves as no better (or worse) than the low, it also elevates the low, namely the poet himself, to the level of his privileged readers. In enacting the imaginative equality of the humble and the mighty, the poet ceases to be merely an instrument of social mediation and seeks to become instead an agent of self-transformation. Mirroring the act of putting the complex into the simple and the high in the low, he arrogates to himself the implicit superiority that enables the act in the first place. I would add that such an exercise in dissimulation is not necessarily ingenuous: Spenser, dubbing himself as the anonymous "Immeritó" in *The Shepheardes Calender*, acknowledges his essential humbleness pending his readers' endorsement of the function he proposes to perform. Like Peter Quince and his rude mechanicals, or Prospero as epilogist, he depends on the assent of his betters to bring off the trick at all. Yet the potential for self-delusion in all this is clearly evident. In claiming the role of mediator the poet implies his own elevation to a position of real authority in which he alone can give convincing voice to an operative myth of social harmony.

The emphasis on the pastoral poet's social status and on pastoral itself as a response to political power aligns it with other reflections on the poet's function in Renaissance courts. It is no accident that the "courtly" pastoral flourishes at a time when Italian humanism was giving way to courtliness (*cortegiania*) – or, as some prefer to put it, "civic" to "courtly" humanism – as a socio-cultural mode more in tune with the new autocratic principalities of the sixteenth century. The new genre of Renaissance pastoral, for which Voltaire observed the Italians "had no models, and in which they have never been surpassed," was largely the achievement of Sannazaro.[6] Sannazaro's *Arcadia* has been called the ideal place for a fifteenth-century humanist.[7] But the revised *Arcadia* of 1504 also reflects the nostalgia and sense of isolation of a *déclassé* courtier at the Neapolitan royal court. Sannazaro's pastoral persona, Sincero, fuses the classical nostalgia of the Renaissance humanist with the dislocation of the Renaissance courtier. This blend of motives is evident in Sannazaro's desire to reconstitute the past on the model of classical Rome: Sincero's vision in Prosa 12, for example, which takes place in a blasted pastoral landscape, is not of the Sebeto but of the Tiber.[8]

Certain motifs common in early Renaissance pastoral recur in Castiglione's *Cortegiano* (1528), where the search of the learned courtier for a vocation is deflected in an elaborate game of disguise and dissembling.[9] Here too, as still later in Tasso, one senses that the cultivation of wit and grace is aimed at preserving the ego from external encroachments.[10] It should be noted that implicit in these Renaissance courtly works, whether pastoral or other, is the premise that beneath his humble mask the author has the capacity to exercise a certain autonomy. In the case of the pastoralist, whether we think of him as fleeing from cultural crisis into an Arcadian "landscape of the mind" or fashioning a calculated stance toward the politically powerful, poetry is an instrument by which the relatively powerless may forge a surrogate power through language. In doing so the pastoral poet may be deceiving himself by mistaking a wholly derivative authority for one intrinsic to himself. Yet occasional exaggerations of his own autonomy notwithstanding, he may legitimately claim to be expressing the shared values of a cultivated elite as well as memorializing its individual or dynastic virtues. Such a claim in turn confers a certain authority on the poet himself. In this light, pastoralism emerges as the quintessential form of courtly culture in its literary aspect.

Yet this more or less established view of courtly literature in general, like that of pastoral, is sharply challenged in recent theory.

Montrose sees Elizabethan pastoral as chiefly instrumental: the poet is a courtier who writes, and his main function is to flatter the real bearers of power by lending eloquence and an air of respectability to their reigning political myths. A "medium" rather than an "analogue" of courtliness, Elizabethan poetry exists to certify the social subordination of all courtiers to an authoritarian power structure.[11] Within this general system, pastoral poetry must be viewed as the ultimate dissimulative mode, "ironic through and through." Drawing on Puttenham's discussion of allegoria, the dissembling trope, Montrose argues that "Puttenham understands literary pastoral to be the characteristic poetic kind of a complex, strife-ridden, and authoritarian civilization – a fallen world of conspiracy and duplicity" (p. 31).[12] Pastoral poets, including Spenser, are "*unavoidably* compromised by the desire to rise and the need to please" (my emphasis). Like Puttenham's pastoral trope, Spenser is a "cunning Prince-Pleaser," part of an elaborate system of strategies by which Elizabeth and her ministers orchestrated her dominance of all classes and factions in England throughout her reign. Hence, when the pastoral poet criticizes courtly conduct, it is at best an intramural affair: by ostensibly attacking abuses of privilege the poet in fact perpetuates the myth of the ideal courtier and so endorses the social structure it exists to sustain.

This view strikes me as unnecessarily reductive. Most readers recognize a certain play, in both senses of the word, in Renaissance courtly literature and a fortiori in the pastoral. This play generally derives from the delicate maneuvering of the courtly writer within a confining yet challenging social milieu.[13] Sir Thomas More's courtier in Book 1 of *Utopia*, or Castiglione's in Book 4 of the *Cortegiano*, uses obliquity and dissimulation as much to reform as to certify the social structure.[14] The function of obliquely addressing a power elite comports especially well with the dissimulative strategies of pastoral, which allow the poet to proclaim his innocence and naïveté while questioning his audience's actions or values. Montrose himself has lately arrived at a similar conclusion. Reflecting in a recent article on his own and others' assumptions about Elizabethan ideology, Montrose writes that

we should resist the inevitably reductive tendency to think in terms of a subject/structure opposition. Instead, we might entertain the propositions that subject and structure ... are interdependent and thus intrinsically social and historical: that...collective structures may enable as well as constrain individual agency.[15]

As this caveat implies, monolithic concepts such as that of an Elizabethan "pastoral of power" deny altogether the habitual assumptions of poetic authority underlying older theories of pastoral. In the name of a severe historical determinism such a construct threatens the long-held view of pastoral as a playful but educative response to social and political issues by a poet who has a ruler's ear. In this scenario, the distinction between poetry and propaganda becomes mere fantasy; the literary shepherd, a literal sheep.

Despite such recent revisions, however – or perhaps because of them – the contemporary challenge to more traditional assumptions about pastoral compels one to question these assumptions once more.[16] The investigation undertaken in the following pages examines literary pastoral in the context of certain broad historical considerations. Towards the end of the Renaissance the overt didactic intention of the humanist allegorical pastoral begins to wane.[17] At this time, especially in the drama, one begins to hear a new note. In the Prologue to Daniel's *Queenes Arcadia*, we are told that pastorals

> best become a claustrall exercise,
> Where men shut out retyr'd, and sequestred
> From publike fashion, seeme to sympathize
> With innocent, and plaine simplicity.[18]

The note of deliberate dissimulation ("seeme") is clear enough. As for "claustrall exercise," More's utopian critique of the nascent capitalism of Tudor England also takes place in a kind of cloister, a privileged space of freedom. This privilege is assumed by men closely associated with regimes whose power they mediate in their writings and on whose pleasure they depend for the very leisure, in their occasional periods of retirement from business, that makes such writings possible.[19] Yet however mitigated by the autocratic courtliness of the sixteenth century, the humanist tradition still permits them the indirect approach of a playfully disguised fiction as a way to criticize and even to influence their patrons.

At least since Vergil, this obliquity has been part of the pastoral convention. To Vergilian pastoral is attributed not only the genre's

5

use of allegory and indirect social criticism, but the very model of a literary career. Vergil's shepherds are thinly disguised poets and protégés who enact the educated Roman's struggle with the burgeoning Augustan regime.[20] This transaction undoubtedly appears more equal than it was in fact. And perhaps partly for this reason Vergil comes to be viewed as the exemplary courtier–poet. His canonical progress through the genres, the *rota Vergiliana*, a staple of Renaissance imitation, is predicated on a mutually gratifying relation of the poet and his patron–prince.[21] This conception of the court poet's authority retains at least the suggestion of an authentic *quid pro quo*. The poet confers gifts of his own that go well beyond the act of flattering an authoritarian regime. In celebrating those in power Vergilian pastoral reflects the assumption that a polity must also be a community and that a community entails more than the simple mediation of power relationships. It also embodies ethical values, including those attached to aristocratic otium. As I will try to show in my first chapter, classical pastoral habitually assumes that part of the poet's function in society is to define and exercise the traditional aristocratic prerogative of contemplation, thereby clarifying the ontological foundation on which the social structure rests. Though strictly speaking he is politically powerless, through his pastoral persona the poet claims a degree of power which he derives from the freedom of a "claustrall exercise" in havens of imaginative retirement that he shares with other courtiers.

This conventional balance in the pastoralist's view of himself is still viable in the Renaissance pastoral, as well as in the ideal of courtliness it reflects. Renaissance poets write and talk about their writing as though their careers amounted to more than a well-dissembled exercise in the pursuit of reflected power. However subordinate their actual situations, the best of the courtly poets presume an educative function. While sharing the exigencies of other courtiers, they are unique in that they can speak, and the power of speech at this time can hardly be exaggerated. It is true that the scope of their speech is not without limits: hence the nearly universal praise of dissimulation.[22] Yet the very anguish attached to the actual limits of their freedom suggests that the notion of absolute, "unavoidable" subservience and flattery is too simplistic.[23] Once again, one might cite a recent pronouncement by Louis Montrose:

An ideological dominance is qualified by both the specific professional and/ or class interests of cultural producers and by the relative autonomy of the cultural medium being worked. In other words, sufficient allowance must be made for the manifold mediations involved in the production and reproduction of an ideological dominance: for the collective and individual agency of the prince's subjects, and for the specific character and conventions of the representational forms they employ.[24]

In Elizabeth's England, as in Guidobaldo's Urbino, literature is part of a larger courtly game. And that game is worth playing precisely because some degree of freedom is an indispensable ornament of any courtly or other viable society, as our knowledge of truly unfree societies serves to remind us. The Renaissance poet is no lawgiver – nor did he dream he was. But his intimacy with the world of power that tolerated, and indeed authorized, his existence permitted him at least a minimal opportunity to affect that world. Those in power listened to him when he spoke; this is borne out by the occasional violence of their reaction when they felt he spoke out of turn. Pastoralism, with its negotiation between the ideal realm of Socratic discourse and the real world of Renaissance courts, was the perfect medium for exercising and reflecting upon this particular "limited life."

In this dispute Spenser is an important case in point. Though physically absent from court, except for occasional visits, during the last twenty years of his life, Spenser's art is motivated, if not compromised, by "the desire to rise and the need to please." The result is a complex relationship between the poet and his courtly audience. Spenser's own assessment of his role views the communal memory of author and reader as the locus for constructing a viable historical mythology. The aim of such a construction is to legitimize the current polity by grounding it in Platonic paradigms of justice and truth and thus to discover the underlying meaning of historical change.[25] The model for this view of poetry is the *Aeneid*, whose immersion in history caused it to be viewed in the Renaissance as ideally fusing action and contemplation. Hence for Spenser in the early books of *The Faerie Queene*, "visionary" moments are also "prophetic" because historical action is the consummation of individual contemplation.[26]

Spenser's effort to recreate Vergil's version of power is ultimately a failure. In Book 4 he is clearly moving away from the centers of power and historical vision toward new internal sources of inspiration, a movement interrupted by his early death (p. 188).[27] Yet if Spenser in his last years is unable to sustain the Vergilian model, retreating from the more optimistic view of the celebratory historical epic, he remains, in his own mind at least, an authoritative source of values, the moral center of his world. From this angle Spenser's career begins to look like Dante's. In various works, but especially in the *Purgatorio*, Dante sees his exile as a long digression from and return to the personal figura of Beatrice, for him the core and penultimate terminus of his creative life. It has been suggested that this conception is derived from the medieval (and Renaissance) reading of the *Aeneid*, and occasionally of the Vergilian corpus as a whole, as an allegory of "man's life in time."[28] This allegory, as we shall see, enshrines in turn the Aristotelian concept of the "estates" or genres of life, in which one normally progresses from action to contemplation. In the *Commedia* contemplation culminates in a personal, figural vision prompted by love; directed toward an embodied beauty, eros becomes the medium of vision, and the figure of the beloved its appropriate object.[29] In Spenser, I shall try to show, such a possibility is already adumbrated by Piers in the "October" eclogue and is fulfilled in his latest work.

Unlike Dante, however, as a Renaissance poet Spenser tends to chart his career in terms of the pastoral. Always the vehicle of his reflections on his role as a poet, Spenserian pastoral oscillates between the claims of the Tudor social myth and those of the literary, specifically the figural, tradition as modified and transmitted by Dante and others. The pastoral – or at least its Vergilian articulation – begins with the flight of Astraea, and Elizabethan courtly pastoral obsessively returns to the "courting" of Astraea in the historical figure of Elizabeth. As this book will argue, in the course of Spenser's career Elizabeth is gradually displaced by a personal figura whose significance evolves with the poet's outlook but who re-emerges in *Colin Clouts Come Home Againe*, Book 6 of *The Faerie Queene*, and the late love-poetry as the mediatrix between his visionary powers and the objects of imitation, i.e. between the self and history or "the world." In short, "Rosalind" (as she is sometimes called) usurps the function of Gloriana in Spenser's personal poetic economy. In the process, Spenser's conception and practice of pastoral undergo a corresponding evolution. Beginning with a Vergilian confidence in the poet's prerogative of educating the

Prince and constructing a cultural community, in his dynastic and national epic Spenser creates an image of power sanctified by his own imaginative idealizations: "ceremonies of innocence," in Yeats' resonant phrase. This version of pastoral is akin to the pastoral of power, though it denies the mere instrumentality of the poet. In the final decade of his life, however, Spenser asserts a more independent and tangential relation to the centers of power, though maintaining a commitment to the poet's unique contemplative function. In this final phase love assumes an increasing importance; the personal figura becomes supreme.

Before turning to Spenser's development as a pastoral poet, I shall explore several theoretical assumptions about both pastoral and the poet's traditional function in courtly culture. In doing so, I shall try to avoid the sometimes cumbersome terminology of contemporary theory, though I hope I have profited from its insights. Instead, I have tried throughout the book to cast my argument in terms of traditional literary–critical and cultural–historical studies.[30] To write in the late 1980s on a standard topic in Renaissance literary studies is to take on the burden of an impressive body of theoretical work from a number of post-structuralist perspectives that has for a decade or so been trained upon the literary and cultural premises and practices of the English and European Renaissance. As will be clear to the reader from the outset, the present book does not primarily seek to add to this body of work. While I do not ignore its practitioners or its provocations, I have been willing to submerge the lively issues of the day in an argument that will strike some readers perhaps, as it has from time to time struck me, as speaking itself from the far side of a chasm that has opened up of late in the literary body politic. To such readers my Yeatsian title, intended to convey at least a whiff of historical irony, may even have a nostalgic ring. Clearly, those of us in literary studies who are not "theorists" (a dwindling company, it sometimes seems) must register as fully as possible the implications of structuralist and post-structuralist inventions. At the same time, the imperative remains to continue the activity of engaging with words written in the past. If the theoretical contributions of the last twenty-five years help to sharpen our awareness of the manifold quandaries and aporias of such a project, so much the better.

In chapter 1, then, I begin by examining the traditional debate, from late antiquity on, about the relative claims of the active and contemplative lives. In this debate the normal supremacy of the *vita contemplativa* is derived from the Hellenic concept of a gentleman (*kalokagathos*) and his cultural development (*paideia*), ideals which in later times it devolves increasingly upon poets to uphold. I then go on to show how Vergil, as read in the medieval allegorical tradition, bequeathes to this debate a literary typology in which the *vita contemplativa* is closely associated with pastoral. The result of this review is to make it clear that antedating the Renaissance pastoral of power is a pastoral of reflection and social rectification, a version of pastoral implicit in Spenser's personal revisions of the mode. The chapter argues, therefore, that the Western literary tradition from the outset entails a tension between the expectation of flattering political power and the moral imperative to maintain a fruitful use of otium. Partly by invoking the example of his predecessors, the pastoral poet as an exponent of the *vita contemplativa* is implicitly licensed to chasten the personal conduct and urge the collective responsibility of his social superiors. This tension is necessarily heightened in the more centralized and autocratic courts of the Renaissance, but the traditional ethical imperative remains viable.

In the remaining chapters I re-examine Spenser's use of pastoral in the context of these considerations, from *The Shepheardes Calender* (chapter 2) and the 1590 *Faerie Queene* (chapter 3), through the pivotal *Complaints* and *Colin Clout* of 1591 (chapter 4), to the 1596 *Faerie Queene* (chapter 5) and the last poems (chapter 6). The argument that runs through these chapters is that the full understanding of Renaissance pastoral depends on our recognizing the importance of the historic link between the literary mode and the philosophical *vita contemplativa*. Spenser's works reveal with increasing clarity that the contemplative life, which is the oldest Western myth of fullness as well as the earliest justification of special privilege, lies at the heart of the pastoral poet's métier. In the parallel evolutions of pastoral, the *vita contemplativa*, and the social function of poetry in aristocratic cultures, one outstanding feature is the dignity of the poet. And this dignity – this authority – continues to rest, the evidence suggests, on his exercising the contemplative prerogative as a potentially fertile collaboration in the cultural forms of production.

It is my contention, therefore, that a pastoral of contemplation balances the pastoral of power in the literary culture of Spenser's time, and specifically in the work of Spenser himself. One might object that the pastoral of power (insofar as it ever existed in the pristine purity Montrose once assumed) is an instrument for the purveyance of "ideology" in the Marxist sense of a false consciousness imposed by a ruling class.[31] But even granting this, I would add that the pastoral of contemplation is also ideological in the more active and fluid sense of "ideology" proposed by Althusser: viz., *any* "imaginary relation of... individuals to the real relations in which they live."[32] Specifically, Spenser's conscious invocation of the Vergilian pastoral tradition, and of the ancient philosophical categories that underlie it, constitutes (in Althusser's terms) one of the "mediations involved in the production and reproduction... of ideological dominance" by which Renaissance poets creatively employ "representational forms." In advancing this argument I am pleading, I hope, not for a self-deluding complacency about the realities of history and power but for a more sympathetic and accurate grasp of poetry's dilemma in the Elizabethan period. My argument is that Spenser plies the various strands of the pastoral tradition and its theoretical substrate in a sustained fictional meditation on his personal status in Elizabethan courtly society. "Personal" is used here as the adjectival form of "persona," the person in question being roughly that of Poet, i.e. a cultural construct feigned by Spenser in order to insert himself into the culture of his age. This book traces the course of that meditation, focusing on the mutations of the pastoral trope as the measure of Spenser's sense of his vocation as a public poet enacting "ceremonies of innocence" which help to form that culture. At the same time, to the degree that so elusive an entity as a "subject" may be distilled from the process of poetic self-presentation, it tries to say something about the private man who produces this public fiction.

I

Vita contemplativa and the pastoral

I

Historically, the concept of a *vita contemplativa* reveals an impressive continuity. From Plato and Aristotle to Spenser and Bacon, thinkers, including poets, argue about the relative validity of several well-defined "estates of life."[1] Despite some significant fluctuations, the contemplative life is generally held to be superior to the active, as thinking is to doing or the intellective are to the prudential functions of the soul. This is true even when, as often, contemplation is considered incomplete without fulfillment in action. The theoretical primacy of the contemplative life is established by Aristotle. It is reaffirmed in Aristotelian terms by Thomas Aquinas when he notes that this life is "not strictly human but superhuman." Already, half a millennium earlier, Fulgentius had complained that the contemplative life, once the province of philosophers, was now being lived by bishops, priests, and monks.[2] But whether as philosopher, monk, or poet, all three of these commentators agree that the activity of the contemplative man ranks among the highest of human possibilities. Indeed, it is that activity in which the merely human shades into the divine.

Perhaps the most enduring aspect of the *vita contemplativa* is its passivity. In Spenser's poetry, a pervasive motif is the longing for a stillness beyond the flux of things. This should not be surprising in a poet who self-consciously allies his major opus with "Philosophy."[3] For it was in speculation about permanence and change that Western thought, i.e. philosophy, began. Questions of reality and appearance, the one and the many, teased Parmenides, shaped the thought of Socrates and Plato, and helped determine the way the Western mind grasped the world for over 2000 years. These speculations imply a primary fix on things that are as they are by nature, as opposed to those that are produced or fashioned by

12

custom or art. Hence in human activities the best that can be said for the varieties of the *vita activa* is that they fulfill the "needs and wants of contemplation."[4] There is an ingrained suspicion of, if not contempt for, that which is achieved by effort. *Theorein*, like *contemplare*, connotes passivity. Both signify the act of looking, but both are also associated with a sacred space or precinct where one yields to the influence of a god. This passive aspect of the act of looking/seeing is still underscored in the medieval distinction between *intellectus* and *ratio*: the former emphasizes the receptive openness of the mind to reality, an activity of leisure; the latter, the labor of thinking.[5] From the outset the case for the contemplative life in Western thought is grounded in a quasi-bucolic ecstasy in which the soul reaches for the eternal. It is a powerful intuition whose intensity has diminished little in the Christian Platonist, Edmund Spenser.

Not surprisingly, in both Plato and Aristotle this bias in favor of contemplation accompanies a conservative attitude toward political activity, as toward human life in general.[6] This attitude is rooted in a privileged mode of existence whose code elevates leisure above labor and imposes the highest obligation of self-cultivation on those who inherit it. Such an assumption underlies Aristotle's original articulation of the three "lives" (*bioi*) of action, contemplation, and pleasure.[7] Though as in Plato it is never quite clear just what contemplation is, one can infer that Aristotle's *theoria* is a transcendent activity carrying the soul beyond the normal limits of discourse or *logos*; a non-temporal, intuitive apprehension of the unchanging, occurring in stillness and leisure, in which the contemplating mind grasps, participates in, and is at one with that which truly exists.[8] Aristotle explicitly connects *theoria* with leisure in the *Nicomachean Ethics* [*NE*] (10.1177a18–b5), adding that leisure must be better than "business" (*askholia*) because we work to attain leisure and not the reverse. Moreover, since such felicity is far beyond our normal expectations of happiness, Aristotle holds *theoria* to be the ultimate apotheosis of man, the mode in which he partakes of the divine (*NE* 10.1127b27–32). These sentiments are echoed in the *Politics*, where *skhole* is said to embrace pleasure, happiness and blessedness and clearly crowns all human endeavor (*Pol.* 7.1329a1).

Nevertheless, Aristotle's preference for the contemplative life, like Plato's, is not unqualified. Both the *Eudemian* and the *Nicomachean*

Ethics posit three ways of life, of which at least two – those dominated by action and contemplation – are valid. Between the *bios politikos* and the *bios theoretikos*, he gives priority to the latter in that it embraces the activities of the higher faculties of the soul, which are the highest expression of human freedom and leisure (*NE* 10.1177a28–35). Yet Aristotle's audience is imbued with the traditional Athenian obligation of the gentleman (*ho kalokagathos*) to fulfill his freedom in action. Thus Aristotle stops short of unequivocally endorsing the *bios theoretikos* (*Pol.* 7.1325a17–b33). Nevertheless, its appeal to him is undeniable. The crux of the matter seems to be the function of power. To the familiar objection to ruling others, namely that it is better to live a free life than one of "mastership" (*despotikou*), Aristotle replies that one can "rule" free men without enslaving them. But he goes on to warn that absolute dominion is vicious because it would entail mastering men whose own *aretê* (virtue or excellence) merits freedom in the natural scheme of things. The inference seems clear: if a non-despotic rule is impossible, as conditions in the fourth century were proving it to be, then aristocratic freedom demanded inaction, withdrawal; to do nothing was at least to do no evil.[9]

The conditions of a disenfranchised intelligentsia continue to exacerbate the aristocratic cultural bias in this debate in post-classical Greece and Rome. More and more, *theoria* is wrenched out of all association with political activity. In one way or another the major schools, even those like the Stoics that tried to maintain a balance of action and contemplation, gradually redefined the *vita contemplativa* as the sole source of satisfaction in the circumstances to which men of intellect had been reduced. The cultivated *apatheia* (absence of pain) of the Cynics (Diogenes Laertius [Diog. Laer.] 6.1.2, 6.29) and the Epicurean *ataraxia* (imperturbability; *ibid.* 10.12 and Lucretius [Lucr.] *De rerum natura* 1.1–30) emphasize the virtues of the contemplative withdrawal from a debased political life that was progressively barring from political activity the classes that had traditionally exercised it. Even the Stoics, who had initially, with Zeno, rejected *apatheia* and political disengagement, came to acknowledge a *bios theoretikos* peculiar to the non-political man, whose aim is to achieve a state of personal felicity based on the well-tempered soul. Hence no less than Epicureans, Skeptics, and Peripatetics, the later Stoics betray a deep compulsion to maintain the superiority of the classical *vita contemplativa*.[10] The common denominator in these post-Aristotelian schools was a new vision of the human condition in which, *mutatis mutandis*, the dominant classical mode of fulfilling peculiarly human needs through political institutions was subverted by a sense of solitude, inwardness, and non-political community (Epicurean *philanthropia* or Stoic *homonoia*) that both broadened and weakened the individual's feeling of membership in an actual social group. In these conditions the residual traces of the *vita activa* were but epicycles designed to save the phenomena of a now-debased, pseudo-Aristotelian "mixed" life. Only with the Neoplatonists, as we shall see, was any effort made to revive a Platonic metaphysics in which knowing and doing were linked in a continuum that permitted something like the classical marriage of the active and contemplative estates.

Of particular importance for the Renaissance is the variant on this reinterpretation of the *vita contemplativa* provided by the Roman Stoic, Seneca. Even more than the Athenian, Latin culture had from the outset resisted the appeal of the contemplative life. Indeed, from their earliest contacts with Hellenism, the Romans viewed philosophy and its practitioners with suspicion.[11] This situation was altered somewhat when, under the influence of the Stoic Panaetius, Scipio Aemilianus and his circle conceded some value to the *vita contemplativa*. The *Somnium Scipionis* in Cicero's *De re publica* gives that author's most emphatic definition of the contemplative life. Concluding with Aristotle's three genres, Cicero admits that *sophia* or theoretical wisdom is higher than *phronesis* or practical wisdom, and contemplative insight into the structure of the cosmos crowns a life of public service. Yet the lure of the contemplative life in Cicero's generation provoked a determined resistance. Cicero himself remains stoutly committed to political activity. In the *De officiis* he had already, in the person of Laelius, criticized the *vita contemplativa* on the grounds that the limits of human intelligence work against it.[12] And in his letter to Cato (*Epistulae ad Familiares* [*Fam.*] 15.4) he applauds himself and his correspondent for "having introduced that true philosophy of the ancients, regarded by some as the hobby of the leisured and indolent [*oti ac desidiae*], into the forum, into political life, yes, almost into the field of battle itself."[13]

By Seneca's time, however, this stiff resistance of old Roman activism to the appeal of contemplation has waned. The Neronian experience shaped Seneca's consciousness in a way that that of Caesar and the Antonians never shaped Cicero's. It is true that

Seneca's pronouncements on the *vita contemplativa* preserve the habitual Roman mistrust of inactivity and reflect the Stoics' traditional opposition to Epicurean withdrawal. In Epistle 94 Seneca divides virtue into *contemplatio veri* and *actio*, but dwells mostly on the latter and its sources in education, relegating contemplation to little more than Aristotle's knowledge of circumstances. And in *De otio*, contemplation (*contemplatio rerum*, 5.1) is viewed as inextricably bound up with action (and even with pleasure): the contemplative man has an obligation to do what he sees ought to be done (6.3). But Seneca has in effect found a way to justify the contemplative life without violating the Stoic commitment to society. So long as the philosopher–scientist is willing to share his learning with others, he is justified in withdrawing from public life (*De tranquillitate animi* [*Tranq.*] 3.3). This is especially the case in old age or under a corrupt political regime, as Spenser's Hermit and Colin Clout respectively will attest. Hence it is no surprise that when summing up the traditionally opposed three *bioi* ("tria genera sunt vitae:... voluptatis, ... contemplationis, ... actionis") he laconically concludes that they all come to the same thing in the end (8.1).[14]

Seneca's revisionary outlook on the *vita contemplativa* is further reflected in the uniquely Roman debate on *otium*.[15] Originally a military notion, signifying release from hostilities, at some point in its evolution the word comes to be contrasted with *negotium*, or the active use of a period of productive peace, i.e. of otium. The elder Cato associates otium both with *luxuria* and with literary activity (*otium Graecum* or *litteratum*), the latter evolving into a period of ascetic withdrawal prior to the launching of greater efforts of eloquence (and therefore of public power). Cicero acknowledges both an *otium honestum*, which is any retirement, voluntary or enforced, not spent in idleness, and an *otium cum dignitate*, that much-vexed phrase from one of his letters which seems to denote the inner harmony of a man of affairs (*Fam.* 1.9.21).[16] In the *De officiis* he excuses his present, externally imposed otium and insists that no productive use of it can possibly rival in merit the *gloria* of a man "who once brought the state repose from civil strife."

But these traditional Republican views of otium are notably modified by Seneca. Seneca is willing to justify otium under a variety of circumstances: when the state is corrupt or unwilling to accept the wise man's services, when he is in ill health, and even when he seeks thereby to avoid suffering the imminent storms of fortune (*De otio*

3.3–5). So long as it benefits as many people as possible, Seneca views this choice as a form of action (*ibid.* 5). Though in Epistle 56 he urges Lucillius to seek in action a cure for *inertia* (no. 9), a little later he seems to prefer *otiosi* to anyone whose "mind…is unstable and has not yet withdrawn into itself" (nos. 11–12).[17] Yet in the final analysis Seneca's retreat into the self is not true contemplation in the Greek sense of personal participation in the essence of things. For him the purpose of withdrawal is not self-transcendence but a "remission" from the *otium negotiosum* of intellectual work in which one may prime the machine for further efforts (*Tranq.* 17.5). The same qualification is even more emphatic in Seneca's younger contemporary, Pliny. For Pliny, even less disguisedly than for Seneca, otium is merely a pause in *negotia*, in which "I read or write or exercise, to restore my mind for work" (1.9).[18] It is most welcome at the end of a life of labor (3.1) but for himself always takes second place to the affairs of friends (*negotia amicorum*, 8.9). As with Cicero and Seneca, the alternative mode of life, that of *theoria* or *contemplatio*, holds no substantial promise of reward worthy of challenging the hope of remembrance for heroic public efforts. Roman science, whether Epicurean or Stoic, lacks the specific world-transcending force of contemplation.

It is not until the rise of Neoplatonism that the classical contemplative life enjoys a true revival. In the later centuries of the Roman Empire the successors of Pliny find their public function usurped by "barbarians" recruited to carry on the work of maintaining the old order while in fact supervising the establishment of a new one. In these circumstances the orators and literati of the early empire become the grammarians and savants who contribute so heavily to the preservation of classical civilization, while the centuries-old debate among the estates of life is resolved, as I have suggested, in favor of a standard mixed life largely indebted to the Stoics. With Plotinus, however, the pattern shifts radically. Like all Neoplatonists, Plotinus rates practical activity of any kind low, upsetting the delicate balance of the two chief estates and merging them into a new *bios kathartikos* in which the function of virtue is reduced to preparing the body for the only truly valuable activity, "vision."[19] Identifying the three Aristotelian *bioi* respectively with the Epicureans (*apolaustikos*), Stoics (*praktikos*), and Plato (*theoretikos*), Plotinus acknowledges both of the last two, but insists that "Action is set towards contemplation" (3.8.6). Even more important, by "contemplation" Plotinus intends something like the original activity of Aristotle and Plato: for him "authentic existence" is constituted by the identification of the mind with God, a participation of the knower in the sole object of knowledge.[20] In contrast to the Ciceronian–Stoic confusion of *cognitio* and *contemplatio*, or the Epicurean reduction of Greek ecstasy to a science, in Plotinus there is a clear resurgence of the quest for a union of mind with Reality, an attempt to immerse the faculty of knowing in the thing known.

Even more germane to the Platonism of the Renaissance is Plotinus' equivocal treatment of action. For Plotinus, who often fuses Plato with Aristotle, contemplation is not only a source of activity, it is an activity itself. The point is crucial to an understanding of Renaissance poets such as Spenser. Plotinus views contemplation as the means by which human beings share in the pure creativity of God. By actualizing potentiality it "introduces beings" and maintains their perfection. This action of *theoria* is not a *praxis* but a *poiesis* or making, a "vision" or "play" that makes manifest the ultimate spiritual realities.[21] In this sense all Nature is a kind of contemplation: it broods, Plotinus says, on the vision of itself (3.8.4). But just as Nature's intuition of God is weak, producing a weak "object," so is most human beings' intuitive grasp of the real. Hence we too, "when weak on the side of contemplation, find in action [our] trace of vision" (*ibid.*). We act, that is to say, from the desire to see our action and make it sensible to others.[22] In short, there are for Plotinus two kinds or levels of action: *praxis*, which is a weak and compensatory variant; and *theoria* or contemplation, a species of *poiesis*, the divine, creative action worthy of the true contemplative. When Plotinus says that "Action is for the sake of contemplation," therefore, he means more than the slow rhythm of life implied by Aristotle (and to a degree by Plato) by which we earn our way to a leisured freedom of world-transcending thought, and much more than the faint echo of that rhythm in the Stoics and Seneca. Instead he intends a brief period of cathartic preparation by means of virtuous action – what Pico in the late fifteenth century will call "propitiation" of the senses and intellect – that issues in a life of true intellectual communion with God and, above all, a sharing of His creativity. For poets like Spenser this elevation of *contemplatio* and its identification with *poesis* is crucial:

in its light the most heroic and earthbound actions may be viewed as adumbrations of the *vita contemplativa*.

As in other respects, the Neoplatonism of Plotinus makes its imprint on the attitudes of early Christian thinkers, especially Augustine, toward the life of contemplation. The otherworldliness of the Gospels, with their admonition to "Love not the world," and Paul's emphasis on the "interior man" may well have been influenced by Stoic, Cynic, and other pagan apologies for the contemplative life. The vocabulary of monasticism – *askesis, philosophia, anachorein*, and later *monachoi* – echoes pagan writings, and Athanasius defends his askesis in the familiar terms of Stoic *apatheia*, as Tertullian had echoed the Cynic diatribes against the world and the Stoic *secessus de populo*.[23] But it is Augustine whose observations on the classical debate give a definitive Christian bias to the Neoplatonist revival of the *vita contemplativa*. Like most of his pagan predecessors in the debate, Augustine consciously resists too casual a renunciation of the world. Uneasily aware of his own radical attraction to the *vita contemplativa*, Augustine invokes Cicero in denying that pure contemplation is possible except in another world, where we may be "blessed with cognition of nature and even with a single science of the gods" (*De trinitate* 14.9). Yet Augustine's distaste for *negotium* as the "curse of time," into which man has fallen from the timeless *otium* of contemplation, leads him to demote Plotinus' action as a compensatory imitation of contemplation to a version of *superbia* or pride.[24] Conversely, contemplation is conceived as the last step in a spiritual exercise that can raise the mind to communion with God, "a certain elevation of the mind [until it is] suspended in God, tasting the joy of the eternal sweetness."[25] This final ascent to "blessedness itself" (1002) removes the last carnal notions from the purified soul so that "man becomes almost wholly spiritual" (1000).

In general, however, Augustine's praise of the contemplative life is qualified in medieval thought by the Christian imperative to practice charity. In his "sentences" on the active and contemplative lives, for example, Isidore of Seville observes that the perfection of the active life is attainable in this life, whereas the contemplative can be perfected only in the next (26).[26] In a similar vein Gregory the Great emphasizes that one can reach the contemplative life only through the active, as Jacob attained Rachel only after living with Leah; while Bernard of Clairvaux stresses the ecclesiastical superiority of Mary over Martha and reads the *Song of Songs* as an allegory of the Church in which the active life of obedience to ecclesiastical authority paves the way for its contemplative consummation.[27] Even Thomas Aquinas, who theoretically places the *vita contemplativa* at the pinnacle of human activities, contrasting the ease of intuitive communion by means of the "intellect" with the arduous labors of "reason," echoes Isidore in insisting that this faculty car achieve its end only with the aid of divine revelation, whereas the practical intellect is inherently adequate to its objectives.[28] Only the poet Dante restores something like the classical equilibrium between the active and contemplative lives. For Dante the two "perfections" of man, being and knowledge, entail the two "blessednesses" of the civil or active and contemplative lives, of which the latter is the "more excellent and more divine."[29] The second perfection is derived from the sciences (2.14.36ff.) and has an ethical force: the Donna of his youthful poems, now reinterpreted as Lady Philosophy, by revealing Paradise shatters the innate vices and thus renews the nature of him who contemplates her (8.20). Dante insists on the equality of the two "paths," identifying the active life with the moral virtues, the contemplative life with the intellectual (14.7). "Felicity" for Dante lies in *mente*, the rational mind, but this embraces both the *animo practico* and the *animo speculativo*, each of which is "dilettosissimo" but especially "quello del contemplare" (22.10). The practical exercise of the mind is its "working virtuously by way of the four cardinal virtues"; the speculative exercise, seeing God through His effects (*ibid.*).[30] In this philosophical work of his middle years Dante lays a theoretical base for his complex *itinerarium mentis in Deum* through the vehicle of love and poetry in the *Commedia*.

It is not surprising that the consummate medieval poet reflects the renewed dignity accorded the contemplative life by Neoplatonism. The same cannot be said, however, of the late-medieval phenomenon generally referred to as humanism. It is axiomatic nowadays that the early North Italian humanists inverted the traditional hierarchy of the estates of life. Yet outside the relatively brief period of "civic" humanism, the medieval (and classical) ranking of the lives remains substantially unaltered. Even the acknowledged father of humanism, Petrarch, displays a problematic approach to the issue. His celebration of solitary self-contemplation, with its distinctly religious flavor, lends his prose and poetry a bucolic character. In his *De vita solitaria* Petrarch recalls most sharply the post-classical and early Christian eremetic contemplatives. Although Petrarch's admiration for Cicero sometimes leads him to praise service to others, his own state of near-accidia forces him repeatedly to fall back on contemplation and prayer. In his most explicit statement on the estates of life, *De otio religioso* 2, Petrarch affirms a modified version of the life of contemplation, in which the proper end of human existence is identified with "God through virtues," a quasi-Aristotelian elevation of the *vita civilis* and *vita contemplativa* jointly over the *vita voluptuosa*. But Petrarch's basic fealty comes out most clearly in the symbolism of Laura and the laurel, his emblems of love and fame, which cannot have failed to influence Spenser in his own love poetry. A symbol of contemplation, Laura serves a function similar to that of the *figura* in medieval love poetry, but radically redefined. Whereas Dante's Beatrice, for example, figurally enacts Christ's redemption of sinners in her lover's personal struggle for salvation, Laura is herself an object of ultimate contemplation embodying the annihilation of world and time. Petrarch is by no means consistent nor even clear in sustaining this conception, and vestiges of medieval figuralism remain scattered through his work. Yet the essence of the Petrarchan *figura* as the ultimate realization or reification of Plotinian *poiesis* – a kind of primitive deconstruction of the notion of metaphysical grounding of the poetic construct – will be available to Spenser in his efforts to ground his own conception of the *vita contemplativa* otherwise than in the political metaphysics of the cult of Gloriana. In the figure of Laura, the contemplative life for the first time threatens to become a secularized religion, in which love and poetry replace Christian wisdom and the creature stands in place of the Augustinian Creator as the proper end of the contemplative life.[31]

In regard to the relative statuses of the two estates, later humanists follow Petrarch's lead. Filelfo, for example, holds the *vita contemplativa* to be the superior life as it supports and leads to the *vita activa*, while Pontano unequivocally exalts the solitary *sapiens* over the prudent *experiens*. Renaissance Platonism, which burgeons in Quattrocento Florence under the Medici, is closely tied to the political shift from the civic to the autocratic organization of power. Ficino's translations and commentaries on Plato under the active patronage of Lorenzo il Magnifico resulted in a highly platonized hierarchy of the faculties of man, at the top of which *nous* contemplates God in the spirit of love.[32] In this syncretic scheme Ficino, like Plato, subordinates moral theory to epistemology. The life of contemplation becomes an amalgam of true knowledge and moral perfection, much as in Book 6 of *The Faerie Queene* the fulfillment of Calidore's heroic quest depends on his epistemological breakthrough under the tutelage of the contemplative poet, Colin Clout (see chapter 5, below). Ficino's mytho-poetic ideal of the well-formed prince reflects the basic powerlessness that was turning the humanist of earlier decades into the ornamental figure of the courtier.[33]

That development is affirmed less obliquely in Pico's famous *Oratio*.[34] Here, as in Ficino and his Neoplatonist precursors, the ultimate destiny of man is communion with God, a participation of *nous* in the divine mind. This consummation is aided by the humanist (and Augustinian) emphasis on will, Pico's basic myth or fable being man's total freedom to develop his native capacities and so secure his place in the scale of being. For Pico, the most highly developed man is the "contemplator," a "reverend divinity vested in human flesh" and thus beyond even the "heavenly" philosopher or man of discursive reason (p. 226). Through the symbolism of the angelic orders, Pico traces a hierarchy of activities in which the active life prepares us for the "leisure of contemplation" that issues ultimately in the mythical union with God in love (pp. 227f.). Hence the disciplines form a natural ascension from the "expiatory sciences" of moral philosophy and dialectic, which cleanse his senses and intellect respectively; to natural philosophy (whose "perfection" is magic, p. 247), in which one alternately investigates and contemplates nature; and finally to theology or the mystical fusion with God, in which "full of divine power we shall no longer be ourselves but shall become He Himself Who made us" (p. 234). Clearly the philosopher's power to effect this ascent, whose immediate source is contemplation of and collaboration with "nature" by way of sympathetic magic, dwarfs the merely political power of the prince. It is the power of the politically powerless, and it resides in a *vita contemplativa* that hovers between a mystical *sapientia* and an emerging science.

Most of the developments in the century dividing Pico from Spenser mitigate the former's Neoplatonic exaltation of the contemplative life. Pico's shading of *contemplatio* toward a cognition of natural forces through an innate sympathy between the mind and nature presages an increasing emphasis in the following centuries on man's natural capacity for wisdom. As intellection comes to embrace both the medieval *ratio* and *intellectus*, and wisdom (*sapientia*) to be defined as a science of divine things and their causes, so contemplation (in Elyot for example) becomes a way in which the fallen soul gains control over first the passions and then the laws of nature.[35] The moral bias of humanism is reaffirmed by the Catholic humanists, Erasmus and Vives; it is paralleled, *mutatis mutandis*, by contemporary Protestant reformers. While Luther countered the increasing stress on freedom among the more optimistic Platonists with his Pauline and Augustinian emphasis on the dependence of the will on divine grace, he and other Reformers nevertheless tended to favor an active faith over pure contemplation. Luther divorces true wisdom or the knowledge of God, impossible in this life except through revelation, from science or the knowledge of created things "outside of God." For Calvin, too, no direct vision of God is possible; we see Him only as mirrored in the beauty of the created universe. Like Bacon later, Calvin rejects the Thomistic search for "natures": though God's mind is reflected in the order of His creation, His purposes are not.[36] Hence, though contemplation of the world's beauty can provide a temporary release into a vague adumbration of another and better world, it cannot offer a satisfactory alternative to the active struggle of virtue in this one.

Yet in the final analysis the Reformation affirmation of the *vita activa* as the dominant mode of human life fails to check those forces drawing thinkers and poets back into the central contemplative tradition. At least through the next century in England, perhaps longer in France and Italy, the injunction to exercise one's mental and verbal powers in the civic life is directed to the service of a state increasingly difficult to conceive as an ethical community. This dilemma is recorded by Castiglione and More at the beginning of the sixteenth century as well as by Edmund Spenser at its end. Despite various deflections triggered by the activist strains in classical Hellenism, Roman pragmatism, and Christian charity, a central continuity appears in the theoretical preference of disparate thinkers over several millennia for the contemplative life. If this bias is repeatedly challenged by an ethical commitment to ameliorating conditions in this world, it is at least as often encouraged by a residual doubt of the substantial reality of the world and by skepticism regarding the attainability of any kind of stable political order. Needless to say, poets at any time are especially susceptible to such doubts as well as to the appeal of a more constant order of things. This is undoubtedly owing in part to their habitual insecurity and social dependence; in this respect Dante, the supreme poet of exile, speaks for his whole fraternity. But poets also have a more specific historical connection with the *vita contemplativa*. Moreover, it is a connection with special relevance to the pastoral genres, and hence to our study of Spenser as a pastoral poet.

II

As we have seen, the domestication of the Hellenic debate on the "estates of life" in Augustan and Imperial Rome came to center in the concept of otium or leisure. Always suspect as an established way of life, during the collapse of the Roman Republic and the reigns of the Augustan and Flavian emperors certain more or less well-defined aspects or categories of otium – *otium litteratum, otium negotiosum*, etc. – were generally granted a degree of respectability. This was the work mainly of quasi-official spokesmen of "high" culture, e.g. moral philosophers such as Seneca or active members of the senatorial class with a literary avocation such as Cicero and Pliny. These representatives of the traditional Roman ruling classes tried to maintain an active posture in a polity where power was increasingly concentrated in a *princeps*. For poets of the period, who came mostly from equestrian or even lower origins, the problem was somewhat different. This difference is shown in their respective views of otium. Where literary survivors of the senatorial order such as Pliny continue to renounce otium in the name of public service, the poets of the time recognize it as a privileged release from the necessity of labor in a political society that offers them little in the way of dignity beyond menial clerkships or military assignments. To a Horace or a Vergil, otium is the *sine qua non* for whatever contribution to society may be possible for men of learning. While it is undoubtedly often a disguised form of self-indulgence, the lackey's reward for trivial services required of him by his patron, it can also be a source of freedom, in his own perception at least, through the exercise of which he justifies his high calling.[37]

A consideration of this phenomenon shows that the poets of late-republican or early-imperial Rome establish a special claim on the virtues of otium which became part of the privileged view of the man of letters inherited by the Renaissance. What I wish to suggest in the following pages is that the residual values of the Hellenic *bios theoretikos*, which were only partly assimilated by the Roman ruling classes, passed as it were by default to the domain of their protégés, the poets. When Renaissance humanism revives and reinterprets the culture of antiquity, this honorific view of otium, with its strong ties to the life of contemplation, is a significant attribute of the literary culture of the ancients reaffirmed by poets and other literati. As I will argue in later chapters of this book, the inherited belief that poets exercise the traditional prerogatives of Athenian philosophers and gentlemen – or perhaps I should say "gentleman-philosophers" – helps to arm poets such as Spenser against the growing assumption in the courts of sixteenth-century Europe that poets are little more than petty courtiers who happen to write. Oddly enough, in the Elizabethan court of the 1590s the wheel has come full circle. For the special value attached to otium in Rome beginning in the first century BCE was originally the invention of poets often newly liberated from physical or social bondage by aristocratic patrons vicariously, and for the most part unwittingly, savoring some small aftertaste of the Athenian contemplative life.

Partly because of their origins, Roman poets thrive on otium. Time to write and freedom from labor or *negotium* are the essence of their trade, and Augustan and "Silver" poets tend to portray themselves, like Ovid, as "shunning affairs, and born for carefree leisure (*secura ... otia*)."[38] The elegiac poets celebrate otium as a gift of Venus and the Muses and exult in their freedom from politics. Certainly Horace and Vergil make no such claim, but their efforts to accommodate poetry to power begin with the acknowledged need for otium. Thus Horace can picture himself as enjoying the "otia secura" that all men toil for (*Satirae* [*Sat.*] 1.1.31ff.), and it is in the *otia* that a "god" has given him that Vergil launches his official poetic career (*Eclogues* 1.6–10). Likewise Martial asks Flavius, a fellow Spaniard, to procure him a "delightful and easy to maintain retreat" that will make him "lazy" (10.104). Some poets may simply mock the laborious features of *negotium* and war, others turn them to their own artistic advantage. Propertius, for example, works up the true heroic fervor – "Surge, anime, ex humili" – to hymn the "Romana castra," only to discover that he himself lacks the spirit to

College of St. Francis Library
Joliet, Illinois

sing Augustus' glory. In the *Georgics*, on the other hand, Vergil repeatedly identifies his own creative otium with the useful labor of rustics.[39]

Along with leisure, a place of one's own, usually a farm or villa, is a stock-in-trade of Roman poetic otium. At times Horace even seems to imply the spatial metaphor implicit in "contemplation" (see p. 13, above), to define a place spiritually so to speak. At the thought of his bit of land, he vows "to find in idle hours sweet oblivion from life's cares" (*Sat.* 2.6.1–2). And in his most famous place-poem, the *Fons Bandusiae* ode (3.13), it is hard not to hear the Orphic note of Arcadian pastoral in the motifs of the unyoked ox and the ilex "set over the hollow rocks from whence leap your babbling waters."[40] A similar redefinition and re-evaluation of time is implied in the Golden Age topos, whose nostalgia centers in the good old days of the Republic and in the figure of the self-sufficient Roman farmer of that time.[41] In the *Georgics* this myth extends to the future as well and points to the *Aeneid*: the necessary, creative fall from a primal virtue leads through men's labors and the horrors of war to the vision of a compensating time of peace and the reconversion of swords to ploughshares (*G* 1.493ff.).

In general, therefore, the Roman poets' conception of otium helps to define their function vis-à-vis the structure of power. Elegists like Propertius strive to transvalue values, making otium itself a positive alternative to the prevailing *virtus negotiosa* of Roman culture and incidentally "softening" it by assimilating the influence of conquered Greece. More typically, the *poeta otiosus* becomes a more or less Epicurean philosopher of otium. Horace is the chief poetic sermonizer on the good life and "even mind," echoed by Martial in the next century.[42] In their most inspired moments Roman poets at their leisure even claim to touch the divine, to enter the sacred *templa* of contemplation. In "Descende caelo" (Odes 3.4), for example, Horace derives his dedication to the Muses from a specific childhood incident when the "fabled doves" protected him, weary and defenseless, against wild beasts, covering him "with sacred laurel and gathered myrtle." Despite his distancing ironies, Horace describes the birth of a poet through the nurturing of creative forces in the protected psyche of a child grown "fearless [but] not without the gods." Whether or not it is a form of contemplation, we encounter here the final gift attributed by Roman poets to their *otia*, a sense of authentic spiritual "life." In one of Martial's epigrams the

College of St. Francis Library
Joliet, Illinois

poet's Muse boasts that "Life [must] acknowledge her own ways" in his poems (8.3). It is because of this quality, another poem concludes, that even at the ends of the earth readers feel the man present in his poems (11.3).

Nevertheless Roman poets, like their Renaissance counterparts, are dependent for their livelihood or dignity on the benefactions of others.[43] To their patrons they owe both security and freedom, with their extension into the sphere of otium or *skhole*. In the conventional public mode the poet may use his talent merely to praise his patron as the Muse, or even the "god," who sustains his life. On a more personal level, however, he may put forth his own special claim to intimacy with the divine powers or with "life," inviting the patron to approach the poet himself as the true source or mediator of power. Thus Martial implies that a poet is something more than merely a "friend" (10.68), and even more pointedly affirms that a free man must first of all possess himself (2.68). The implication is that the Greek ideal of a gentleman's uniquely privileged life has been preserved only by materially dependent poets. This may be simply a face-saving ploy by one oppressed with obligations; yet elsewhere Martial insists that it is only by living freely that the rich *eques* can properly acknowledge the gods' gift of wealth (1.103). To a friend at leisure in Spain he writes, "it is not shameless for life to seek the leavings once fame has enough" (1.49.41f.). But as the Roman quest for fame is rarely satisfied, it is the poet himself, Martial implies, who must occupy the space it leaves for mere living.

Within the narrow world of their privileged otium, then, Roman poets typically strive to enact the prerogatives of the leisured classes as defined by Hellenism, i.e. *skhole* and *theoria/contemplatio*, in effect forfeited by their betters in the more austere Roman milieu. As preservers of the contemplative life they fill a gap in the ancient world between the Greek and Christian cultural dispensation whose diverse, though on the whole positive, attitudes towards contemplation we have already examined.

In this connection it may be useful to reflect upon a distinction drawn by Hannah Arendt between the sense of immortality and that of eternity. The former, she writes, dwells in and accepts time, within which the active man seeks to perform deeds (including writing) that will outlive their agent. The latter denies time: in contact with it the contemplative man seeks to enter into and experience the realm of the unchanging (*The Human Condition*, pp. 18–21). There is no doubt in which dimension official Roman culture had its being. In one of his letters (9.3), Pliny contrasts the "rewards of immortality" (*praemium aeternitatis*) with the lure of "that rich and deep leisure" (*pingue illud altumque otium*). Although Pliny's word is *aeternitas*, it clearly denotes what Arendt calls "immortality," for he goes on to say that every man must either fix his thoughts on his mortality and live "a life of toil and effort," or else "relax quietly and not…wear out his short existence with vain endeavours." Despite the restricted scope for heroic action in Pliny's world, it is symptomatic that he nevertheless counts himself among those who choose to seek "immortality" in the active life. To their patrons' pursuit of this elusive *fama*, *gloria*, and *aeternitas* Roman poets freely lent their pens in the full range of public poetry from eclogue to panegyric to epic. Yet the same poets' more intimate utterances, often in direct addresses to the patrons themselves, suggest that they did their best to keep alive the sense of the eternal as well. Part at least of the poet's function in the Roman world was to exemplify and commend his peculiar version of the contemplative life.

Poets and other men of letters in the Renaissance faced a cultural situation in many ways similar to that of the Roman celebrators of otium. In some respects, this similarity was intense. Because of the high visibility of Petrarch, as well as Boccaccio's successful promotion of Dante's memory in Florence, literary Tuscanism had achieved an unusually prominent place for letters in the culture of "civic humanism" in fourteenth- and early-fifteenth-century Italy. Added to the importance of the rhetorical and philological training they shared with other humanists, these phenomena made it appear for a time that poets might well be the legislators of the lettered world. It is during the fairly rapid decline of civic humanism in the small republics of Northern Italy, and the evolution of these states into *principati* under the rule of strong autocrats and burgeoning family dynasties, that writers, playing a waning political and even cultural role, begin to echo motifs of the Roman decadence. For the fifteenth-century shift in the power structure created a new brand of patronage founded less on civic virtues and service to the state than on aesthetic cultivation. Political conduct in general and literary activity in particular became intensely personal. Lorenzo de' Medici, for example, conducted an invisible tyranny, ruling by means of a clientele and sitting atop a hierarchy of his creatures of different social ranks.[44] Hence the humanist hero of the earlier period, epitomized by the late-fourteenth- and early-fifteenth-century chancellors, is succeeded by the "intellectual as hired hand," whose prevailing mood fuses "social aimlessness," opportunism, and urbanity, qualities idealized in Castiglione's Courtier.[45] It is true that humanists and poets continued to contribute heavily to the propagation of a sense of community, often by means of various versions of pastoral. Thus the peculiar proletarian cast of Laurentian culture, with its coarse songs sung by actresses in peasant costumes, aided in the binding of all classes to a common cultural mythos.

Nevertheless, the feeling persists that the new poets and intellectuals of these regimes are the creatures of despots, to whom they owe their social beings. In Florence, for example, a distinction must be made between protégés of Lorenzo either raised up from obscurity to a career in letters like Poliziano or primed for such a career from infancy like Ficino, and others such as Alberti, the Pulci, or Pico, who came from noble families.[46] Naturally, how a poet viewed his status at court or gauged his personal freedom was partly a function of his claim to privileges of birth or family position. Similarly, at Ferrara under Ercole d'Este there was a separation of functions between noble amateurs who write, such as Boiardo, Ariosto, and Ercole Strozzi, and professional men of letters who live by the pen, not to mention more subtle differences between a feudal lord such as Boiardo and a "cultured bourgeois" such as Ariosto.[47] Of course, even for the former not all the evidence suggests abuse. In all periods the Medicean patrons displayed varying degrees of affection for their protégés. Despite his humble and modest status as tutor to Lorenzo's children, for example, the brilliant Poliziano "lived with Lorenzo on terms of the closest intimacy [, and] retained the freedom and self-respect of a scholar while residing in the palace of the greatest man of Florence."[48] Similarly, Alfonso d'Este of Ferrara took over Ariosto's maintenance following the poet's refusal to accompany Cardinal Ippolyto to Hungary, promising him leisure and possibly enabling him to build the cottage in which he finished the *Furioso*.

As one might expect, therefore, the literary responses of Renaissance poets to their treatment by patrons ranged from the most abject praise to dignified chastisement. Even flattery is not always distinguishable from a more central function of the courtly poet, the articulation of shared cultural values. In the court of

Lorenzo de' Medici, patronage was an integral part of his personal and dynastic myth, in whose propagation Lorenzo himself was a full partner. Hence in Poliziano's dedication of his *Miscellanea*, remarks on literature that he claims to have first made to Lorenzo on their horseback rides together and then been urged by the latter to write down, the author acknowledges that his book "takes its authority" from him to whom it is commended.[49] On the other hand, there is some evidence of conscious resistance by writers to the public roles they assume. Most Renaissance criticism of a patron or regime is necessarily oblique. The Florentine historians Machiavelli and Guicciardini, for example, exploit Roman historiography's potential for comment on contemporary events. Ariosto's Satires occasionally attack the machinations of the papal curia, tyrants, and oppressive ministers, while even his Italian comedies, so closely associated with the official Este cultural program in the first decade of the sixteenth century, borrow plots from Plautus and Terence to give a political cast to Roman comedy's central theme of rebellion against parental authority. In dialogues too, social criticism can be rendered and then disclaimed. An example is Stefano Guazzo's *Civile Conversazione* (1574), a text heavy with implications for Spenser's England. In this work the speakers, Guglielmo Guazzo and his physician Annibale Magnocavalli, openly debate the virtues and vices of princes. Utilizing the time-honored genre of humanist dialogue, Guazzo, like Ariosto, can have his satirical cake and eat it too.[50]

It is when belated Renaissance humanists find mere criticism of despotic regimes inadequate, however, that they most blatantly echo ancient appeals to the contemplative life. In Florence, for example, when the Pazzi conspiracy had consolidated support for the Medici, the aristocratic Alamanno Rinuccini withdrew from active politics, adopting in his *De libertate* (1479) the Roman–Stoic defense first articulated by Seneca of the retired life as a legitimate response to tyranny.[51] Nevertheless, the most common form of renunciation by writers is purely literary; and the literature of the Italian Renaissance, in both its humanist and its courtly phases, is replete with verbal gestures of detachment from political power. This tendency toward withdrawal is already apparent in Alberti, whose later writings increasingly emphasize domestic activities at the expense of political ones, a reversal of the classical bias.[52] Even the greatest productions of courtly literature display this urge to self-definition by symbolic flight. In Sannazaro's *Arcadia*, the Vergilian pastoral, purged of political overtones, is reduced to a purely lyrical form in which the woods of Arcady have no logical successor in court or city; while the *Cortegiano* celebrates the renunciation of power and glorification of the private self.[53] Less than a generation later one senses that this phase of Renaissance culture is nearly over. This suspicion is supported by Guazzo's *Civile Conversazione*, a work that reflects the beginning of the metamorphosis of Castiglione's aristocratic courtier into the seventeenth-century ideal of the gentleman, In the last book of the work the whole pattern of courtly renunciation of, and withdrawal from, the exercise of power is openly mocked in the "Game of Solitude," in which each of the dialogists must announce a place and a reason to shun "bad company" and append an appropriate proverb for his or her life of solitude. In the end the players answer riddles to earn their release from solitude to dinner. Thus has a major aspect of the history of Renaissance culture been reduced to the neat paradigm of a parlor game.[54]

In the centralized Elizabethan regime, with its reliance on patronage and literature as instruments of policy, the status of poet–courtiers and other men of letters strongly resembled that of their counterparts in the "courtly" phase of the Italian Renaissance, as distinguished from the humanism of the fourteenth and early fifteenth centuries.[55] In the early decades of Elizabeth's reign her patron–politicians marshalled all their forces, including the newly-discovered power of the printing press, to consolidate the new regime, much as Lorenzo de' Medici had done following the Pazzi conspiracy in Florence a century earlier. While emulating European princes in adorning the regime with humanists and classical learning – as much the insignia of power in Renaissance courts as Platonism is its philosophical code – the Tudors in addition emphasized the moulding of middle-class opinion, strongly Protestant in its bias, as reflected in the high proportion of "utilitarian" works published well into the early Elizabethan decades. At the same time, the elaborate progresses by which the Queen exposed to her subjects her personal presence and the symbolic potency of her court began in the 1560s, reached a climax in the famous three-week Kenilworth entertainments of 1575, resumed again in the 1590s, and continued even into Elizabeth's last years.

Poets clearly made a major contribution to this effort. A

generation before the English masque was invented, prominent court poets were lending their pens to the glorification of Eliza. Sidney, who had earlier incurred her displeasure by going beyond his commission on a diplomatic mission abroad, was asked by Leicester in 1578 to rehabilitate himself in his sovereign's graces by writing *The Lady of May*. John Lyly's services at Kenilworth helped secure for him the patronage of Burghley, which in turn made possible the writing in 1579 of *Euphues*, one of the first literary expressions of the Elizabethan courtly ideal. In the same year Spenser himself, who had been living at Leicester House, anonymously celebrated "Elisa" in the pastoral–courtly mode of *The Shepheardes Calender*. Well on his way to what might have proved to be a triumphant career, he offended the Queen, and perhaps Leicester himself, by the ultra-Protestant fervor of his eclogues and of *Mother Hubberds Tale*, written and possibly "called in" in 1579–80, and most likely reflecting the prolonged Alençon marriage negotiations of those years.[56] Later, as the Elizabethan court took on increasingly the symbolic features of Renaissance culture, the more courtly forms of literature came into prominence, including the inevitable complaints about the stinginess of patrons.[57] Finally, though anti-courtly satire and moral tractates against the abuses of courts and courtiers can be found in any courtly literature as a kind of minimal return of the repressed, there is a notable resurgence of these genres in the 1580s and 90s.[58]

Spenser himself, of course, will be the chief exemplar in this book of poets' responses to the evolving conditions of Elizabethan courtly culture. To understand more clearly the context of Spenser's development, however, it is worth examining some other contemporary evidence pointing to a revaluation of courtly values in the light of the Roman precedents and Italian analogues previously discussed. For Spenser and his contemporaries too, the ancient debate about the active and the contemplative lives and the concomitant revaluation of otium form the backdrop of the literary resistance of individuals to an emergent autocracy.

There is little doubt that Castiglione's idealized image of the courtier had a profound impact on court life under Elizabeth, especially in the early decades of her regime, when she was forging the delicate network of influences and institutions alluded to above.[59] English courtiers adopted the Castiglionesque paradigm even as they vied for favors and played the Queen's peculiar version of the game of courtly love. Sidney turned this game into high art, capping with the flamboyant chivalry of his death a largely unsuccessful performance in which he was barred from prominence by the lot of the marriage-game and by his own honest miscalculations of Elizabeth's sympathy with the radical Protestant cause. Gradually, however, the great examples of high ambition and its fate had to have an effect on the attitude of the "ruling class" toward life at court. Although it was the very end of Elizabeth's reign that saw the fall from favor of her most charismatic courtier, the glittering Essex, there is abundant evidence that the 1580s and 90s were in general a period of deep questioning of the courtly ideal. Perhaps the realization slowly dawned on the younger generation of courtiers that beneath the pose of unambitiousness that had masked the struggle for personal power in the previous generation lay the real subservience the monarch required of her men. The courtier had renounced all desire for power; the Queen, taking him at his word, let him play out his role, keeping the real power to herself and turning for advice to the faithful and truly unambitious Burghley.

Whatever the cause, another model of civility made its appearance in England almost on the heels of Castiglione's, though it did not immediately rival the latter's influence. Although written half a century after the *Courtier*, in 1574, Guazzo's *Civile Conversazione* first appeared in English translation in 1581, just twenty years after Hoby's Castiglione. Superficially of the same genre, Guazzo's book presents a more down-to-earth image of society, appealing less to an elite of self-styled courtiers than to the emerging type of bourgeois gentleman mirrored in the book. It is impossible to say with certainty that Spenser knew Guazzo's work, but his friend Lodowick Bryskett knew it and incorporated it into his own *Discourse on Civill Life*. In any case, the aim of Guazzo's book is certainly close to that announced in Spenser's "Letter to Raleigh," which may reflect the influence of a more "civil," less courtly ideal already in the air in the early 1580s. Whenever this influence began to be felt, it seems that its effect was to present a vision of civility wider than that of the courtier and to temper the lingering nostalgia for Castiglione's ideal with a strong note of anti-courtliness.[60]

An insight into this re-evaluation of the older courtly ideal may be gleaned from the reflections of a typical courtier of the younger Elizabethan generation, Sir John Harington, the translator of Ariosto. Virtually raised at the court of his godmother Elizabeth –

his parents were a courtier and a natural daughter of Henry VIII –
Harington "perhaps understood the Queen as well as any man in her
last years."[61] She had readily pardoned him for his part in the Essex
expedition to Ireland, and he managed to stay out of serious trouble
thereafter by adopting the mask of a harmless clown, at the same
time circulating his candid and sometimes biting epigrams. In the
latter he displays the wit and detached civility of an ideal courtier,
acknowledging, like Castiglione or Puttenham, that "dissimulation"
is part of the game of courting.[62] On the other side of the coin,
Harington's private notebooks and letters reveal an undercurrent of
discontent with courtly life. Periodically retiring to his modest estate
at Kelston, he registers the personal frustrations of his "unambitious" career: "I have spent my time, my fortune, and almost
my honestie, to buy false hope, false friends, and shallow praise"
(*Nugae Antiquae* [*NA*] p. 168). Clearly, beneath the public masks he
wore at court, Harington preferred to think of himself as a bluff and
principled gentleman.

Harington's private myth fuses the pastoral motifs of retirement,
leisure, and contemplation. An epigram addressed to Essex "when
he lay at Greys and protested to live retyred" balances the
philosophical ideal of retirement with the writer's own hard-nosed
sense of the dangerous realities Essex is encountering. Other writings
show an attraction to the classical ideal of otium, and Harington
characteristically distinguishes an enervating "idlenesse" from a
contemplative ease that "rayseth the soule to the trew love of God
and inflameth it with a desyre of virtuous actions" (*NA* p.199), a
distinction Spenser was contemporaneously incorporating into his
Faerie Queene. Harington's late, conventional *Prayse of Private Life*,
ostensibly a free translation of Petrarch's *De vita solitaria*, is filled
with echoes of Cicero and Seneca in praise of otium.[63] In his private
reflections on the Queen's death, written at home in Kelston in 1603,
this otium takes on the inevitable coloring of Elizabethan pastoral:

Here now will I reste my troubled mynde, and tende my sheepe like an
Arcadian swayne, that hath lost his faire mistresse; for in sooth, I have loste
the beste and faireste love that ever shepherds knew, even my gracious
Queene, and sith my goode mistresse is gone, I should not hastily put forth
for a new master.   (*NA* p.180)

For a man of Harington's limited means, the habit of courting was
hard to shake, and he put forth in vain for the favor of the new King.

Nevertheless his intimate writings give fairly reliable testimony to the doubts and resistances at work in this *homme moyen sensuel* of Elizabethan courtly society.

As in Harington's court jottings, so in the more pedestrian tract literature of the period, akin to the conduct books or manuals of courtliness, there is a discernible drift toward pastoral and contemplative values. Earlier in Elizabeth's reign the emphasis had been on public service and the obligation of younger men to come to court. This is still the bias in Pettie and Young's Guazzo, despite "William's" passionate defense of the contemplative life. There is a shift in emphasis, however, in an anonymous dialogue, *The English Courtier, and the Cuntrey-gentleman*, published in London in 1586 and dedicated to Sir Francis Walsingham.[64] While acknowledging the traditional three estates of life of the "Philosophers" – "contemplative," "active," and the life of "pleasure" (Aiii^v) – this text cites Cicero and others (Biv^v) in support of living in country houses. Similarly, Bryskett's *Discourse of Civill Life*, published in 1606, but almost certainly written in the 1580s and based on Cintio's *Tre Dialoghi della vita civile*, begins by invoking the Ciceronian tradition in defense of community and "convention" in the style of Guazzo.[65] But prefaced to the main discourse, along with Bryskett's own original dedication of the treatise to Lord Grey, is Sir Robert Dillon's long defense of Bryskett's retirement as a kind of *otium studiosum* in which he serves his country by writing an edifying book in support of the active life.

By contrast with these more or less balanced humanist works, Nicholas Breton's *The Court and the Country* (1618) suggests that in the next generation there occurred a more radical change in attitude.[66] Here the issue is truly joined, though neither Breton's "Country-Man" nor his "Courtier" is able to persuade the other of the superiority of his own way of life. The work is dedicated to one Sir Stephen Poll, Knight, who combines "knowledge of the court" with a "sweet retired Life at home" (A2^r), and the aggressive anticourtly persona of the country gentleman allows Breton to vent a whole gamut of diatribes against courtiers – those "hangers on upon those that sometimes in great places have an humor to fatten fleas" (B3^r) – and conversely to idealize the country as a "Paradise" where one seeks and finds "content."[67] Though superficially sharing the conventional balance of Bryskett's *Discourse*, Breton's litany of attractions to the life of court rings hollow in the face of the passionate conviction of his countryman. At the very least, in the intervening years feelings about this *paragone* have heated up, driving the adversaries toward irreconcilable extremes.

The foregoing discussion may serve to suggest something of the ambivalence with which Spenser's contemporaries viewed the Elizabethan and Jacobean courts. Even in the age of James I the Castiglionesque ideal is still alive. But alongside it have sprung up Harington's Albertian norm of a more authentic life in the bosom of the family and the freedom of one's own estate, Bryskett's Ciceronian ideal of literary otium as a preferred version of the active life, and the ultimately revolutionary values of a Guazzian "civil society" as a noncourtly form of polite intercourse. These modifications of High Renaissance courtliness are all creatively embodied in the literary career of Edmund Spenser. Spenser launched that career at a time when the desire for personal preferment and artistic success subjected the neophyte poet to the stresses of the Elizabethan patronage system, when the limits of expression were being tested both by court poets and by the greater courtiers who protected them, and when anticourtly poetry carried a large share of the burden of resistance to the more repressive aspects of Tudor civilization. In their reaction to the conditions of their existence we have seen that Renaissance poets could draw on a long-standing theoretical preference for the *vita contemplativa*. That preference, however, buttressed by the poet's special relation to the traditional estates of life, is in turn bound up with the pastoral mode and genres, and with the Renaissance reading of Vergil.

III

From what we have already seen of the historical debate about the hierarchy of "estates of life" and the pivotal relation of *skhole* or otium to the life of contemplation, it should come as no surprise that in both its philosophical underpinnings and its literary evolution the pastoral is closely associated with the *vita contemplativa*. Thus, when Bacon points out in *The Advancement of Learning* that as a shepherd Abel naturally figures forth the contemplative life, he is reflecting a well-established connection.[68] Renaissance literary theorists like Scaliger had linked the genre with the earliest, agricultural stage of civilization.[69] Bacon too notes that the "two simplest and most primitive trades of life" were the shepherd's and the husbandman's.

But if the "election went to the shepherd, and not to the tiller of the ground," that fact has less to do with an assumed historical priority than with what Bacon takes to be the essence of the shepherd's life. In Bacon's allegorical reading of the Biblical episode, Abel and Cain constitute "an image of the two estates, the contemplative state and the active state [*imaginem duarum vitarum, contemplativae nimirum et activae*]." And he adds that "by reason of his leisure, rest in a place, and living in view of heaven," the shepherd is "a lively image of the contemplative life [*typus est vitae theoricae*]." Bacon's characterization of the shepherd's life is worth underscoring. The three attributes he singles out go to the root of the contemplative associations of pastoral; whatever else he may be or do in the long evolution of the mode, from its inception the pastoral shepherd must have otium, he must be still and in a fixed locale, and his surroundings must be open to and mirror the essential order of things.

The spirit of quietism that lay behind the philosophical genre of the *vita contemplativa* also, in the Hellenistic period, produced bucolic poetry. Of course one encounters this spirit in earlier literature, from the proto-shepherd Proteus' noon-hour idyll among his seals in the *Odyssey* (4.400ff.), a model for Vergil's sixth eclogue, to the designation of the same hour as the "time for exaltation and discovery of the self" in Plato's *Phaedrus*.[70] But following the collapse of the Greek polis the ultimately Aristotelian *vita contemplativa* or *theoretica* (Bacon's *theorica*) is gradually transformed into a new *vita solitaria* centered in the countryside. The post-Socratic philosophical tradition continually stresses the importance of a country setting as a necessary condition for the contemplative life. For Epicurus it behooves the wise man to "love the country" (*philagresein*) (Diog. Laer. 10.120). In contrast to the quintessentially "political" settings of the Academics and Peripatetics, in which pure speculation expresses the aristocrat's privilege of transcending his social obligation to share in the life of the city, the Epicurean garden symbolizes the ideal situation of all men: a wholly unpolitical, individualistic solitude outside both the polis and the family. Even the Stoics, as we have observed, in rejecting total withdrawal from the city and the active life, emphasize the value of temporary retreat to the countryside, whose leisure enables the speculation necessary for performing good acts.

The link between the quiet countryside and the *vita contemplativa* is broadly reflected in Hellenistic and Roman literature. In Alexandrian prose and poetry the refuge from power in some form of self-cultivation is conveyed in the *limen* or "safe harbor" motif – a motif of more than passing importance in Spenser as well, as we shall see – which Menander often associates with the quiet life and retirement into the country. A strong death-wish is seldom far from the surface, but Bion and others substitute *hesychia* or peace for death as an antidote to one's evil fate.[71] From the Scipionic period on, the literary topos of withdrawal to the country and to the self is associated with the senatorial and equestrian classes' increasing sense of alienation from the center of political power.[72] Vergil's *Eclogues* register a strong note of shock at the radical inversion of a traditional political order during the civil wars, and his *Georgics* further record a tension between Stoic service to the state in the form of didactic poetry and withdrawal into Epicurean moral "science" (see *G.* 2.458–512, for example). In the first century CE, as we have seen, passive resistance to a mode of political involvement rendered more ceremonial than effectual by the emperors becomes an insistent motif in Seneca and Pliny.

At the same time these tendencies were coalescing in the Hellenistic invention of bucolic poetry. The Theocritean theme of *hasychia* (= *hesychia*, peace or rest in the countryside) in Idyll 7.126 reflects the ideal of the "theoric" life of Zeno and Epicurus. Thomas Rosenmeyer sees it as embodying the "central hope" of Stoicism and Epicureanism, a "stillness" at the heart of Theocritus' new view of man in the world.[73] Neither an escapist retirement into the private life nor bitter retreat into "conversation with oneself" (p. 69), Theocritean otium, according to Rosenmeyer, connotes "a fulness in its own right" (p. 71), a "fixity which endorses the pulse of life" (p. 92). As Spenser will imply in Book 6 of *The Faerie Queene*, this withdrawal into the center of the human and natural world is a creative prelude to the resumption of normal human activities, and embodies a momentary freedom from the passions that is sanctioned by nature. At its inception the Baconian leisure, rest in a place, and contemplation of the heavens lie at the heart of European pastoral.

The association of pastoral with contemplation is not lost sight of in the Renaissance. Although the encrustation of motifs alien to the classical mode often obscures this connection, it can be recognized even in so quintessentially a Renaissance work as Tasso's *Aminta*, where the traditional note of Arcadian leisure may be heard in the familiar "Golden Age" chorus in Act 1. Other archetypal pastoral works or passages awaken echoes that go back to Aristotle. Thus the famous debate between Musidorus and Pyrocles in Book 1 of Sidney's *Arcadia* recalls the qualified preference for contemplation over action in Book 10 of the *Nicomachean Ethics*, an echo that lends support to those who have felt Musidorus, the putative shepherd, to be in the right.[74] A pastoral interlude cast in the Platonic–Aristotelian mode provides a contemplative refreshment of the spirit, both distinct from and in the end contributory to the life of practical wisdom and moral virtue.

By the time it reaches Tasso and Sidney, of course, the pastoral literary tradition has been enriched by elements of a platonized Christianity. This process may be observed already in the allegory of Christian pastoral, for example in Origen's third-century commentary on the *Song of Songs*, whose pastoral imagery Origen takes to imply a Christian version of the *vita contemplativa*.[75] The bridegroom (a king who elects to become a shepherd) chooses the best place for his flock (the chosen people). Here he rests at midday, when "the light is poured out in the world most copiously," an early intimation of the Neoplatonic Creator whom Origen links with the twenty-third Psalm (p. 122). According to Origen, God's activities on behalf of man are reflected in the pastoral life of the believer:

That first life, the pastoral, was a preparatory one, in order that, being set in a green place, he might be brought up on the water of refreshment. But the things that follow have to do with progress and perfection [Origen compares John 10:7 and 11:9].

Origen's Christian-allegorical version of pastoral, like the Epicurean one of Theocritus, posits a pristine contemplation somehow more perfect and inward than the life of action for which it is a preparation. Like Eden, the pastoral *locus amoenus* becomes the arena of a restorative and nourishing gnosis. As in Homer and Plato, Epicurus and Theocritus, this locale is associated with the noon hour, which Origen glosses as "the secret places of the heart" where the soul comes to a "clearer light of knowledge from the Word of God" (p. 125).

Origen's shepherd, like Bacon's, exercises his leisure in view of heaven. A millennium later Boccaccio will arrogate this Christian pastoral otium to poetry itself. Observing that poets have at all times preferred "solitude because contemplation of things divine is utterly impossible" in cities and courts, Boccaccio compares poets with hermits and "other reverend and holy men" who "serve God with a freer mind." These men live in the woods, and Boccaccio goes on to describe the conventional *locus amoenus*, concluding that "there the flocks and herds, the shepherd's cottage or the little hut untroubled with domestic cares [are all] filled with peace and quiet."[76] Spenser might easily have been recalling these words in his descriptions of hermits and shepherds in *The Faerie Queene*. To Boccaccio the poet's implicit kinship with the country, and with the *vita contemplativa*, is part of a general preference for poetry over theoretical philosophy. He even goes so far as to pre-empt contemplation for the former, in this respect sharing his friend Petrarch's surprisingly modern privileging of signifier over signified (see p. 21, above). Looking for an example to clinch his association of poetry with the life of solitude (14.19, pp. 88f.), he instinctively turns to Vergil.

Vergil's unique status in the medieval literary tradition made his career paradigmatic for later poets. It is perfectly conventional, for example, for Spenser as the "New Poet" to launch his own serious course of publication with an eclogue book and to preface his epic with an echo of the traditional seven-line proem to the *Aeneid*: "Lo, I the man…"[77] The Vergilian order of composition was also associated with a progression from primitive to more highly developed stages of human civilization. This association, probably derived from Book 2 of the *Republic*, is reflected in several epigrams on Vergil written by Maffeus Vegius, author of the notorious thirteenth book of the *Aeneid* in the fifteenth century:

> Pastor oves, et arator agros: et proelia miles
> Instruxi aeterno clarus honore Maro. (1)

> (As shepherd I, famous Maro, have brought sheep,
> as farmer fields, as soldier battles into eternal fame.)

More succinctly, Vergil's Muse "Per silvas et agros ad fera bella venit" (comes through woods and fields to savage wars, 2), and Vergil himself "Silvas, rura, acies cecini" (sang of woods, fields, armies, 3).[78] No doubt this view of the genres simply reflects the widely held belief we have noted in Scaliger and Bacon that as the pastoral phase of civilization precedes the agricultural, so pastoral poetry must have been invented earlier than georgic, and both earlier than epic.

It is not easy to say just how or when this tradition got started, though it was certainly well established by the end of antiquity, perhaps by Vergil himself.[79] Even less clear is the precise point at which the genres began to be connected allegorically with different "estates" of life. Within a century of Vergil's death Tacitus is already identifying the bucolic tenor of his poetry with the Aristotelian *bios theoretikos* (*Dialogus* 12–13). A few centuries later Donatus subjects the *Eclogues* to a rigorous system of allegorical classification, while Fulgentius identifies each of the first three eclogues with one of the traditional states of life.[80] Eventually this is extended to the Vergilian corpus as a whole. Thus an anonymous thirteenth-century manuscript tells us:

Et sciendum est quod Vergilius considerans trinam vitam, scilicet contemplativam, voluptuosam, et activam, opera tria conscripsit, scilicet, Bucolicam per quam vitam contemplativam demonstrat, et Georgicam per quam vita voluptuosa intelligitur ... et Aeneidos per quam datur intelligi vita activa.[81]

(And it must be understood that Vergil, reflecting on the triplex life, viz., contemplative, pleasureable, and active, wrote three works, viz., the *Bucolics*, wherein he presented the contemplative life ... the *Georgics*, wherein is understood the pleasureable ... and the *Aeneid*, through which we are given to understand the active life.)

Here the identification of pastoral with contemplation falls within a progression from the contemplative to the active life. This schema, however, does not necessarily reverse the Aristotelian hierarchy discussed earlier. While locating contemplation at the very pinnacle of human existence, where man enters into the divine, even Aristotle had observed that the philosopher must return to a life of active citizenship. Throughout the long debate – in Seneca, in Plotinus and Augustine, in the medieval Fathers and the Renaissance humanists – the purely analytical, abstract hierarchy of *genres de vie* reaching upward from action to contemplation accommodates a chronological progression from contemplation to action, and often from action to contemplation. Likewise, from its inception Vergilian allegoresis mimes a presumed movement in the life of man from a prior state of felicity to consummation in some form of the active life.

Normally, however, it is not the poet's career but that of his epic hero which bears the burden of Vergilian allegoresis. A direct descendant of the Stoic and Neoplatonic allegories of Homer, which allowed post-Socratic scholars to save the appearances of the canonical works of classical Hellenism by positing the theory of *hyponoia* or hidden meanings, the allegorical approach to Vergil founded by Donatus and Fulgentius comes to focus on the *Aeneid* as a figuring forth of man's journey through this life. This emphasis on the *Aeneid*, however, by no means precludes either pastoral or contemplation. From the outset the poem was held to entail an "epic duplex" blending outstanding exemplars of the active and contemplative lives, and hence implying a place for pastoral themes and episodes even within the heroic ambience. In the Christian allegoresis of Homer, Odysseus came to symbolize the Christian's (or Christ's) sufferance of this world on his way to his heavenly home.[82] Similarly, by combining Homer's two heroes – Odysseus in the first half of the poem, Achilles in the second – Vergil fits the man of contemplation or "science" and the man of action into a single coherent scheme of human life.

One further implication of the method deserves special attention. In the fifteenth century Christoforo Landino proclaims that in the *Aeneid* Vergil has revealed the "*summum bonum* of man," namely the "contemplation of the divine."[83] In order to receive this wisdom, however, the soul of the reader must first be "inwardly cleansed" of impurities so that those "virtues pertinent to life and mores" may be established (p. 53). As a member of the Florentine circle of Lorenzo de' Medici, Landino no doubt reflects the platonizing hierarchy of human activities observed above, in which moral philosophy and dialectic are "expiatory sciences" that prepare the soul for natural philosophy (= contemplation of the creatures) and theology (= union with the divine). The important point to note in the present context is the inference Landino draws with respect to allegory. Landino explains his omission of politics from the *Camaludensian Discourses* by claiming that he is concerned only with the "inner sense" of the *Aeneid*. This is further clarified by his comment in the Preface to his 1488 edition of the poem to the effect that its double sense addresses two kinds of reader: the literal sense instructs the active man in (and presumably moves him toward) political virtue, while the allegory instructs the contemplative man in science.[84] From this we can see that for Landino at least there is implied in the very notion of allegoresis an invitation to the *vita contemplativa*. That is to say, a fundamental premise of poetry as veiled philosophy, and specifically of the *Aeneid* as a duplicitous vehicle for conveying hidden truths, is that whatever concessions its surface may make to the exigencies of action, the core of its content is contemplation.

From its creation to the Renaissance, then, the *Aeneid* was read as a philosophical allegory on the life of man. The pattern of exegesis, one that varies little in succeeding centuries, is established in the sixth century by Fulgentius. The initial *arma virumque*, which Fulgentius identifies with the *virtus* and *sapientia* of Christ in I Corinthians I:24, summarizes human progress from birth to the active use of wisdom.[85] Developing these terms in reverse order, Books I–6 deal with the growth of Everyman from infancy through childhood and adolescence to adulthood; whereas Books 7–12 show how the fully matured man exhibits virtue in government and war by arming himself for goodness, defeating violence, and implementing wisdom. Book 6 is by far the most important part of the poem. Like all his successors, Fulgentius gives it the lion's share of his attention. This portion of Aeneas' journey constitutes the hero's entrance into the contemplative life, his initiation into the "secrets of knowledge" (p. 130).[86] The descent into creatures in Book 6 establishes the fundamental connection of Vergilian allegoresis with the *vita contemplativa* as the apex of the philosophical life. To medieval allegorists the *descensus ad inferos* crowns the education of the Christian warfaring hero. It represents a critical moment of entry into one's intellectual inheritance in preparation for the active life.

This passage into the *vita contemplativa* is closely tied in turn to the crucial motif of filiation. Fulgentius casts his allegoresis in the form of a fable in which Vergil's ghost comes to him to explain, in the manner of an indulgent schoolmaster, the doctrine he had hidden in his poem.[87] By the same token, in his account of Book 6 it is through facing the dead and certifying their deadness (the vain embrace of Anchises) that Aeneas turns to the fulfillment of his wisdom in virtuous action. In this two-fold acknowledgment of paternal *traditio* or inspiration, Fulgentius identifies an element of un-anxious influence, or permissible appropriation, at the heart of the allegorical reading of ancient epic. Dante will make the most of this aspect of the tradition in his commitment to the fatherly Vergil as his primary guide through the Other World of the dead. And even Spenser, whose acknowledgment of his own filiations, like his use of allegory, is more disguised than Dante's – no such spiritual guide materializes in *The Faerie Queene* – will be aware nonetheless that in his varying quests no man travels alone. Indeed, as I will be arguing in succeeding chapters, the strong motif of poetic filiation associated for Spenser with the constellation allegory-pastoral-contemplation is a dominant factor in explaining his ability to transform the Elizabethan pastoral of power into his own contemplative variety.

There is a clear kinship between Dante's practice in the *Divine Comedy* and his conscious subscription to the Fulgentian program of allegorical interpretation of the *Aeneid*. Dante's own reading of Vergil occurs in Book 4 of the *Convivio* and most nearly parallels that of Bernardus Silvestris, to whom is generally ascribed the twelfth-century *Commentary on Vergil's Aeneid*.[88] In the first six books adolescence is figured by the hero's entrance into "the wandering wood of this life [*la selva, erronea di questa vita*]," an obvious starting-point for Spenser's Red Cross Knight as well as the Pilgrim of the *Commedia*.[89] Books 4–6 present in sequence maturity (*gioventute*) under the aegis especially of temperance, another suggestive parallel with *The Faerie Queene*; old age or prudence, Aristotle's *phronesis* (27.5); and decrepitude (*senio*, the encounter with Anchises), which Dante glosses as a return to God "as to a haven" in which one blesses one's past life. These remarks suggest that in addition to the fourfold allegory of the theologians, Dante's epic shaping of the soul's itinerary was influenced by Vergilian allegoresis. And since the tradition of reading Vergil in this way continued beyond Dante's time to Spenser's, it would seem equally plausible that a journey that begins in the Wood and Cave of Error and ends soon after a redemptive vision of the soul's ultimate destiny from the Mount of Contemplation, or after a similar vision of the Graces on Mt. Acidale, would have been deeply shaped by the long-established understanding of the *Aeneid* as a great philosophical quest.

There is no question that the medieval habit of allegorizing Vergil continued unabated into the Renaissance. The fourteenth century continued to pursue the allegorical method and to find Vergil essential. Petrarch, who evidently acquired the "habit of allegory" from Fulgentius, repeatedly adds moral comments to the *Aeneid* in his personal manuscript, as well as citing the moral exposition of the departure from Troy in a letter to Francesco d'Arezzo and in the *Secretum*.[90] Petrarch is emulated in this practice by fifteenth- and sixteenth-century literati such as Maffeus Vegius, Poliziano, Sanna-zaro, Mantuan, and Alemanni. In general, Renaissance revisions of medieval Vergilian allegoresis reflect those in the debate on the active and contemplative lives. In some instances, where medieval theorists had generally urged the contemplative and active lives over the voluptuous, their Florentine successors emphasize the need for a balance among all three. Normally, however, Renaissance allegorists favor the more dualistic conception of a fundamental struggle between divine intellect and bestial matter, in which man's "fated" fall into the body can be redeemed only by the mind's detaching itself from earthly disturbances and thus attaining a kind of "temporal beatitude." This can lead either to a choice of the active life, in which one employs reason (*ratio*) illuminated by mind (*intellectus*) in perfecting the earthly life, or to the mind's directly experiencing truth and beauty through contemplation.[91] These tendencies are reflected respectively in the humanist comments of Francesco Filelfo and the extended Neoplatonic exegesis of Christoforo Landino.

Filelfo's relatively brief remarks on the *Aeneid* are contained in two letters to Ciriaco d'Ancona, the first (written in 1427) focusing mainly on Vergil, the second (1443) on the Platonic three-part division of the soul that underlies that reading.[92] The first letter establishes that the allegorical reading of Vergil continues into the humanist period, accommodating the epic to the Renaissance understanding of the Greek philosophical tradition. In Filelfo's account the poem as a whole embodies the humanist fusion of the *vita contemplativa* and *activa* (p. 35), with the contemplative life as the necessary foundation of the active, and *sapientia* and *prudentia* respectively as the informing virtues. Filelfo follows the orthodox lines of Fulgentius and Bernardus Silvestris. Extrapolating from the *arma virumque*, he identifies the Aeneas of Books 1–6 with *sapientia*, that of Books 7–12 with *prudentia*. In developing *sapientia*, Aeneas must struggle through the serial ordeals of birth, adolescence, the pleasures of love, and so forth until he reaches the last stage, *perspicientia tota* (p. 41). The active life depicted in the last six books includes the display and praise of justice, fortitude, and piety and achieves its consummation in Turnus' death (p. 42).

Filelfo's analysis of his key terms in the second letter to Ciriaco places him squarely in the Aristotelian tradition. He explicitly identifies the two key faculties as "scientificam" and "ratiocinativam," clearly the equivalents of Aristotle's *to epistemonikon* and *to logistikon*.[93] For Filelfo, as for Aristotle, the problem is to reconcile the division of the virtues into moral and intellectual kinds with a claim for a cognitive element in the former. Like Dante in the *Convivio* (4.17), Filelfo defines *prudentia* (= Aristotle's *phronesis*, or practical wisdom) as "a mediator between the moral and intellectual virtues." Yet though *prudentia* governs the active life, it is useless if it is not "imitating" *sapientia*, which sees the truth *in caelo* (p. 39). *Prudentia* is crucial precisely because whereas the source – or, as Spenser will put it, the "sacred nursery" – of virtue is perfect vision, its end is "civil felicity" (*ibid.*). Filelfo's philosophical account of Vergil's allegory reflects early humanism's grasp of the necessary balance between purely contemplative faculties and activities and those that mediate between gnosis and praxis. In his letters on the *Aeneid* Dante's "two felicities" are given a restatement within the Renaissance–Humanist ambience.

Though written only a few decades after Filelfo's letters, Christoforo Landino's extended commentary on the *Aeneid* in his *Disputationes Camaldulenses* reflects the substantially different intellectual climate of the Florentine Platonic revival.[94] Viewed against a millennium of Vergilian allegoresis, Landino's interpretation reflects the Platonic theory of poetry noted earlier, in which allegory itself appeals to the contemplative man, as well as a shift from the balanced claims of the two major estates of life to a preference for the contemplative.[95] Landino's interpretation stresses not the allegory of the *Aeneid* but that of Aeneas: the unfolding of the poem's spiritual meaning follows the historical chronology of the hero's journey rather than the order of the books. Hence the entire argument about the estates of life is confined to Books 1–6, thus obviating the need (but also excluding the possibility) of interpreting Books 7–12. The overall scheme of his itinerary is the flight from sensual pleasure, avarice, etc., toward contemplation, identified with Italy. Having escaped the sensual flames of Troy, the avarice of Thrace, and the niggardliness of the Harpies (Dante's Hoarders and Wasters reborn), Aeneas must struggle at Carthage against the desire to rule, symbolized by Juno, and the surrender to worldly ambition signified by the marriage to Dido. Resisting the lure of the civic "task," Aeneas leaves Carthage, makes his final break with the life of the senses (leaving the rebellious women in Sicily), and enters into the contemplative life (i.e. arrives at Italy).

Several implications of Landino's revisionism are worth stressing. Unlike the typical Fulgentian Everyman-hero, Landino's Aeneas is identified explicitly as the exceptional man. Such a man alone is capable of achieving the superior existence, which is of course the *vita contemplativa*. This alteration explains Landino's exclusive focus on Aeneas' journey to Italy rather than on the total content of the *Aeneid*, in which the *descensus ad inferos* traditionally represents the acquisition of self-knowledge necessary for the active or civic life. As Landino's Sybil warns the hero, even when the storms of active life are past, he must suppress the desire for those things that the contemplative life rejects – chiefly, we infer, the desire to engage in civic activity. This repudiation by one of Lorenzo's protégés of any lingering trace of "civic humanism" in the emerging courtly culture of Florence also throws light on Landino's third major revision of the traditional exegesis: the identification of Dido not with carnality but with the civic life's distraction from contemplation.[96] As with Pico's hierarchy of the sciences, the platonizing culture of the late Quattrocento in Florence tends here to deflect humanism from active participation in political power toward fulfillment in the contemplative life, i.e. from *praxis* to *gnosis* as the consummate activity of man.

This tendency of the "literary wing" of the Florentine Academy to reject the civic emphasis of the previous two generations of humanists may imply less an inherent flight from the world than an adjustment to the new role of, and new demands on, men of letters under the emerging *principati* that I discussed earlier. Ficino can urge upon Lorenzo the *discordia concors* of the well-rounded hero who shuns the choice of any one of the three estates of life to the exclusion of the others.[97] But for Lorenzo's courtiers the safer way seems clearly to be the *vita contemplativa*. Fifty years earlier Filelfo could still read the *Aeneid* as promoting contemplation as a preparation for an enlightened humanist active life. While paying lip-service to this ideal, Landino draws on the Platonic undercurrents of Ficinian poetic theology to argue that the superior man shadowed in the *Aeneid* will eschew the temptations of politics in order to focus his intellect on seeking the way home to God.

Filelfo and Landino provide the Renaissance foci for the meaning of Aeneas' archetypal journey, often filtered through its deliberately allegorical appropriation by Dante in the *Commedia*. They also suggest the importance of the allegorized Vergil for later Renaissance poets such as Edmund Spenser. Spenser will make his own contribution to this tradition. For him, too, the *vita contemplativa* plays an important part in the life of the poet, even the poet aspiring to participate in the public life of a Renaissance court. His work reflects the tension implied in the two versions of that role embodied in the allegoreses of the *Aeneid* by Filelfo and Landino. In this chapter I have tried to trace the connection between Vergilian allegoresis and the ancient philosophical debate about the estates of life, as well as the association of that debate with literary pastoral, either as an independent genre or as incorporated into the intellectual patterns of heroic poetry. Spenser's awareness of his place in this tradition is registered throughout his career, officially launched in 1579 by the publication of *The Shepheardes Calender*, his first and most sustained pastoral work. There the poet's relative optimism about the project he is initiating is couched in his adaptation of the Vergilian eclogue with its socially positive bias. Later works repeatedly return to the pastoral mode as the central vehicle for reflection upon the poet's role in his society. But as the nature of that role is redefined, Spenser's conception of the pastoral is continually revised, and its fundamental contemplative associations are increasingly affirmed. The contours of this evolution form the substance of the remaining chapters of this book.

2

Colin's début

When Spenser orchestrated his public début as a poet, the surface of
the performance, at least, exhibited all the decorous sparkle of
Renaissance artifice.[1] Set against the studied humility of the
anonymous Immeritó, petitioning the learned and chivalrous Sidney
for protection, are the extensive claims made for the "new Poete" by
E.K. in his dedication to Harvey, the same commentator's elaborate
exegetical machinery, and the poet's own deliberate progress in his
self-presentation from "A Shepeheards boye (no better...)" ("January") to the self-assurance of his Horatian and Ovidian epilogue.[2]
Implicit in this performance, though only glancingly stated here and
there by E.K., is the Vergilian paradigm of this début: "So flew
Virgile, as not yet well feeling his winges" (p. 418). By presenting
himself in a pastoral persona, as yet unworthy even of a name,
Spenser lets stand the implication that he is thus far a nobody, a
cipher embodying and wholly defined by the long pastoral tradition
from Theocritus to Marot, from the "Roman Tityrus" to "Colin
Clout."[3]

The apparatus of dedication, plea for patronage, and citing of
contemporary personages and events signals to the informed reader
that the "new poet" is an individual of a modest social status, who
must be taken up by a Maecenas and made into a somebody before
he can be named in public. On the other hand, within the work the
pastoral names and allusions to the tradition, as well as its
conventional issues and themes, insist on his essential filiation to the
line of poets, deriving principally from Vergil, in which Immeritó
seeks to – and by writing in fact does – take his place. In short,
one might conjecture that there is an implicit contest of authorities
going on in the *Calender* between the desired patron, behind which
figure stands the entire power structure in Spenser's society, and the
Vergilian precursor, i.e. between political context and intertextuality.[4]
In this most publicly staged of débuts Spenser appears formally on

the scene at one and the same time in the guise of a beggar for favor and as a boaster. Like the Socratic Eros born of poverty and plenty alluded to in his favorite Ovidian tag, "Inopem me copia fecit" ("September" emblem), Spenser combines plenitude and emptiness: he is filled with the legacy of his pastoral forebears and yet avers a need for material sustenance.[5] If he lacks patronage and social status, he also incarnates a literary tradition that begins, ironically, with the same ambiguous dependency and the same promise of a return on the solicited investment.

This emphasis on the dialectic of poverty and plenty complements several approaches that have been taken by recent critics. Of these, two are worth mentioning here. The first is that of Harry Berger, who resolves the apparent ambiguity of Spenser's self-presentation in the *Calender* by divorcing the poet from his pastoral persona.[6] If we allow that already the mature poet of 1579 evinces a retrospective superiority to the simplistic "idyllism" of Colin Clout, the act of writing the poem becomes in effect Spenser's somewhat condescending bow to his own earlier "fledgling imagination" ("Mode and Diction," p. 147). That is to say that Spenser adopts the pastoral genre for his début in order to repudiate its inherent nostalgia or (in Berger's phrase) "longing for paradise," to reject the mode itself though not its artifice. A somewhat different approach, taken by Louis A. Montrose, emphasizes Spenser's own real ambivalence, as reflected in the "dialectic between Colin's rejection and Immerító's aspiration," but replicated also in the various antitheses expressed on every major issue raised in the several eclogues.[7] This fundamental ambivalence grows out of the poet's own reservations as a suitor for aristocratic favor. It implicitly acknowledges the counterpoise of humble petitioner and self-assured boaster in the work as a whole. By granting that the ambiguities of the *Calender* may stem from Spenser's own inner divisions, rather than from his unequivocal dissociation from his pastoral persona, we are able to view in a positive light his choice of the pastoral for his first important work.[8] We are now in a position to read his self-inscription in the Vergilian line as an implicit acknowledgment and revision of the inherent duplicity of pastoral which surfaces and is gradually thematized through the long evolution of the mode.

It has been said that in pastoral "the only royal way to the good life is to have it every way."[9] This premise can be discerned already in Theocritus, where Vergil clearly found it implied. But it is Vergil himself who incorporates this "pastoral duplex" (to coin a phrase) into the very structure of his *Bucolics*. This intention is announced in the Hic/Ille debate of his first eclogue, in which the two shepherds represent respectively those who have benefitted and those who have suffered under the newly installed Augustan regime. They are also (*pace* Servius) both personae of Vergil himself, separately as poet and as landowner, and compositely as the collective voice of those now threatened with silence. This aspect of pastoral is evident in Spenser's approach to the eclogue-form. Like his major precursors in the genre, Spenser views pastoral structure as a kind of map or guide to the "landscape of the mind."[10] In the *Calender* he consciously emulates Vergil's innovative weaving of free-standing eclogues into an eclogue-book, the constituents themselves often enfolding multiple points of view, achieving almost by authorial fiat an associative unity graspable only in the work as a whole. Though Spenser's immediate models are less often Vergil than Mantuan and Marot, and though in any case he always works significant changes on his models, his feeling for the form of the total work, as well as for its political/cultural assumptions, proclaims his Vergilian kinship. That kinship resides largely in a balanced structure that reconciles opposed tendencies, allowing the simple conventions of pastoral to convey the full complexities of life, and particularly of life as viewed from the underside of clientage in Tudor courtly society. In short, Spenser's adaptation of Vergilian bucolic constitutes an endorsement of pastoral as at least potentially an adequate vehicle for a poet suspended between the emptiness of his petition for favor and the fullness of his literary inheritance. At the inauguration of his career as a courtly poet, Spenser evidently endorses by appropriation the Vergilian prototype of the "pastoral of power." I have argued above that the Vergilian vehicle itself historically implies the identification of pastoral and otium with the philosophical *vita contemplativa*, and enacts the Augustan poet's usurpation of the traditional prerogative of a ruling elite. But at least on the visible surface of Spenser's intention in *The Shepheardes Calender*, there is no hint of a revisionary pastoral of contemplation. While the *Calender* is far from lacking in problematics, Spenser's initial public strategy in donning the Vergilian mantle is fully – i.e., pastorally – naïve. Before proceeding to examine Spenser's adaptation, it is worth glancing at the evolution of the bucolic structure, inherited from Vergil, which he adapts.

I

A strong feature of the classical eclogue collection is the *media via*, or midpoint on the road to Arcadia, where competing views of life are traditionally reconciled.[11] It is a point in fictive space (and a moment in time) at which reality and imagination intersect, and the limited possibilities of human existence are transfixed by the dream of a fulfillment without bounds. The motif lies very near the heart of the pastoral vision. For the mode that Theocritus and Vergil perfected, and that had so rich an afterlife in European letters through the Renaissance, is at bottom a vehicle of imaginative accommodation in a world of non-Euclidian space where parallel lines meet and the shepherd–poet may indeed have it every way.

The motif makes its début in Theocritus' seventh Idyll. Here, in the crucial if ideologically neutral meeting between Theocritus' own avatar in the poem, Simichidas, and the demonic goatherd, Lycidas, we see the genre itself placed in a realistic perspective. The crux of the episode is the engagement of the Theocritean persona in a singing-match with his bucolic counterpart by which he earns gifts that seem to endorse his own poetic authority. It is a kind of laying-on of hands, and it occurs halfway on the road (*tan mesatan hodon*) from town to the country estate of Simichidas' friends, a place whose material abundance symbolizes the gifts of nature to civilization.[12] The encounter at this juncture of the Pan-like, laughing herdsman and the urbane protagonist is very striking. When the songs have been sung and the gift of friendship bestowed, the former returns to his rustic pursuits, the latter to a feast in honor of Demeter.[13] Beyond the poem, the rites of a humanized nature will soon be consummated. But the poem itself is a literary rite of the "natural" man.[14]

This emphasis in Theocritus on a balanced conjunction of antithetical modes is both extended and refined by Vergil. The tension between reality and the pastoral convention in the *Bucolics* as a whole is epitomized in the ninth eclogue by the meeting of Lycidas and Moeris exactly halfway (*hinc adeo media est nobis via*) on the road to town.[15] Vergil is clearly drawing on the Theocritean example – hence his borrowing the name Lycidas – though he deepens the implications of the encounter both by having his singers go toward rather than away from the city and by giving more symbolic play to the Theocritean tomb that marks the spot.[16] Yet if here, as in Eclogue 10, Vergil's singers return in the end to the familiar comforts of town as the *umbrae* of night descend, the implicit denial of the possibility of total freedom in nature does not necessarily imply the end of pastoral song, i.e. of fashioning an ideal landscape of the mind. Vergil's handling of the *media via* motif reflects his view of pastoral in general. Eclogue 9 ends with a postponement of singing till the return of Menalcas. Though "time bears away all things, even memory," another singer is awaited who will renew the song. The immediate political circumstances, epitomized by Meliboeus' exile in Eclogue 1, undoubtedly cast a pall of anxiety over Vergil's various poet—personae in the *Bucolics*, as many commentators have observed. Yet song itself, it is implied, will survive even in Rome, and it remains psychologically rooted in the idealized Arcadian countryside. Despite his more sombre emphasis, Vergil is at one with Theocritus in holding that the recognition of realistic limits does not entail the rejection of the pastoral vision.[17] Vergil has added to the coherence and immeasurably deepened the resonance of his Alexandrian model, but he has not substantially altered the basic pastoral myth. The world of pastoral is an autonomous if precarious world of the speculative imagination. As we have seen, it textualizes an imaginative space to which the mind can withdraw, "annihilating" ordinary experience paradoxically both to nothing and to "thought" (as Marvell will have it), and from which it then returns to the quotidian emotional, cultural, and political contexts. It was invented by Theocritus, who found it no more capable of literal habitation than does Vergil.[18] For both poets, poetry is born in the limited freedom of the creative imagination symbolically located halfway on the road between a purely textual country and a "political" (or, to be precise, post- or megalopolitical) town.

The Shepheardes Calender fits securely into this Vergilian milieu. Despite its debts to the satirical–allegorical strain of Renaissance humanist pastoral – the tradition of Petrarch, Mantuan, and Googe – Spenser's overall conception of the mode is clearly "Arcadian."[19] His adoption of the calendar-motif, itself a medieval innovation, is frequently explained as a way of emphasizing the contrast between the biological cycle and the linearity of human life.[20] Since the only escape from this predicament is its imaginative transcendence, the work is said to move from pastoral simplicity (we go round like all of God's creatures) to heroic complexity (though physical beings, we are doomed to die and must therefore realize our spiritual destinies). There is certainly some warrant for this view of Spenser's poem. But to treat this rhythm as though it always and necessarily implied a repudiation of pastoral fantasy in the light of passion and death is to misconceive the nature of the mode.[21] Spenser, like Theocritus and Vergil, follows the ambiguous "royal" way of pastoral. For these poets Arcadia is the place where all paths meet, all lines of thought converge.

In the *Calender* that convergence takes place centrally in "June," the structural hinge or fulcrum of the work that appears to be its thematic centerpiece as well. Occurring virtually halfway through Spenser's calendar year, it is also the middle eclogue of three in which Colin appears in his principal role of thwarted lover, and is therefore the medial example of the Plaintive kind.[22] Significantly, it is the only one of the three in which Colin is not physically alone. "January" and "December" are more or less pure complaints. Though accompanied by single stanzas of anonymous narration, before and (in the case of "January") after Colin's monologues, there is no hint of dramatic action, no encounter with another character in either of them, but only the lovelorn shepherd's lament. In "June," however, the plaintive essence of *The Shepheardes Calender* is set forth in a carefully articulated dramatic dialogue between Colin and his chief foil in the work, Hobbinoll. I wish to suggest that as Theocritus divides his sympathies between Lycidas and Simichidas, and Vergil his between Moeris and Lycidas, so Spenser, projecting himself equally into Colin and Hobbinoll, forges an even balance between the forces of dissolution and those of continuing cohesion imaged in the fictive landscape.

The crucial encounter takes place in a classic pastoral setting. This setting in turn becomes a major vehicle for the theme of the eclogue, Colin's exile from Arcadian bliss as a result of unhappy love. The opening lines, spoken by Hobbinoll, at once evoke the traditional *locus amoenus*, the pleasance where two shepherds meet to sing:

> Lo *Colin*, here the place, whose pleasaunt syte
> From other shades hath weand my wandring mynde.
> Tell me, what wants me here, to worke delyte? (ll. 1–3)

The beckoning shades, the breezes singing to man's delight – beginning with the opening verses of Theocritus' Idylls these are the standard features of the pastoral place. True, the middle line raises the spectre of a self-deconstructing avowal of pastoral common-places: "wand[e]ring" may well imply the nostalgia and instability of a self-deluding mind, perennially seeking escape from reality, "annihilating all that's made." Yet the line itself is ambiguous enough to check any unequivocally skeptical reading. *This* green shade has "wean[e]d" the speaker's mind from "other shades," the verb declaring its own myth of maturation – a progressing to the One from the many? – to be weighed against Colin's "antipastoral" version later in the poem. In this Eden of priority, nature envelops the speaker and his friend in its music. Each item in the landscape, visual as well as aural, contributes its own note to the overall harmony, together constituting a concordance of the whole. For Spenser's audience, whose ears were well attuned to Platonic and Pythagorean ideas concerning music, this is enough to conjure up a pristine state in which the harmony of things is literally audible. The general tenor is that which Leo Spitzer (following Heidegger) finds implied in the untranslatable German word *Stimmung*: "the unity of feelings experienced by man face to face with his environment," something "fused with the landscape," which in turn is "animated by the feeling of man."[23] It is a quality that, from Vergil on, is inseparable from pastoral. Behind it, as we have seen, lies the philosophical genre of the contemplative life, rooted in a quest for just such an originary state.

In such a place Colin finds his friend, and Colin himself acknowledges it at once as "that Paradise...whych *Adam* lost" (l. 10). Its praises occupy much of the first half of the eclogue, in which Hobbinoll invites Colin to cast off his cares and enter into the "pierlesse pleasures" of a state in which nocturnal demons are banned and all is light and measure (l. 32). But against this conventional backdrop of pastoral harmony Colin identifies himself from the outset as an exile, deafened to these Arcadian concords by his own inner discord:

> Thy lovely layes here mayst thou freely boste.
> But I unhappy man, whom cruell fate,
> And angry Gods pursue from coste to coste
> Can nowhere fynd, to shroude my lucklesse pate. (ll. 13–16)

Spenser's reader would have no difficulty in identifying the ghost of Vergil's first eclogue that haunts this opening.[24] And if the melodramatic allusion to "angry Gods" seems to obtrude a heroic note into Colin's bucolic dismay, there is again a time-honored precedent in pastoral for the divine hounding of a shepherd to the boundaries of despair: the story of Daphnis in Theocritus 1, the archetypal hero–victim of pastoral's tragic underside, hounded to exile (and death) not by political change but by a mysterious reservation enfolded in his own psyche.

The bulk of "June" presents Colin's alienation through a continued debate with Hobbinoll. In answer to the latter's invitation to seek "harbrough [harbor]" in the pleasant valley, our hero can only recall his innocent childhood and the first, tragic stages of his love. This was the time when he too could hear and echo life's harmonies, which for him resolved the minor dissonances of love. The mention of song inspires Hobbinoll in turn to recall Colin's music in its grandest, most Orphic effects, when its echoes "made the neyghbour groves to ring, / And taught the byrds...[to] / Frame to thy songe their chereful cheriping, / Or hold theyr peace, for shame of thy swete layes" (ll. 52–6).[25] In the central stanzas of the poem he tells how the Muses themselves once forsook "theyr yvory Luyts and Tamburins" in deference to the "silver sound" of Colin's "oaten pype." But when they saw who it was that so outplayed them,

> They drewe abacke, as halfe with shame confound,
> Shepheard to see, them in theyr art outgoe.   (ll. 63–4)

These lines conclude the pastoral agon proper; the rest of the eclogue, save for a single concluding stanza, consists of Colin's final reply.

Though Colin pre-empts our attention in "June" with the story of his fall from pastoral innocence, it is Hobbinoll who ends the poem, as he began it, by asserting his own continuing state of grace. Having listened in sympathetic silence to Colin's long tale of woe, he devotes his final speech to a conventional end-of-the-day farewell that is also a quiet benediction on the pastoral milieu:

> But now is time, I gesse, homeward to goe:
> Then ryse ye blessed flocks, and home apace,
> Least night with stealing steppes doe you forsloe [delay],
> And wett your tender Lambes, that by you trace.
>
> (ll. 117–20)

Hobbinoll's parting words carefully close the frame on Colin's unhappy exile by emphasizing the unvarying felicity of the pastoral setting. And if the poem's opening lines evoke the beginning of Vergil's first eclogue, this closing stanza even more emphatically recalls the ending of his last, the lament for his friend Gallus (himself a type of Daphnis), cut off by love from the poet's own repose.[26] The echo is especially clear in the motif of returning home, sometimes taken to be Vergil's farewell to Arcadia: "ite domum saturae,... ite capellae" (*Ecl.* 10.77).[27] Vergil's lines, I will argue, are hardly as gloomy as they are often made out to be; but Spenser's, or rather Hobbinoll's, are if anything even more positive. Flush in the face of Colin's unhappiness, they reaffirm the "blessed" condition of his own flocks and, by a familiar pastoral metonymy, of their guardian:

> O carefull *Colin*, I lament thy case,
> Thy teares would make the hardest flint to flowe.
> Ah faithlesse Rosalind, and voide of grace,
> That art the roote of all this ruthfull woe.
> But now is time, I gesse...   (ll. 113–17)

Pastoral convention dictates that Hobbinoll show sympathy for his love-struck friend. But Hobbinoll has gone well beyond sympathy: he has virtually identified himself with Colin's "case" and (himself a kind of pastoral woods) echoed his passion. But he has not allowed that passion to destroy the general repose of which he is the poem's chief beneficiary and exemplar, just as Tityrus, reclining in his leafy shade, is that of Vergil's *Bucolics*. Hobbinoll's final speech re-establishes the pastoral's fundamental appreciation of man's natural sufficiency and of his ability to enter with ease into the full stream of life, even within the external or internal constraints imposed respectively by the political or the human situation.

Spenser's intention in all this is revealed in the gratuitous bit of "rhyming" that frames the poem. As we have seen, Colin's first speech in "June" begins with an acknowledgment of his friend's pastoral bliss:

> O happy *Hobbinoll*, I blesse thy state,
> That Paradise hast found, whych *Adam* lost.   (ll. 9–10)

Hobbinoll's answering line more than a hundred lines later completes this blessing by tying Colin's lamentable "case" to his own blessed state. The two key lines neatly contain the body of the poem, enclosing the main theme of Colin's exile in a mutual refrain of blessing and lament:

> O happy *Hobbinoll*, I bless thy state...
> O carefull *Colin*, I lament thy case.

Juxtaposed in this way, these salutations throw into relief the eclogue's internal balance, which is so characteristic of the pastoral tradition to which Spenser subscribes. Once the rhyme is heard, a deeper consonance emerges. Colin, the care-worn exile blasted by love, blesses the pastoral world and its changeless serenity; Hobbinoll, happy heir to that world, laments its loss by Colin. Each participates in the other's condition, taking its characteristic note into his own song. In the end, blessing and lament constitute a *discordia concors* on the theme of Arcadian happiness.

It is important to recognize this structural feature of "June" if we are not to misread the eclogue and, in turn, *The Shepheardes Calender*. Critics of the "antipastoral" persuasion are prone to view Colin as the voice of reality and ripe wisdom, courteously condescending to his still-innocent friend. Disillusioned by love, and no longer a naïve child of pastoral nature, Colin has put away childish things. In his fall from innocence he can only dream helplessly of those "carelesse yeeres" (l. 33) before sex, or allude by negation to the shepherd's proverbial ability to transmute love's losses to memorable song. But his very reiteration of these conventional motifs, it seems to me, serves to highlight the pastoral norms from which Colin has departed. The plot of "June," as we have seen, repeatedly alludes to the pastoral topos of easing love's pain through music. In Theocritus that topos is sometimes conveyed with a kind of homespun and obscene shrillness in the singing-match. But here the note is the true Arcadian one of Vergil's *Arcades ambo* (*Ecl.* 7.4). The shepherds are intimate, mutually responsive friends, and the lover is invited to cool his ardor with the consolations of song. In this case the therapy fails, and when Hobbinoll resumes his normal role in the end, we are all the more aware of what Colin has lost. A similar effect results from Colin's famous lament for his dead master, "Tityrus," who is praised, ironically, for having known how to "wayle hys Woes, and lightly slake / The flames, which love within his heart had bredd" (ll. 85–6). Whether he is blaming Rosalind or the absence of Tityrus for his own incapacities, Colin's complaint, like Hobbinoll's earlier reminiscence, reiterates the pastoral poet's normal function: to "learne these woods, to wayle my woe, / And teache the trees, their trickling teares to shedde" (ll. 95–6). As with his prototype, Orpheus, and as with Spenser's later pastoral sojourner, Calidore, love is the serpent that stings the shepherd into action and engenders song.

As a whole, therefore, "June" maintains the validity of pastoral song. This is the burden of what may be its best-known lines, those in which Colin recalls his destiny as pastoral singer in its more positive aspect, thus waking echoes that go back to Daphnis in Theocritus' first Idyll. In answer to Hobbinoll's vision of Colin triumphant over the Muses, Colin himself adopts the conventional modesty of the pastoral singer: "Of Muses *Hobbinol*, I conne no skill." He insists, moreover, that his personal contribution to the general concord has come from an impulse that is self-delighting:

> I never lyst presume to *Parnasse* hyll,
> But pyping lowe in shade of lowly grove,
> I play to please my selfe, all be it ill. (ll. 70–2)

As stricken lover, the pastoral shepherd must flood the landscape with the music of his pain. And when, like Tityrus or like Colin himself previously, he performs that role, his singing imposes itself on nature as a gift returned to its giver, so that the wild beasts flock to him and the woods resound. But Colin now is "not, as I wish I were," and at the end of his complaint he bequeaths his former function to happier shepherds who will "beare witnesse" to his fall and preserve his memory (ll. 105, 108). Though his career is presumed to be over, he becomes a source of inspiration to others who, in telling his story, will maintain the continuity of the pastoral community. And this of course is precisely what Hobbinoll proceeds to do in the speech that closes the poem.

Against Colin's defeat, I would argue, his exile from "paradise" at the height of the joyous season of fulfillment, must be weighed Hobbinoll's and, in a more devious way, Colin's own reaffirmation of the pastoral norm. This encounter informs the eclogue's internal composition, which focuses on a balance of opposing sentiments fused by mutual sympathy. Within the ambience of pastoral friendship, the meeting of Colin and Hobbinoll repeats those in Theocritus and Vergil between shepherds definitively divorced from Arcadian felicity by the forces of love or fortune and those able to preserve that felicity in their songs. Further, it mirrors the complicity of the latter with and their dependence on the former. In reaffirming the pastoral norm at the end of "June," Hobbinoll is complying with Colin's own wishes and carrying on the function originally his.

This aspect of their relationship is borne out by the eclogue's many classical echoes. Of these the most important is Colin's derivation from Vergil's Gallus, and behind him Theocritus' Daphnis. Although the opening exile theme recalls Tityrus and Meliboeus, Hobbinoll's farewell and return home with his "blessed flocks" evoke Vergil's elegy for Gallus. An important implication of this echo is that Spenser, unlike some modern commentators, has clearly grasped the limits of Vergil's artistic capitulation to the destructive conditions of life. There can be no doubt that Vergil registers fully his awareness of the forces, political and psychological, external and internal, that challenge the mind's thrust toward an imaginative/contemplative priority. Whether he believes that any such priority exists is a question we cannot consider here. But he does, both here and in his later poems, exercise the poet's presumed authority to resist these alien encroachments, as if overcoming their threats were possible. Similarly with Spenser. We saw that Hobbinoll insists on his own "blessed" condition in his address to his sheep. Vergil's epithet for *his* flock in Eclogue 10, *saturae*, satiated or fat (Rieu translates: "You have had your fill"), if slightly less subjective than Spenser's, nevertheless fully connotes the ripeness or sense of fruition that mitigates the tragedy of Gallus.[28] Hobbinoll's ultimate serenity incorporates the Vergilian affirmation of pastoral continuity despite the blows of fortune. Thus it registers Vergil's "gravis umbra" (10.76) as well the related "si nox pluviam ne colligat" of Eclogue 9. But it insists on keeping Colin's pathos in proper perspective.

In short, the dominant Vergilian resonance in *The Shepheardes Calender* is that of pastoral wholeness, a fundamental *concentus* of opposing views. To apply what may still be our most useful definition of pastoral, in *The Shepheardes Calender* Spenser tries to convey the complex intuition that "life is essentially inadequate to the human spirit, and yet a good life must avoid saying so" (Empson, *Some Versions*, p. 110). In pastoral, as Empson goes on to say, "you take a limited life and pretend it is the full and normal one." It is this pretense that makes Spenser's major personae avatars repectively of that archetypal satyr, Lycidas, or his offspring Tityrus – i.e. the pastoral singer as contented man – and of Daphnis or Meliboeus, noble sufferer and exile. Together these two types circumscribe Spenser's pastoral landscape; in their discordant harmony they compose their author's "generous distaste for the conditions of life."

II

To this Vergilian pastoral paradigm Spenser appends his personal signature. A great deal has been written about the intention of his calendar-form.[29] It is clear that the irregular alternation of kinds leads us through a circular tour from winter to winter but also progresses from a unique springtime to a wintry quietus. Thus Colin does and does not end where he begins. Spenser, on the other hand, as a novice poet in 1579 on the threshold of his public career, is suspended between the fellowship of dead poets and the lure of advancement through patronage. Like Fulgentius or Dante in more heroic contexts, he can summon the ghost of his spiritual father Vergil as a more maternal, nourishing presence to neutralize or placate those looming patriarchal figures, his potential patrons – much as Horace invokes his childhood Muses/doves to warrant an authentic vocation which protects the son of a freedman from the political powers that may deny the poet even so much as a name. The anonymous author of *The Shepheardes Calender* is both Colin Clout and Immeritó, i.e. content and aspiring. These paradoxes are formally circumscribed in Spenser's careful counterpointing of elements of progression and revolution, lines and circles, in his articulation of the work as a whole.

An overview of the *Calender* may be of some help here. The most linear of E.K.'s ranks is the Moral. Here the constant reiteration of a Mantuanesque or humanist admonitory note heightens their intrinsic hysteria as they march grimly from the youth–age skirmish of "February" to "May's" distrust of deception, "July's" overt iniquities, and the sad fall of Morrell in "September." Opposed to this linearity of paranoia and mistrust is the essential stability of Willye's radically pastoral ease in the Recreative eclogues. "March" and "August" preserve most faithfully the Arcadian pastoral's sense of timelessness in a contemplative space, although the latter is challenged but not defeated ("Vinto non vitto," Willye's Emblem) by Colin's plaintive sestina. Poised between the progressive and regressive or static attitudes of these kinds is the peculiar mixture of the two in the Plaintive triad: Colin, who enters the poem as old–young man, is still hopeful (at least in his Emblem) in "January," finds all hope spent in "June," and resigns himself to the exigencies of death in "December." This overview suggests that Spenser extends the *media via* balance of "June" to the other eclogues in the collection, where its fundamental classicizing poise informs the structure of the work as a whole. In order to give voice to his personal and cultural apprehensions and to make a qualified affirmation of his readiness to undertake the traditional obligations and risks of the poet's role, he adopts the inherent inner balance of Vergilian bucolic.

Naturally, the main focus of Spenser's self-dramatization in the *Calender* is Colin, whose exaggerated disablement by frustrated love in "June" I have shown to be offset by Hobbinoll's reaffirmation of pastoral sanity. In the first of the Plaintive eclogues, "January," Colin's deviation from the pastoral norm is suggested by his "reading" the sunny late-winter landscape as a wasteland and by his excessively tragic response to the Vergilian descent of evening. The prime model for Colin's love-plaint is Corydon's lament for Alexis in Eclogue 2. But Corydon's hard-won self-knowledge leads him to see nightfall as an admonition of his own protracted lunacy, whereas Colin, who has already implicitly rejected one aspect of the pastoral norm by breaking his pipe, tacitly enacts the deathlike aspect of sunset by leading his "sonned sheepe" back with "hanging heads" that mirror his own despair.[30] If Colin's Emblem ("Anchóra speme") seems to qualify this despair, abetting the narrator's sympathetic evocation of the pathetic fallacy in his closing observation, at the center of the eclogue Colin himself gives some hint of a more balanced outlook on his own plight. Just after he has projected his grief into the mild scene by turning the melting icicles into sympathetic tears, Colin anticipates the bless–lament rhyming of "June" by recalling his first encounter with Rosalind:

> A thousand sithes I curse that carefull hower,
> Wherein I longd the neighbour towne to see:
> And eke tenne thousand sithes I blesse the stoure,
> Wherein I sawe so fayre a sight, as shee.   (ll. 49–52)

The stanza ends with the hint of a healthy recognition of the true nature of love: "Ah God, that love should breede both joy and payne" (l. 54). At the heart of Colin's despair is the more adult perception that love, like most things, brings mixed effects, an insight subsequently drowned in the young man's self-indulgent grief.

While I do not agree with Harry Berger that Colin's attitude is intrinsically tied to that "pastoral milieu" and its generic psychological narrowness, it seems clear that the drift of the Plaintive sequence – excluding for the moment "November," which features Colin as singer rather than as pastoral lover and exile – parallels that of the Moral up to a point.[31] "December" repeats "January" not only in meter but in Colin's appearing *solus*, excluded from any possible solace by his pastoral better half, Hobbinoll, who in "June" had at least been able to share his sorrow and lament his case.[32] Colin again addresses his complaint to the shepherds' god, Pan, who in his "greene cabinet" is all the more a *deus absconditus* to Colin in his own wintry isolation. Colin's retrospective survey of his life turns the seasonal metaphors of the *Calender* into a clownish rehearsal of the Hellenistic Ages of Man. In spring a "heedlesse" youth, his unavailing love has taught him in summer the need to fortify himself against the ills of the world, an attitude half-mocked by another pastoralist, Robert Frost, in "Provide, Provide." Even so prepared, he finds his autumn harvest to be the falling of unripe fruit and the reaping of a "weedye crop of care," leaving him now old without ever having known the delights of youth and ready to hang up his pipe for the cold winds to "blaste."

Colin has changed from "January" to "December," but only in becoming the more himself, as the emergent voice of "January's" narrator, himself still anonymous, confirms by now giving him his name:

> A Shepeheards boye (no better doe him call)
>
> ("January," l. 1)

> The gentle shepheard satte beside a springe,
> . . .
> That *Colin* hight...   ("December," ll. 1,3)

The question of his own nomination still pending as the *Calender* ends, Spenser has projected into its structure this imperative of earning one's name. Whether the significance of Colin's name is purely textual – the sum of his attributes as revealed to us by the intervening poems – or intertextual – involving Spenser's debts to various precursors, including Skelton – its attribution here confirms the paradigmatic dimension of the *Calender* for its emergent poet.[33] In enacting his inherent character, Colin adumbrates the pessimism in the face of life's perils of his counterparts in the Moral eclogues. The sequence of this rank pivots around an increasingly exaggerated opposition of extreme points of view. In each case the eclogue turns on a public issue of the day and features a Colin-like shepherd, normally young and callow (the exception, "May," proves the rule by incorporating this type in its fable), who is vulnerable to a threatening world. Collectively, their tone approaches paranoia. Indeed, the very hysteria of these inadequately equipped shepherds militates against our accepting their attitudes as salutary; while their interlocutors, though sometimes cast as the official villains, always espouse plausible and sometimes even preferable positions. Finally, the series culminates in a return to a qualified Vergilian norm.[34]

In the first of the Moral eclogues, "February," Spenser keeps in focus the issue of a young man's learning to cope with life's complexities. E.K. introduces its theme as the intransigence of youth, but even he shares Cuddie's scorn of old Thenot's "crookedness and unlustinesse," as his reading of the Emblems bears out.[35] Of course Thenot is right in recognizing that the younger man makes trouble for himself by leaping at the first signs of spring, thus losing heart too soon when February's cold winds return (ll. 33–50). Yet despite his impatience, Cuddie is still a "springing youth" happy in his love for Phyllis. On what will be the central issue for Colin Clout, Thenot's stoical wisdom is of no use at all: to him "all that is lent to love, wyll be lost" (l. 70). This flat rejection of love seems as extreme in its way as the more political aspects of his fable of the oak and briar. If he is right in implying the folly of those ("upstart courtiers"?) who would begin their own rise by destroying their would-be protectors, there is more than a hint in his rhetoric of a blind sanctification of whatever is old and established:

> For it had bene an auncient tree,
> Sacred with many a mysteree,
> And often crost with the priestes crewe,
> And often halowed with holy water dewe.   (ll. 207–10)

We may suspect the specific malice of left-wing Protestant iconoclasm in this portrait of an over-inflated pillar of society, but we may also guess that in general Spenser endorses his younglings' impatience with the rigidity of their elders.

E.K. introduces "May" even less equivocally than he had done "February." In line with the announced "Satyrical bitternesse" of the Moral kind, he presents the poem as a straightforward piece of anti-Roman satire. Yet Palinode's echoing of the conventional opening of the spring eclogues – even old Thenot had begun "April" with a mild criticism of Hobbinoll's woefulness – affirms a reasonable human standard of innocent joy in the renewal of the year that makes Piers' assignment of such "follies" to "Younkers" seem prudish at best. Piers manages to redress the balance by turning our attention to ecclesiastical matters, thus tapping the presumed sympathies of a large part of Spenser's audience including his putative patron, Sidney. But in the final analysis Piers' fable conveys a paranoic fear of experience that bars the proffered "concord" of the innocent-seeming Palinode, whose very name implies a challenge to Piers: how can the pastoral song be sung in an atmosphere so clouded with mistrust? The overall balance of the eclogue is signalled by the perfectly matched word-play of the Emblems' half-lines from Theognis:

Palinodes Embleme
Pas men apistos apistei.

Piers his Embleme
Tis d' ara pistis apisto?

The untrustworthy man distrusts everything, observes Palinode; what faith in the faithless? replies Piers. The Greek construction *men/de*, as Spenser and his humanist-educated friends would know, confirms this perfect equivocality; even E.K. is content with paraphrase, adding coyly, "And thys is all that they saye," thereby completing the title's rhyme.

"July," on the other hand, reveals no comparable ambiguity. As E.K.'s brief Argument notes, it commends "good shepeheardes" like Thomalin and vituperates the "proude and ambitious" kind like Morrell. Once again the long central diatribe is put in the mouth of a somewhat hysterical young swain. But this time Thomalin's paranoia is harder to dismiss, partly because he can summon the late experience in Rome of no less a witness than Palinode to support his assault on pastoral "misusage." Against this testimony Morrell's scornful stock response carries little weight. But "July" also injects a new motif into the sequence of Moral eclogues, one borrowed from "June" and announced visually in the woodcut: that of high versus low places. In "June" the hills are associated with Colin's courtship of Rosalind (perhaps because she was from the north), while Hobbinoll claims the lowly Edenic dales. In "July" the aspiring hills become the emblem of Morrell's ecclesiastical presumption to affluence and power, Thomalin keeping to the site of traditional pastorly humility. This interpolation of the Mantuan-esque aspiration topos into an Arcadian context places the latter under a considerable strain. After all, as Morrell points out, hills *are* better for sheep, and in pastoral poetry shepherds normally take their innocent ease while their flocks roam about on hillsides. Thomalin may be in the right, but his stubborn rejection of the topographical conventions of Vergilian pastoral brings us closer to an irreparable breach between the Mantuanesque Moral eclogue and its Arcadian ancestry.

This possibility is, I believe, tacitly acknowledged in "September." The fourth of the Moral eclogues tempers the sharpening polarities of its predecessors and brings the Moral kind back into its original Vergilian–Arcadian ambience. On the level of action, "September" is the most extreme of the set. From the fabular warnings of Thenot and Piers, and the disillusionment of Palinode as reported by Thomalin, we arrive now at the dramatic presence of the defeated Diggon Davie, who narrates his own dissolution under the influence (in E.K.'s words) of the "loose living of Popish prelates." Diggon too recalls Colin Clout. Like Colin he has voluntarily exiled himself from the paradise of Hobbinoll, who is significantly his interlocutor here as well as Colin's in "June." His disillusionment with what he has seen and lost is premonitory of Colin's no doubt, though it is not until *Colin Clouts Come Home Againe* that we will see Colin, like Diggon, return home stung, embittered, and the wiser for it.

On the other hand, in place of the polarized interlocutors of "February," "May," and "July," Hobbinoll maintains the funda-mental balance of "June," in this paralleling Willye's stance in the Recreative eclogues as well. Recalling "June" also is the Vergilian dimension of Hobbinoll's role. In a sense Diggon Davie is a

Meliboeus type, one half of the primal pastoral pair of Eclogue I. Unlike Meliboeus, though, Diggon has brought about his own troubles by seeking to better his fortunes in a "farre countrye" (Argument). Hobbinoll's initial reaction to Diggon's plaint is less than generous. He flounders about searching for the right consolatory note, first urging Diggon to speak more plainly, then when he has caught the other's drift, warning him to be more circumspect and to accept the unavoidable vicissitudes of life. Hobbinoll has no consolation to offer for the injustices of the world toward Diggon. But as Tityrus had done with Meliboeus, he can offer his friend the modest "comfort" of his cottage until the latter's "Fortune" turns. In this resolution Spenser again displays a fundamental tact and poise, balancing the sympathy and sanity of the pastoral convention against the practical inadequacy of its traditional consolations. Once more he rescues the convention from discredit by tactfully acknowledging its inherent limits.

As A. C. Hamilton and Harry Berger have argued, the Plaintive and Moral eclogues both seem to be opposed in the *Calender* to the central "recreative impulse" (Berger) of "literary self-delight and aesthetic detachment."[36] Against the parallel extremisms of the poems we have just examined is set the Recreative restraint of "March" and "August." In both eclogues this restraint is provided by Willye, pitted in "March" against Thomalin, in "August" Perigot, both of them parodies of Colin who receive solace for their love-pangs from the inscrutable Willye.

In "March" Willye's function centers on his vicarious participation in Thomalin's clownish *innamoramento*. Spenser establishes Thomalin as an inexperienced youth whose naïve hostility toward Love will lead to his downfall. Like Colin he lacks the maturity to cope with his state. But like the Colin of "June" rather than that of "January" or "December," Thomalin is not alone. Cast in the Hobbinoll role of sympathetic listener, Willye urges his partner to tell his tale and then comments on it, avowing "pittie [for his] plight" (l. 103). Their essential concord is stressed in the Vergilian closure of hastening homeward under nightfall, and in their complementary Emblems. Both speakers reaffirm the ambivalence toward love of Colin's one insight in "January": love is honey and gall, and excludes wisdom. The recreative balance of "March" is buttressed by the hint of Willye's own innocence. Even he knows Love only from his father's report of a similar tussle, and on that occasion the god was unarmed.

Willye's stabilizing role is elaborated in "August" by the addition of that quintessential pastoral topos, the singing-contest, the only instance of it in the work. If Perigot parodies Colin ("whilom thou was peregall to the best," Willye reminds him, l. 8) in that his pastoral felicity is threatened by Love, Willye succeeds, as Hobbinoll had failed to do with Colin in "June," in prodding the love-struck shepherd into song. It is through the hilarious "undersong" by which Willye mimics and thus exorcizes Perigot's love-languors that he achieves this act of fraternal consolation, jibing him out of his doldrums with the clownish lilt of their rollicking roundelay, and arriving in the end (as Cuddie's judgment attests) at an Arcadian concord of kindred spirits. In this respect "August" may be read as the ultimate comic distillation of Vergilian pastoral in *The Shepheardes Calender*. There are indeed echoes of Theocritus in the poem, as E.K. notes, in the description of Willye's cup as well as in the conventional third shepherd as judge of a singing-contest designed to relieve the pangs of a shepherd in distress. But it is the amoebaean song itself, an essentially original invention, and particularly the irrepressible Willye's absurd rhymings and baffling rhythms, that make "August" such a sheer delight:

> PERIGOT. It fell upon a holly eve,
> WILLYE. hey ho hollidaye,
> PER. When holly fathers wont to shrieve:
> WIL. now gynneth this roundelay.
> PER. Sitting upon a hill so hye
> WIL. hey ho the high hyll,
> PER. The while my flocke did feede thereby,
> WIL. the while the shepheard selfe did spill. (ll. 53–60)

As in "March," this shambling tune makes havoc of the earnest narration of an *innamoramento*.

Answering this roundelay are the lugubrious sonorities of Colin's sestina, the consummation of Spenser's pastoral *poésie à écho*, the passionate shepherd's cry that fills all nature with song, reducing the variegated tones of the phenomenal world to a monochrome of self-reflexive textuality.[37] The reigning pathos of the genre, as well as its traditional links to the landscape, are suggested by five of the sestina's key end-words – *woe, crye, sound, part,* and *sleepe.* The sixth, *augment,* re-enforces the essential action of the poem, in which repetition equals amplification, and inner and outer states of alienation magnify each other exponentially. Does this "shrieking," "silvery," echoing sound drown out the lighter music of Perigot and Willye? As Touchstone might say, let the forest judge. Just as the Plaintive triad of "January," "June," and "December" may strike some readers as dominating the structure of *The Shepheardes Calender* as a whole, so here the formal complaint may seem to put to rout the purely ludic roundelay. There is a certain parallel here with "June" as well. Whereas there Hobbinoll is induced to "lament [the] case" of Colin Clout, here the love-struck Perigot, whom Willye was to cure of his "fond fantsies," is constrained in the end to "admire ech turning of [Colin's] verse." On the other hand, just as Hobbinoll in "June" makes it clear that he, and with him the pastoral world, will endure in spite of Colin's fall, so Willye in "August" tacitly excludes himself from the chorus of applauders of Colin's sestina.[38]

But there is really no need to crown a victor in this debate. As usual, the pastoralist will have it both ways if he can. The two songs in "August" deal with love, the traditional threat to pastoral joys, in a recreative manner: the roundelay by its joyous patter, the sestina by its erotic sublime. In this contrast they represent different modes of the Arcadian spirit, both implicit in the bucolic genre from the outset. I might, anticipating the argument of chapter 3, label these modes (or moods) comic and pastoral, if doing so did not implicitly privilege the element of solemnity in the latter. But however one calls them, in their diverse ways both achieve the same end: to repair in the dimension of music the rent fabric of human experience. Thus even while adapting his Vergilian model to a medieval and Christian form, Spenser reaffirms the ancient function of pastoral song.

III

The three eclogues remaining to be discussed – one ("November") E.K.'s favorite, the others the favorites of most of the rest of us – appear to stand outside the principal kinds identified in the General Argument, despite E.K.'s assigning them each to one of those ranks: "April" (implicitly) to the Recreative, "October" to the Moral, and "November" to the Plaintive. What sets them apart is their unusually reflexive content, their heightened consciousness of genre. "April" and "November" feature the chief specimens of Colin's art in the major pastoral kinds of panegyric and elegy; "October" furnishes the main discussion of the social role of the poet. One might say that the Recreative and Plaintive members of this triad constitute the praxis, and the Moral member the theory of Spenser's pastoral muse.

In terms of the present argument, the most important of these poems is "October," but the other two cannot be ignored. "April," which has been written about so admiringly, obviously recreates that unviolated state of pastoral felicity to which Hobbinoll will allude in "June," as well as recreating, by textualizing, the Queen as its authorizing and enabling Presence. Here we see Colin – or rather hear him, for he has absented himself from the poem's present, which is therefore already past to him – at a time when he is not yet stricken by love, performing his indispensable ceremonies of praise. Chief among the latter is his metamorphosing "*Eliza*, Queene of shepheardes," not only into the more prosaic and homely "*Elisa*," but into song itself, the offspring of Pan and Syrinx:

> For shee is *Syrinx* daughter without spotte,
> Which *Pan* the shepheards God of her begot...

> *Pan* may be proud, that ever he begot
>   such a Bellibone,
> And *Syrinx* rejoyse, that ever was her lot
>   to beare such an one.   (ll. 50–1, 91–4)

She is the very music, as well as the Muse, of a mythic love transmuted to art. At the same time, proleptically this eclogue makes the most positive Vergilian bid in the entire work to place the poet himself in the pastoralized social world of his audience. Having made Eliza into Elisa, he bids her "ryse up...decked as thou art / in royall aray" (ll. 145–6).

These "flowers" (the normal Elizabethan term for the devices of rhetoric) are those magically constituted by the singer himself in this most sonorous of Elizabethan flower-poetry and these most sinuous of the *Calender*'s verses. Colin has dressed his beloved Elisa much as Florizel will "prank up" Perdita and Spenser himself will "duly have...dect" his bride in the *Epithalamion*, the latter an important displacement from the public to the private sphere which will occupy us shortly (see chapter 6). But in the present work, it is precisely the distinction between poetic texture and political context that Spenser is attacking. As we shall see in chapter 4, the tapestry in *Muiopotmos* reduces the figure of the poet to the butterfly enmeshed in a text of another's weaving, ambiguously conceding ultimate authority, even "poetic" or recreative authority, to the spider, emblematic of goddesses and queens, wielders of political power. Later still, in *Amoretti* 71, the poet allows himself to be cast as the cunning spider waiting to "snare" the hapless bee but, miming the paradox of erotic surrender, now inscribed by the lady herself in her pastorally adorned "drawen work."[39] But at the present stage of Spenser's exploration of the poet's social function, there is little to suggest any such self-conscious paradoxicality. If Elisa is "decked...in royall aray," this betokens no original act of creation by her poet, but only a secondary re-creation of her prototype "as thou art," i.e. "royall." She *is* the

> Queene of shepheardes all:
> Which once he made, as by a spring he laye,
> And tuned it unto the Waters fall.   (ll. 34–6)

Despite Hobbinoll's ambiguous syntax, it is only "his laye" (i.e. *her* lay, l. 33) and not "*Eliza*" that Colin has made. Indeed, as the last line quoted implies, the act of re-creating or re-presenting Eliza in the flowers of verse is analogous to "tuning" his song to that of an originary nature. But in this case, as we have seen, Eliza herself, daughter of Pan and Syrinx, is Song.

This self-conscious display of Colin's self-negating pastoral artistry is framed by allusions on the part of the actual personae of the poem, Thenot and Hobbinoll, to his disastrous love. Hobbinoll, referred to slightingly by Colin in "January," here first appears in the *Calender* as the friend turned "frenne [enemy]" from whom Colin's affections have been "alienated" by Rosalind (Argument). In the end the two speakers join in a litany of regrets at the cost to poetry of Colin's "folly" in loving what he "cannot purchase," namely Rosalind. The issue is defined as a conflict between the public and private aspects of the pastoral myth, and the former is clearly favored. We may recall that in "June" Colin will deny the "Muses" but affirm his own self-delight. "April" states the antithesis by showing us the fertility of his muse as against the blighted sterility of his affections. Moreover, even within Colin's song Rosalind herself is granted an honorable place in the celebration of Elisa as a fourth Grace in the ceremonial dance around the shepherds' Queen and her piping swain:

> Lo how finely the graces can it foote
> >   to the Instrument:
> They dauncen deffly, and singen soote,
> >   in their meriment.
> Wants not a fourth grace, to make the daunce even?
> Let that rowme [space, place] to my Lady be yeven:
> >   She shalbe a grace
> >   To fyll the fourth place,
> And reigne with the rest in heaven.   (ll. 109–17)

We will see this situation significantly altered in Book 6 of *The Faerie Queene*, where the same Fourth Grace now *supplants* the Queen. But in "April" it is at best a modest secondary authority, derived from the only authentic subject–object of the poet's song, Eliza, that can earn Colin's lady a place in "heaven." In every sense, therefore, "April" represents the apex of Spenser's pastoral myth in *The Shepheardes Calender*: a wholly pastoralized community in which love and poetry thrive, with the Queen as its center and source and the poet its priest and chief celebrant.[40]

Colin's role in "November" is equally conventional. The pastoral elegy, like the panegyric, is a vehicle for giving ceremonial form and therefore a public voice and place to private sorrow.[41] Nevertheless, the unique appearance here of Colin as a singer in the formal sense – his songs in "April" and "August" are sung by others in his absence and against a chorus of comments on his wasting – helps to draw the *Calender* towards its final closure on the note of Colin's personal alienation from the pastoral world and the loss of his former place in it. Colin can sing publicly of death and achieve the elegy's normal resignation to it because he is himself on the way to identifying death as the only certain goal of life. "November" not only duplicates "December" in E.K.'s ranking; it is its appropriate public prelude.

This is perhaps why Spenser chooses to include in the collection an elegy on the death not only of a private person – and a young one – but of someone who, if she is a historical personage at all, is so unimportant in the world that even E.K. must confess her identity to be "altogether unknowne" to him (Argument). Unlike Vergil's fifth eclogue, in which the pattern of lamentation and resignation terminates in the apotheosis of Daphnis (presumably Julius Caesar), to become a guiding light to the bereaved community, "November" finds consolation for life itself in the "joyfull" discovery that there is no "assurance" in earthly things. At the heart of Colin's dirge is a profound ambivalence. Early on he can utter the banality, "Now is time to dye." But although his struggle with the fact of untimely death brings him beyond this facile posturing, it is notable that Colin has no words outside his song once it is done. In response to Thenot's conventional praising of that effort, Colin is silent. If his "woe is wasted" here, in the next eclogue his life and youth are equally so. It is not only an arrested and stunted pastoral world to which "November" and "December" bid farewell, but all "earthly things, and slipper hope / Of mortal men" (ll. 153–4). Nowhere do we have any sense that Colin has been reconciled to life, even a life that includes the recognition of death.

"April" and "November," then, embody the two poles of Colin's public function as a poet. And one could infer that Spenser is making full use of the linear aspect of the calendar-form to exhibit his hero's "progression" from an ideal of pastoral community, in which he shares his public recreation of the Queen, to a narrowed focus on the individual's spiritual destiny that renders the idea of an earthly community, even one constituted by the consolations of song, all but irrelevant. The key to this putative development in the *Calender*'s tone and attitude is "October." Here, it has been persuasively argued, a panoply of obstacles is displayed barring the young poet from fulfilling his traditional social role.[42] That Cuddie is in some sense a parodic counterpart to Colin seems beyond reasonable doubt, though whether E.K. utters his famous phrase of characterization – "the perfecte paterne of a Poete" ("October" Argument) – without irony is at least questionable.[43] But more importantly, Spenser has doubly distanced himself from Cuddie, first by substituting him for Colin, whose future is the real issue of the poem, and then by letting him play out his serious ideological position with an increasingly comic accent. The net effect is to make the case against a satisfying poetic career under current conditions while at the same time humorously cajoling those who have the authority to settle the matter into complying with the poet's aspiration to place. In short, while it is true that Spenser acknowledges the obstacles to his own advancement, he ties that advancement to the possibility of (morally) right reading, appealing to any potential Maecenas around to step in and fulfill the *Calender*'s Vergilian paradigm.

From the outset, Spenser hints at Cuddie's serio-comic relation to Colin Clout. Like Thenot in "November," Piers exhorts Cuddie to "hold up thy heavye head" and help pass the time with cheering songs. But whereas Colin's poetic blight results from his unhappy love, Cuddie is wearied and silenced by sheer lack of recognition – one of many touches in the work that imply that Colin's love-sickness is a cipher for a different kind of disease.[44] Everywhere else in the *Calender* we are invited to view Colin's difficulties in terms of a wholly private grief barring him from an advancement that otherwise awaits his bidding. In "June," for example, Colin's assertion of the "metarecreative" motif of self-delight in the face of Hobbinoll's exhortation to pursue his Muse underscores the private/public antinomy in the poem and connects the idiosyncratic choice of the private sphere with the aberrant Colin's wasteful love. By contrast, in the paradise of Hobbinoll, the poet's natural function is not (*pace* Berger) merely self-delighting; it is fulfilled in the wholly pastoralized celebration of the larger community epitomized by the "April" lay, centering in the worship of the Queen.

In "October," however, through the mediation of the clownish Colin-clone, Cuddie, Spenser considers the possibilities for a poet *not* isolated from his vocation by a disabling love. As Helgerson has observed, Spenser quite candidly details these external barriers, rooted in the state of Elizabethan society itself.[45] The poet cannot live on the praise of his peers; yet those able to reward him furnish neither patronage nor the material for the traditional heroic and amatory genres. There seems to be no social ground for a worthy public poetry:

> But after vertue gan for age to stoupe,
> And mighty manhode brought a bedde of ease,
> The vaunting Poets found nought worth a pease,
> To put in preace emong the learned troupe.
> Tho gan the streames of flowing wittes to cease,
> And sonnebright honour pend in shamefull coupe. (ll. 67–72)

Piers counters with the suggestion that Cuddie turn his "aspyring wit" from "Princes pallace" to "heaven." Cuddie replies that this is more Colin's forte, and it is indeed what the latter seems to do in "November." But at this point "October" takes a new tack, as Piers and Cuddie debate the place of love in a poet's psychic landscape. The tone becomes increasingly comic as this dispute goes on, but the question is of course central to Colin's story. Both speakers recognize true poetry as an aspiring art. The issue is whether love imps or clogs a poet's wings. Piers espouses Spenser's own doctrine of heroic love as it is stated in *The Faerie Queene* and elsewhere: "For lofty love doth loath a lowly eye" (l. 96). Love, according to this view, is a metaphysical quality, radiating from Eliza herself, whose presence will transform Elizabeth's courtiers into Gloriana's knights, and her lowly pastoral poet into one of her bards. Cuddie's Love is the "Tyranne" of Colin's experience, and in keeping with his jaundiced view of the contemporary cultural climate he waxes ironic about the current requirements for soaring poesy – "The vaunted verse a vacant head demaundes" (l. 100) – and closes out the debate with his unintended parody of the fashionable poetic frenzy fueled by "*Bacchus* fruite." In this, as in other contestations in the *Calender*, the "right" values are not all on one side. Cuddie's penetrating critique of the present conditions for public poetry is enough to certify Spenser's sense of realism about his dilemma. The point is that even as he voices his doubts through Cuddie, the poet craftily undermines his doubting persona, thereby allowing his affirming persona to reap the benefit of Spenser's doubts. The "perfecte paterne of a Poete" becomes a perfect poetic windbag.

Spenser's trilogy of eclogues on poetry and its present state rounds out his treatment of his own poetic novitiate in *The Shepheardes Calender*. Behind the smokescreen of Colin's self-alienating, aspiring love lie the social ills that complicate the worthy poet's normal Vergilian progression toward at least a modest niche in the halls of power. Spenser makes unmistakably clear his apprehension of these external obstacles, even as the apparatus of the *Calender* announces his suit for recognition and bid for preferment. Spenser's carefully mediated ambivalence on this crucial issue of the poem is in keeping with its lesser ambiguities; as always, he tries to have it both ways. On the one hand, the poet is a mere private individual, nameless and placeless, and therefore "base begot with blame" like his works ("To His Booke"). On the other, he brings to his prospective audience the entire legacy of learned poetry celebrated throughout the pastoral tradition, including its associations with and claims on behalf of the *vita contemplativa*. That audience has given evidence of being incapable of either seeing themselves idealized as exemplars of heroic virtue or providing patrons to the poets who would thus portray them. Yet they can by recognizing and rewarding Immeritó rectify the latter fault, and by listening to and learning from his poems supply the lack of virtue as well.

The Shepheardes Calender utilizes the complexities and ambivalences of pastoral to state Spenser's claim to public recognition. Clearly, the work harbors a deeply felt suspicion that the poet must write for himself, that his true fruition is inseparable from private emotional satisfactions. Yet for all his realistic doubts concerning the possibility or even desirability of social and professional advancement, in creating the "new Poete" Spenser issues a qualified and supremely poised advertisement of the role he wants to play. It is a bid addressed with the requisite mixture of humility and aplomb. Containing both a plea and a promise, on balance the *Calender* reasserts the Vergilian poet's confidence that poetry can provide a secure ethical foundation for public and private virtue, and that without the poet the commonwealth will thrive uneasily at best. As he strove to justify that confidence in the first books of his heroic poem, that other Vergilian paradigm – the allegorical epic as the record of a philosophical quest – was to emerge on the surface of his intention.

3

The Faerie Queene (1590)

Spenser had already at least begun *The Faerie Queene* when he was formally introduced to his public in *The Shepheardes Calender*.[1] The question facing us here, therefore, is not of a "development" in his use of pastoral in the former work but rather of incorporating the major generic myth of the *Calender* into his heroic poem. It is a question already implicit in the *Calender* itself and explicit in "October," where the fundamental ideality and surface simplicity of pastoral come up against the complex resistances to a serious moral art inherent in Elizabethan courtly culture. How this tension is resolved by Spenser in the first installment of *The Faerie Queene*, published in 1590 during his brief return to England, is the focus of the present chapter.

That Spenser intends his reader to be aware of a continuity between his pastoral and epic works is indicated by the first stanza of *The Faerie Queene*:

> Lo I the man, whose Muse whilome did maske,
>   As time her taught, in lowly Shepheards weeds,
>   Am now enforst a far unfitter taske,
>   For trumpets sterne to chaunge mine Oaten reeds,
>   And sing of Knights and Ladies gentle deeds;
>   Whose prayses having slept in silence long,
>   Me, all too meane, the sacred Muse areeds
>   To blazon broad emongst her learned throng:
> Fierce warres and faithfull loves shall moralize my song. (1.Pr.1)

Echoing the vocabulary of "October" and "June," this introduction, self-consciously Vergilian despite the mediating echoes of Ariosto's *Orlando Furioso*, conjures up the unfulfilled anonymous poet of the *Calender*, whose individual character is masked in conventional trappings and who puts on the pastoral tradition at the prudent bidding of time while awaiting recognition and a name. In addition to the dissembling repudiation of his "Muse" in "June," the stanza echoes the ambiguous challenge of "October" to revive heroic poetry in far from heroic times. "Enforst" (by whom or what?) to exchange his bucolic pipe for epic trumpets, the humble singer undertakes to pursue the twin themes of public celebratory verse urged by Piers on Cuddie: "bloody Mars," the work of "those that weld the awful crowne" ("October," ll. 39–40), and, in the slacker interstices of heroic action, "love and lustihead" (l. 51). Like the *Calender*, the opening stanzas of *The Faerie Queene* entertain the notion of the poet's heroic effort to revive past glories by taking on the burden of epic verse, despite a temperament implicitly more suited to pastoral.

What lies behind the exercise in *occupatio* entailed in his use of the *humilitas* trope? As many readers have sensed, it is the anxiety of Spenser's renewed bid for recognition, this time despite his removal from court and without the benefit of the conventional dissimulated humility of pastoral.[2] In the 1590 *Faerie Queene*, Spenser makes an intense effort to incorporate the pastoral myth into his heroic poem.[3] As in the *Calender*, the fundamental tension between the two modes, and between their respective points of view, remains; but now it is – I suggest deliberately – folded into the texture of the poem. That tension has its roots in the dialectic of the active and contemplative lives, as dramatized in the choice of the public versus the private arenas, a dialectic which, as we have seen, was well recognized in Vergilian allegoresis as intrinsic to epic poetry. Spenser's overall solution in the first installment is to portray a continuity between the rival claims by implying that the contemplative life is the indispensable foundation, if not indeed the end, of the active. In effect, he makes a case for his own activity as a poet as the informing source of heroic virtue in love and war.

This intention, however, is not realized without strain – if indeed it is realized at all. For one thing his first hero, the "clownish" Red Cross Knight (the epithet is Spenser's in the Letter to Raleigh), is himself something of a tyro and, like his precursors in the *Calender*, evinces a strong streak of paranoia that runs counter to the basic pastoral openness. Hence one of the contending impulses in Spenser's pastoral economy is channeled into Redcrosse's adolescent encounters with life, and especially with the world of delusive appearances. To a large extent Book I tells the story of how the urge to heroic action must be mitigated and refined by the visionary insights of contemplation, ultimately the poet's. Book 3, on the other hand, begins by assuming the epiphanic perceptions of the transcendentals that underwrite human action. With its focus on the more intimate, especially the sexual side of the struggle, it forges a new role for pastoral. By the end of the installment, Spenser has worked out a fusion of heroic and pastoral modes that implicitly promotes the importance of poetry as a vehicle for retrieving and anatomizing the fundamental motions of the spirit, and locating them within the normal constraints of civilization. The 1590 *Faerie Queene* therefore constitutes Spenser's most ambitious and hopeful claim for poetry's contribution to the community of readers: that its ceremonies of innocence sanction that community's highest collective ends.[4]

I

After his modest début, the narrator of *The Faerie Queene* quickly merges into the conventional apparatus of epic invocation, culminating in his address to Elizabeth (Pr.2–4). With the book's protagonist the story is different. Redcrosse, like his author, is a novice facing the challenges of the "world." Although his clownish demeanor is not linked to his humble origins at this point in the narrative, it is apparent from the outset that he is an inexperienced and awkward youth, vulnerable to various unspecified pitfalls but of an earnest nature, like so many of his ilk in the *Calender*, that betokens difficulties in negotiating even the simplest turnings in his road:

> Right faithfull true he was in deede and word,
> But of his cheere did seeme too solemne sad...   (1.2)

The forthrightness and *corage* are part of his equipment too, so that it is not surprising that this naïf is the antithesis of the typical worthies of the day ironically characterized by Piers in "October": those "doubted Knights, whose woundlesse armour rusts, / And helmes unbruzed wexen dayly browne" (ll. 40–2). Elizabethan chivalry there is shown to be "doubted" indeed (dubious as well as redoubtable), and the rusty, woundless armor epitomizes its dormancy. By contrast, Redcrosse too is an untried knight, but by reason of his youth. Like Immeritó and *The Faerie Queene* narrator (though not now its author), our hero appears on the scene nameless. Symbolic of an honorable legacy, *his* arms, as yet distinct from the man, display the "old dints of deepe wounds" sustained in his predecessors' battles. Though a novice warrior himself, he carries a concrete testimony to the tradition of heroic activity he is about to enter into. When he has completed his initiation and is about to fulfill his quest, this anonymous tyro will have cast off the generic sobriquet of the Knight of the Red Cross and earned his specific identity as St. George, *geourgos*, the heroic man of earth.

Such a consummation seems unlikely enough in the light of Redcrosse's basic character. Much of his story in Book I, in a sense virtually all of it, turns on his struggle with his own nature. If Redcrosse shares the clownish innocence of his prototypes in *The Shepheardes Calender*, they are traits not easily accommodated to the kinds of experience he will undergo in pursuing his appointed task, a problem Milton will palpably wrestle with in *Paradise Lost*. Rather, at least up to canto 10, they suggest the blunders and painful moral education read from Fulgentius to Landino in Aeneas' allegorical journey "home." Specifically, in order to qualify himself as an active warfarer against spiritual evil, he must undergo a voyage into, and beyond, the *vita contemplativa*, which is at the same time a journey into self-knowledge and an *itinerarium mentis in Deum*. The naïveté of Colin in the Plaintive eclogues, or of Cuddie, Piers, and Thomalin in the Moral, whether confronting complexities of the heart or of politics, when translated out of the pastoral arena dooms its possessor to distress or despair. So it is with Redcrosse. His initial encounter with Error is essentially a young man's initiation into the difficulties of "reading" the deceptively simple road-signs of the moral life, and in the half-light at that. His boast that "Vertue gives her selfe light" (1.12) is belied by the "litle glooming light, much like a shade" cast by his armor (1.14). Though successful in the end, he exposes the weakness of an overconfident inexperience, as Una's more cautious admonitions let us know:

> Be well aware, quoth then that Ladie milde,
>   Least suddaine mischiefe ye too rash provoke:
>   The danger hid, the place unknowne and wilde,
>   Breedes dreadfull doubts...   (1.12)

But the knight does prevail, and it is one of his humblest qualities, the innate fear of shame manifest in his answer to Una, that ultimately sustains him.

This inherent sense of dignity is brought out at the low point in his battle with Error, when Redcrosse is beset by her noxious odors and foul offspring. The knight is likened to a shepherd at sunset attacked by gnats and brushing them off "with his clownish hands":

> Thus ill bestedd, and fearefull more of shame,
>   Then of the certaine perill he stood in,
>   Halfe furious unto his foe he came.   (1.24)

For Redcrosse, heroic fury is a direct expression of his "shame." In Spenser's view, the pastoral figure is justified because a critical component of his hero's fortitude is precisely that which he owes to his innate simplicity. Redcrosse is not threatened by the intricacies of error; to him its manifestations are a mere annoyance. It is the shame of defeat or of retreat that arouses his ire and brings him quickly to success. Even Una is slightly amazed that such temerity can succeed (1.27).[5]

On the other hand, the defect of such a virtue is self-evident, and Spenser takes some pains to portray his hero as possessing humility without self-understanding. Redcrosse soon finds himself in more tricky interior mazes which he cannot so readily fight his way out of. Again Spenser reminds us of the extreme pastoral simplicity of his knight, now with Duessa on the edge of Fradubio's wood, when he evokes the type of wary shepherd from which Redcrosse has departed, who "often there aghast / Under them never sat, ne wont there sound / His mery oaten pipe, but shund th'unlucky ground." But Redcrosse, "soone as he them can spie, / For the coole shade him thither hastly got... / There they alight, in hope themselves to hide / From the fierce heat, and rest their weary limbs a tide" (2.28–9). As in the moral eclogues of the *Calender*, wariness does seem called for in these treacherous circumstances – Redcrosse has already of course fallen prey to his ignorance of his own sexual nature in the scene in Archimago's hut – and Spenser proposes no alternative between the opposed extremes of naïveté and constant dread. As he and Duessa enact the pastoral topos of seeking refuge from the noonday sun, the first eerie cries of Fradubio introduce an episode that reveals to everyone but Redcrosse himself the trap into which his innocence has betrayed him.[6] From here to the House of Pride and Orgoglio's dungeon is a swift and apparently inescapable path, from which his total redemption will require instruction in the art of spiritual or mystical contemplation.

Like the risks of simplicity, the perils attending pastoral otium are a hallmark of Book 1. Indeed, the pathos of Spenser's initiating hero arises from our sense of his oscillation between an almost hysterical chivalric drive and a compensating desire for ease. Over and over again the latter, the impulse to accept one's nature and the limited conditions of life, leads to catastrophe. The tendency is especially apparent in Spenser's treatment of the rest-motif. We saw earlier that not only does Christian pastoral incorporate the pagan motif of a restorative shady refuge from the heat of the noonday sun, but the poetry of late antiquity frequently applauds the seeking of a temporary haven from the labors of the active life. Spenser himself will employ these topoi repeatedly in Book 6. Yet in this most Christian of "legends," involving the most earnest of his laborious knights, the urge to escape the heat of activity and seek haven in a cool pleasance repeatedly brings Redcrosse to new levels of impotency and defeat.[7] Worse yet, the action of the poem suggests that he is most vulnerable to the lure of this natural desire when he has been most faithfully executing his heroic vocation. For example, though he may share unwittingly the chivalric pridefulness of Lucifera's castle, as suggested by his obeisance to that queen following his conquest of Sansjoy (5.16), he does defeat his adversary. He has tried to do what is perhaps impossible: to maintain contempt for the court's extravagant display while still pursuing their common ideal of glory.[8] Not fully comprehending the source of his self-differentiation from these specious external images of heroism, he allows his conduct to negate the differences. The ideal *vita activa* still lacks its foundation in a Christian humanist version of the *vita contemplativa*.

In any case, it is precisely following his eleventh-hour escape from this dilemma, in a moment of spiritual triumph, that Redcrosse falls prey to the need for solace and rest. Duessa finds him unarmed beside a fountain, in a pastoral *locus amoenus* replete with "cooling shade," "trembling leaves," and the "sweet musick [of birds], to delight his mind" (7.3).[9] There

> they gan of solace treat,
> And bathe in pleasaunce of the joyous shade,
> Which shielded them against the boyling heat,
> And with greene boughes decking a gloomy glade,
> About the fountaine like a girlond made. (st. 4)

"Pourd out in loosnesse on the grassy grownd" (st. 7), Redcrosse is as ignominiously taken capitive by Orgoglio as is Verdaunt when Guyon rescues him from the hot clutches of Acrasia in 2.12.

Spenser will revert once more to the rest-motif, which signifies an unredeemed conception of *otium*, before he finally achieves a temporary resolution of the problem in the cantos of Redcrosse's illumination. In many ways the Despair episode mirrors that of Error with which it frames the narrative of the hero's downfall. Once again, accompanied by Una, Redcrosse enters a dark place to test himself prematurely against an elusive foe. But this time he is much reduced from the cocky novice of canto 1, whereas his adversary embodies his own deepest flaws.[10] Given the fall from innocence that Redcrosse has undergone, it is no great feat for Despair to probe the self-doubt at the core of Redcrosse's Calvinist consciousness. But Spenser also connects this spiritual malaise with the tension throughout the story between the young knight's desire for heroic exploits and his residual attraction to retreat and rest. In "February" the weathered Thenot observes that Cuddie's over-eager desire for release from winter's rigors fosters further impatience with the world's ways. Likewise Redcrosse, who has too often blindly set himself tasks beyond his present powers to endure, now reveals a part of himself that has always sought refuge in oblivion and the cessation of effort. The promise of this consummation all but conquers the knight. Despair croons:

> He there does now enjoy eternall rest
>   And happie ease, which thou doest want and crave...
>   Sleepe after toyle, port after stormie seas,
> Ease after warre, death after life does greatly please.   (9.40)

Once again, this time with Una's active intervention, Redcrosse escapes, to embark upon a much-needed course of instruction. But what remains foremost in the reader's mind is how determinedly Spenser has set up his antithesis between heroic activity and the contemplative impulse. In a sense, the Despair episode complicates and deepens the previous ordeals suffered by Redcrosse in various analogous labyrinthine ordeals. In canto 1, though "wrapt in *Errors* endlesse traine" Redcrosse can hardly be said to have experienced the existential quandaries of "error." His real erring in her mazy wood is little more than an epitome of his vocation as a knight-errant. When he has overcome his adversary, he solves the literal maze with sublime ease (1.28). Similarly, though on the plane of sensuality, his fall to Orgoglio does not result from any act of conscious reflection or cogitation. But with Despair, we are for the first time aware of an impulse in Redcrosse toward introspection. As in the Fulgentian model of the allegorical epic, he is on the threshold of the contemplative life. But his first, untutored act of contemplation – indeed, of ratiocination of any sort, it would seem – proves nearly fatal. So extreme is the dichotomy of action/contemplation in Book I that according to Una even this act of reflecting on his spiritual condition is to be shunned:

> Come, come away, fraile, feeble, fleshly wight,
>> Ne let vaine words bewitch thy manly hart,
>> Ne divelish thoughts dismay thy constant spright. (st. 53)

For three-quarters of Redcrosse's odyssey the *vita contemplativa*, which will play such a major part in Spenser's own spiritual economy, is assigned this perfidious function. Up to the point where the hero's own understanding of his experience catches up with ours in the final cantos, Spenser is content to limit his role to a self-defeating parody of chivalric inexperience and moral and spiritual naïveté.

Contrasted with Redcrosse's almost obsessive commitment to the active life, and the perils associated for him with the contemplative, is the epiphanic pattern reserved in Book I for Una. Una functions at times as a character in her own right and with her own human limitations: witness the moving account of her "reunion" with Archimago disguised as Redcrosse in canto 3. And of course she plays an important ancillary role, as we have seen, in the trials of Error and Despair, a role expanded exponentially by the three daughters of Caelia in canto 10. But in between, while she is separated from Redcrosse, Spenser uses Una in two pastoral scenes that bear out the mode's association with vision or contemplation. Indeed, it is largely these passages that comment upon and qualify the hero's rigorous adherence to the heroic ideal up to the moment of his fall.

Both scenes take place in the deepest woods and involve subhuman denizens of a pastoral peaceable kingdom. And both involve the unveiling of the maiden and a literal epiphany, or shining forth, of her essential nature. In canto 3, in what can be viewed as an antithetical foreshadowing of Redcrosse's surrender to weariness in canto 7, Una, tired and abandoned by her knight, seeks repose in a forest pleasance. As she lies down "in secret shadow,"

> From her faire head her fillet she undight,
> And laid her stole aside. Her angels face
> As the great eye of heaven shyned bright,
> And made a sunshine in the shadie place;
> Did never mortall eye behold such heavenly grace.   (3.4)

Thus exposed, she is suddenly assaulted by a "ramping Lyon" who just as suddenly, "with the sight amazd" of Una's uncovered beauty, instinctively recognizes "her wronged innocence" and "simple truth" and becomes her fawning servant, until he is killed by Sansloy later in the canto. As will be the case in Book 6, the "natural," primitive creature is in closer touch with the truth of Una's beauty than are the various human beasts gathered around the predatory Kirkrapine and blind Corceca. But to those of unclouded vision like the Lion her radiant meaning is clear.

Several of these sylvan seers appear in sequence in canto 6, perhaps the most thoroughly pastoral canto of *The Faerie Queene* before those involving Pastorella in Book 6. Once again the episode turns on the behavior of ironically opposed characters: Sansloy, whose "beastly sin" of barely controllable lust is papered over with the flimsiest show of civility as he courts Una; and Sir Satyrane, one of Spenser's most intriguing pastoral characters. Somewhere in between lie those literal beasts the satyrs, embodiments of untrammeled libido in the Italian pastoral drama, but like the lion here magically defused and returned by the presence of Una to a kind of primordial, anappetitive serenity.[11]

The episode begins when Sansloy, rapidly losing patience with Una's stubborn virginity, rudely tears away her veil. The effect contrasts with that on the lion:

> Then gan her beautie shine, as brightest skye,
> And burnt his beastly hart t'efforce her chastitye.   (6.4)

As the narrator cries for the heavens to see and avenge "this hideous act," "Eternall providence" answers the narrator's prayer in a "wondrous way": Una's shrieks interrupt the "rurall meriment" of a flock of satyrs. This "rude, misshapen, monstrous rablement...

come incontinent" to rout and (the pun leads us to expect) supplant the incontinent Sansloy. But when they actually see the disheveled virgin, blubbering and "dolefull desolate,"

> All stand amazed at so uncouth sight,
> And gin to pittie her unhappie state,
> All stand astonied at her beautie bright,
> In their rude eyes unworthie of so wofull plight. (st. 9)

Once Una has overcome her fear of the satyrs,

> They all as glad, as birdes of joyous Prime,
> Thence lead her forth, about her dauncing round,
> Shouting, and singing all a shepheards ryme,
> And with greene braunches strowing all the ground,
> Do worship her, as Queene, with olive girlond cround. (st. 13)

The episode becomes even more like a stock pastoral idyll as the satyrs' merry songs fill the woods (and are echoed by them) while, "leaping like wanton kids in pleasant Spring," they present their new idol to their old god, Sylvanus (st. 14).

Una, however, is a Christian lady, and even her conquest of Sylvanus and his troop, and consequent displacement of the wood-nymphs in their regard, cannot console her for her failure to raise their spiritual sights above idolatry.[12] Whereupon, enter Sir Satyrane. As his name implies, Satyrane is closely akin to the bestial-innocent satyrs. The bastard son of a satyr, begotten by force on a lady married and passionately attached to a "loose unruly swayne" significantly named Therion (bestial), Satyrane is one of those natural types we will meet over and over again in Spenser's most pastoral book, Book 6. Nourished in the hard discipline of the wilderness, he there develops his innate courage and fearlessness into the noble savagery of a natural hunter.[13] As he outgrows or subdues his literally bestial adversaries, his "courage" makes him lust after bigger game. So he seeks "forreine foemen" to try his martial skills on, and thus "through all Faery lond his famous worth was blown" (st. 29). Yet Satyrane always returns to his "native woods," the source of his name and his virtues; it is during one such homecoming that he sees and rescues Una from her futile mission among the idolatrous satyrs. Like his cousins, Satyrane instinctively acknow-ledges Una's virtues, though "her wisedome heavenly rare" provokes his wonder not worship (st. 31). Unlike the satyrs,

Satyrane is half-human – in Book 3 we will come to know him as a man of the world – and thus capable of nurture. Hence he "learn[s] her discipline of faith and veritie," and when he has gained her trust enough to be told of her separation from her lover, he leads her away.

Since in terms of the plot nothing comes of this sustained primitivist pastoral of Satyrane and the satyrs – Una is soon joined by Arthur and united with Redcrosse – I believe we must see it as part of that radical thematic bifurcation of Book 1 discussed earlier. As Redcrosse heedlessly marches deeper and deeper into spiritual darkness, a victim largely of his own inadequately enlightened dedication to heroic endeavor, Spenser utilizes the pastoral epiphanies of Una to the lowly, less than fully human creatures of the woods as a way of pointing to the kind of access to originary Presence denied his hero. It is only on the festive but innocent animal spaces of the pastoral woods that the contemplative virtues shine forth, radiating outward from Una herself and touching the instincts of the lion, the satyrs, and the savagely chivalric, half-bestial knight of nature, Satyrane.[14]

Only after his close brush with Despair exposes his helplessness, is Redcrosse himself allowed to expand beyond his aggressive activism and embrace the contemplative life, as well as experience the epiphanies by which Spenser represents its claims. As if imitating the normal pattern of the allegorized *Aeneid*, in which the Achillean hero earns his entry into the life of contemplation, the last three cantos of Book 1 mend the breach between the estates of life that has hitherto obtained. Redcrosse's ultimate heroic action is framed by two episodes of indoctrination into a mode of being which is antithetical to that in which he has existed up to this point.

The primary vehicle of Redcrosse's initiation into the *vita contemplativa* is, logically enough, Contemplation. Following a well-established medieval tradition of Christian mysticism ultimately derived from Prudentius, Spenser conducts the patient knight's spiritual education and rejuvenation according to the three-fold process of Purgation, Illumination, and Perfect Union.[15] The revelations of the hermit Contemplation follow the hero's instruction in Holiness and Mercy. After emphasizing the need for good works, the hermit leads Redcrosse to a vision of the New Jerusalem, pointing out to him the "way" that leads, "after labours long," to eternal rest (10.52). This epiphany is, in a way, the last in a series of such invitations to repose – the trees of Fradubio's woods, the fountain of sensuality, and Despair's lullaby are the major forerunners – that the knight undergoes. Thematically, it is the archetype and source of the others: the true Jerusalem of "peace" and rest manifests the real goal of his striving.

On the other hand, Contemplation himself reminds Redcrosse that the active life is sanctified by the aims and values revealed by the contemplative: Cleopolis' glory is authentic and has its origins in that of Jerusalem. Redcrosse wants to embrace the contemplative life forever:

> O let me not (quoth he) then turne againe
>   Backe to the world, whose joyes so fruitlesse are;
>   But let me here for aye in peace remaine,
>   Or streight way on that last long voyage fare,
>   That nothing may my present hope empare.   (st. 63)

True to both the classical and Christian hierarchies of the estates of life, having ascended to the highest rank of human felicity he does not see the point of coming back down.[16] Under the hermit's gentle prodding the knight does at last accept his obligations to Una and Gloriana but vows to "shortly backe returne unto this place / To walke this way in Pilgrims poore estate" (st. 64).[17] For this he is rewarded by the final phase of his reconstruction as a total hero of Holiness, one that blends action and contemplation in a single "unitive way": he is told his real name, his British and peasant origins, and his great personal and racial destinies.[18] Still dazed from his vision (st. 67), and fully expecting to return soon to this sacred place, he rejoins Una and they depart.

In canto 12 Redcrosse experiences a more complex initiation. In the interim he has returned to his quest and freed Una's parents from the dragon. Presumably as a result of his indoctrination on the mount of Contemplation, he has been able to conduct this heroic action and endure its attendant hardships with a quiet assurance about ends. His reward is betrothal to Una in a restored Eden that merges the estates of life in a festive foreshadowing of the pure repose that will ultimately crown all his efforts. Canto 12 of Book 1 is Spenser's Earthly Paradise, replete with the renewed innocence of a world redeemed from evil.[19] The victorious couple are greeted there by Una's released parents, attended by "comely virgins ... fresh as flowres in medow greene" (12.6). Children frolic wantonly, and all gaze like overgrown infants on the fallen dragon. The whole scene is suffused with an innocence which suggests that evil and the consciousness of it are a bad dream now dissipated into thin air.[20]

For Redcrosse, the focus of this idyll is his betrothed, whom he now sees for the first time as she really is, the dark habits of her mournful journey through Redcrosse's own land of unlikeness now cast aside like the pall of guilty adolescent sexuality he had borne under the unacknowledged tutelage of Archimago:[21]

> For she had layd her mournefull stole aside,
> And widow-like sad wimple throwne away,
> Wherewith her heavenly beautie she did hide,
> Whiles on her wearie journey she did ride;
> And on her now a garment she did weare,
> All lilly white, withoutten spot, or pride.   (st. 22)

Redcrosse's chivalric commitment to the active life, as informed by his brief ascent to the contemplative in the House of Holiness, has earned him a new vision. Once again, but this time with regard to this world and its natural delights, the scales fall from his eyes: "Oft had he seene her faire, but never so faire dight" (st. 23).

Only in such a setting can Spenser find a legitimate place for the third of the traditional estates, the *bios apolaustikos – vita voluptuosa*, or life of pleasure.[22] The wedding festivities peak in a sensual outflowing almost unparalleled in *The Faerie Queene* and uniquely unqualified with innuendo. The sumptuous nuptials are redolent of a redeemed sensuality:

> Then gan they sprinckle all the posts with wine,
> And made great feast to solemnize that day;
> They all perfumde with frankencense divine,
> And precious odours fetcht from far away,
> That all the house did sweat with great aray.[23]   (st. 38)

To the pleasures of sight and smell are added those of sound, as the mundane scene is suffused by the "trinall triplicities" of cosmic harmony (st. 39).[24] There is no apparent limit to the lovers' "exceeding merth," and the once prurient hero's "heart did seeme to melt in pleasures manifold" as his labors are crowned with a sexual fruition felt for once to be consonant with his sense of duty.[25]

In this pastoral of erotic fulfillment, there is no conflict among the triplicities of Spenser's anatomy of the estates of life: the contemplation of sheer beauty, its fruition in pleasure, and the obligations of the active life. Nevertheless, the latter remains in the ascendant:

> Yet swimming in that sea of blisfull joy,
> He nought forgot, how he whilome had sworne,
> In case he could that monstrous beast destroy,
> Unto his Farie Queene backe to returne:
> The which he shortly did, and *Una* left to mourne.   (st. 41)

Una's father has previously enrolled himself in that growing roster of inviters to repose. Echoing Redcrosse's own sentiments on Contemplation's hill, he has offered to reward Redcrosse's efforts by making his kingdom a permanent refuge "of ease and everlasting rest" (st. 17). Having escaped a "sea of deadly daungers," the hero is invited to plunge forever into one of sensual delights. But Redcrosse, who before the dragon-fight could dream of a quick return to mystical contemplation, now resists the peremptory lure of a renewed prelapsarian sensuality. He has tasted the joys of contemplation and vowed his allegiance to a chastened life of pleasure; now he reaffirms his six years' obligation to the active service of Gloriana.

What Spenser seems to be implying here is that ideally the three estates subsist concurrently, each complementing the others in a full life. The question, however, will be asked again, and the answers will change, particularly in Spenser's later works. For the moment, as he completes the first stage in the cumulative journey of his perfect hero, Spenser fulfills his conception of pastoral as a socially redeeming ceremony of innocence. He employs the restorative features of the pastoral ambience and its contemplative transcendence of false appearances to construct a paradigm of heroic struggle issuing, on the personal level, in a fusion of the three traditional estates of life and, on the social, in the reconstitution of the communal ideal of primitive Christianity.

This achievement is re-enforced by Spenser's characterization of the narrator. An interested observer who has been alternately cautionary about Redcrosse's errors and sympathetic with Una's distresses, the narrator of Book 1 emerges in the final canto as engaged in a journey of his own explicitly paralleling that of his characters. The narrator's destination is never stated, though we infer that it will be the end of the entire poem.[26] At the outset of canto 12 he identifies his own voyage with that of the happy couple – or rather with the Red Cross Knight's, since for Una the Earthly Paradise is the end. Spying their common "haven nigh at hand, / To which I meane my wearie course [corse = corpse?] to bend," he acknowledges his own need, comparable to Redcrosse's at the fountain or Una's in the wood, for rest:

> There this faire virgin wearie of her way
> Must landed be, now at her journeyes end:
> There eke my feeble barke a while may stay,
> Till merry wind and weather call her thence away.   (12.1)

Whereas the Lady can accept permanent repose here, the story-teller, like his protagonist, will find only a temporary respite before renewing his labors. The motif is repeated in the final stanza of Book 1:

> Now strike your sailes ye jolly Mariners,
> For we be come unto a quiet rode,
> Where we must land some of our passengers,
> And light this wearie vessell of her lode.
> ...And then againe abroad
> On the long voyage whereto she is bent:
> Well may she speede and fairely finish her intent.   (12. 42)

By means of this nautical simile Spenser endorses his own commitment to a continuing struggle toward a still remote goal. Though he shares Redcrosse's attraction to pleasure and contemplation, even as he coasts into his first port of call Spenser renews his journey as a poet toward some ultimate rest.[27]

I want to suggest that behind this personal version of the heroic odyssey lurks a hint of the old Vergilian paradigm. It has been proposed recently that Book 1, the story of St. George, is Spenser's "georgics," the initial adventure of *The Faerie Queene* constituting a missing link between the bucolics of *The Shepheardes Calender* and the extended heroics of the following books.[28] Redcrosse and his successors must learn the need and value of labor – and, I would add, the proper place of pleasure – and Spenser's own working out of his labyrinthine narrative is tantamount, both for himself and his reader, to an induction into a strenuous and taxing art.[29] This hypothesis has considerable implications for Spenser himself. From the proem's pointed allusion to his former pastoral guise to the self-conscious application of one of the book's central motifs to his own narrative persona in canto 12, Spenser keeps his private dilemmas largely out of sight. But he remains nonetheless deeply implicated in the issues of Book 1, particularly in the question of the rival estates so intimately bound to the poem's generic layers.[30] If he is trying to reconstruct a model for blending the three estates by fusing the three Vergilian genres in an image of action informed by contemplation and admitting of sensual pleasure, it is not surprising that he signals his personal stake in the issue by self-consciously aligning the journey of his poem with that of its hero. He will do so again, most blatantly in Book 6. At the present juncture, however, he is willing merely to display the possible mediation of a "georgics": a poetry and a civilization of work closely tied to a sense of origins in a place, that place itself figuring as the source of learning and balance. Such a georgic ideal is located midway between the pastoral realm of pure contemplation and the epic's celebration of violent action and imperial destiny. *Faerie Queene* 1, therefore, may be qualifiedly viewed as a way-station on the poet's personal itinerary. That itinerary leads from a reluctant recognition of the idyllic norm of inner harmony and self-delight to a full-fledged commitment to public service with its more tangible if ambiguous rewards.

II

For whatever reason – whether because of Spenser's election of an Aristotelian model for temperance (actually continence), or because of the order of composition, or something else – Book 2 contributes little that is new or different to Spenser's use of pastoral.[31] To a considerable extent, Guyon duplicates the extreme resistance to rest or pleasure of the unreconstructed Red Cross Knight, while the book as a whole recalls in its structure the strict dichotomy of action and passion, of aggressive heroics and debilitating erotics, of the Moral eclogues and the earlier cantos of Book 1.[32] Its violent climax features an almost total inversion of the pastoral delights of Redcrosse and Una's nuptials, as Guyon smashes the "sea of blissful joy" in which Verdaunt and others have swum. But Book 3 is a wholly different affair. The spectre of classical *akrasia* once laid to rest, Spenser returns to the more intimate areas of the moral life in search of the constructive aspects of love and chastity. In short, he resumes the terminal themes of Book 1 on a more determinedly this-worldly and even social plane. At the core of his vision in this book is the chastely loving Britomart's search for both sexual and dynastic fulfillment.

The narrative strategy in Book 3 to a certain extent parallels that of Book 1. Once again the chief tension in the book is between epiphanies of permanent truths hidden from ordinary experience and the texture of that experience itself. The visionary aspects of the book's titular virtue are conveyed mostly in the idealized explications of its three heroines: the revelation of Britomart's sexual destiny in Merlin's glass in canto 3, the brief unfolding of Belphoebe's virginity in canto 5, and Amoret's education in true "womanhed" in the Garden of Adonis in canto 6. In each of these instances an ideal aspect of chastity is represented in its essence and we are made to feel the permanency of the virtue despite its actual vicissitudes. In cantos 7–12, on the other hand, Spenser is less interested in archetypes than in the phenomenology of erotic experience. Having revealed to us in the first half of the book the ideals that govern and warrant human eros, he can in the second half turn his attention to tracing the contours of erotic experience from its ideal aspect in Cupid and Psyche (Cupid disarmed, Psyche therefore erotically unthreatened, and their offspring innocent Pleasure) to its harsh reality in the House of Busyrane.[33] To a considerable extent, this study of erotic love centers on Florimell and her counterpart Hellenore; its climax is the Malbecco episode in canto 10, an essay on the pastoral of erotic fulfillment in the guise of a classical-courtly comedy of manners.[34]

Although the permanent features of chastity are allowed throughout to emerge dramatically, they do so predominately in the first half of the book. Despite the important differences among the paradigmatic heroines, all three exist on the same platonic level and are equally parts of the ideological superstructure of Spenser's anatomy of chastity.[35] This paradigm is communicated to the reader through detached and "readable" allegories involving, to borrow a pregnant phrase from Isabel MacCaffrey, ideal characters "in the kingdom of archetypes."[36] In each instance the epiphany of the heroine's exemplary virtue is conveyed through spatial images or places – *sacra templa*, as it were – set apart from the surrounding landscape and marked by one or another kind of visionary illumination.

The first of these epiphanies is Britomart's *innamoramento*, executed in two phases to accentuate respectively the personal and social dimensions of the event.[37] Narcissistically admiring herself in her father's magical mirror, the heroine, who knows already that she must bind her life with the "knot" of matrimony, sees her destined mate, Artegall, in a vision and is infected with the love-disease. Her malaise is then converted to activity by the wise Glauce, who conducts her to Merlin's cave. There the wizard, seeing through the dissembling "womanish guile" of the tale Glauce has concocted, laughingly announces to Britomart the "good fortune" beneath the seeming catastrophe of her condition, and from his "world of glas" reveals to her the true identity of her bridegroom-to-be – though living in Faery Land, like Redcrosse he is an Englishman – and the glorious destiny they share.[38] Assured that her infatuation is sanctioned by "eternall providence" (3.24) as the instrument of a grand dynastic plan that will issue in Elizabeth's Welsh line, Britomart, again at Glauce's suggestion (3.52), sets out to find her promised husband. Britomart's perfection has been shown to derive from the dynastic promise revealed to her in Merlin's Cave, thus placing her normal feminine instincts in a controlling social and familial framework. Hence she is able to translate her love into heroic action, sustained from the outset by a visionary revelation of that action's ultimate meaning. Although Spenser will frustrate the reader's expectation of seeing the consummation of this match in his heroic poem, there is no suggestion in these cantos of any ironic detachment of the narrating poet from this dynastic theme.

On the face of it, both the setting and the meaning of Belphoebe's virginity, the subject of the next epiphany, appear to be far removed from Britomart's socially grounded chastity. Yet it is represented in another version of Spenser's platonic pastoral. In the total picture of Spenser's chastity, virginity seems a sterile alternative to the promised fruition of Britomart. But while Belphoebe shadows the private aspect of the Queen, the episode transparently figures forth Raleigh's suit for Elizabeth's favor. Hence her virginity, like Britomart's chastity, has its public aspect, Elizabeth's militant virginity being the cornerstone of her efforts to ensure a peaceful succession.[39]

Nevertheless, or perhaps one should say for that very reason, Spenser trumpets Belphoebe's virginity at the very moment that she is trying to treat Timias' love-disease while withholding from him the "soveraigne salve" that might cure him (5.50). The Rose of her femininity is the one gift she will not give "th'unworthy world forlore," and Spenser pulls out all the stops in his rhapsody on this stingy virtue. Belphoebe's Rose can flourish only in a uniquely private space at the calm heart of an inviolable nature:

> Ne suffred she the Middayes scorching powre,
> Ne the sharp Northerne wind thereon to showre,
> But lapped up her silken leaves most chaire,
> When so the froward skye began to lowre:
> But soone as calmed was the Christall aire,
> She did it faire dispred, and let to florish faire.   (st. 51)

At the heart of his celebration of heroic, married love Spenser insists that Elizabeth's virginity in no way conflicts with her courtesy, any more than with the great principle of fecundity whose vocabulary pervades the following stanza (st. 52). Both share pride of place in her "Heroick mind":

> So striving each did other more augment,
> And both encrease the prayse of woman kind...
> So all did make in her a perfect complement.   (st. 55)

Virginity is the ur-chastity that warrants the more fruitful variants of Britomart and Belphoebe's more susceptible twin sister, Amoret. At the same time, Belphoebe also shadows the political and public dangers inherent in the Queen's too flagrant exposure of her essential femininity.

It should be noted in passing that the platonic and aristocratic bias of this courtly pastoral is underscored by Spenser's allusions to Theocritus. Both here and in Book 2 (3.20–42) Belphoebe's heroic virtues are associated with the *locus amoenus*, far from court, in which she appears. Yet Spenser goes out of his way to distinguish the site of Belphoebe's epiphany from the woods of unredeemed natural virtue in which we encounter the satyrs in 1.6 and the treacherous foresters in 3.5. The connection of the latter with the idyllic pastoral of Theocritus is signalled in the episode of Florimell's "Chorle," the Witch's son in canto 7. Here, as elsewhere in *The Faerie Queene*, the pastoral of the "savage" woods is about natural man. Unlike the literary shepherds or courtly pseudo-shepherd Calidore in 6.9–10, the rustic "clown" is incapable of perceiving the moral forms of Nature visible to the refined contemplative soul. Like his mother, the Churl is blind to love – though she is "moved" by Florimell's beauty, which she thinks must be divine (3.7.11), her kindness is no more inspired by understanding than is her son's lust – and therefore inevitably subject to "uncivile" passion (st. 19). For this reason he is portrayed as a pastoral shepherd of the Theocritean type, as viewed through the lens of the courtly "Arcadian" pastoral tradition from Vergil to Sannazaro and Sidney. Denied the gentleman's prerogative of achieving contemplation of the higher forms, his otium becomes mere laziness (st. 12). A true rustic must labor; if he doesn't, he is a "laesie loord." The use of Theocritean pastoral as a code for this aristocratically conceived peasant or villain is evident in the Churl's clownish, bumbling gift-giving (st. 17; cf. Theocritus 3 and 11, and Eclogues 2 and 8), and in his mother's equally ineffectual efforts to cure his love-malady (st. 21; cf. Theocritus 11), which is more appropriate in tone than its counterpart in canto 2, where Glauce seeks vainly to thwart the higher purposes working through Britomart's love-pangs.

The third and most sustained pastoral epiphany of Book 3, the Garden of Adonis, unfolds Amoret's chastity or, as Spenser usually calls it, her "womanhed." Without getting bogged down in the question of the ultimate philosophical orientation of the account – whether Platonic, Epicurean, or Deconstructionist[40] – we may observe that this "allegorical core" of Book 3, though occurring midway through the book, terminates the sequence of positive epiphanies by which the virtue of chastity is unfolded.[41] More obviously allied with Britomart's heroic love than with Belphoebe's virginity, the ideal of womanhood that Amoret acquires in the Garden connects the erotic life with its basic biological function. On the other hand, it does not arm Amoret herself against the psychic pitfalls with which it is entangled in life. This problematic of eros will form the substance of the second half of Book 3.

The Garden itself is introduced as Venus' "joyous Paradize," her favorite haunt on earth and the site of her perpetual love-tryst with Adonis. Here Adonis himself, "All be he subject to mortalitie, / Yet is eterne in mutabilitie, / And by succession made perpetuall" (6. 47). Time, the universal foe, is in the garden, threatening its denizens (st. 39); but Nature can overcome Time by procreative "succession." Hence, under the aspect of eroticism as Nature's sole weapon in her war with Time, Eros himself is rendered in his inherent pastoral innocence as Adonis' carefree playmate:

> Who when he hath with spoiles and cruelty
> Ransackt the world, and in the wofull harts

Of many wretches set his triumphes hye,
Thither resorts, and laying his sad darts
Aside, with faire *Adonis* plays his wanton parts.   (st. 49)

Cupid disarmed is a well-known emblem of Platonic love; but here
he signifies instead a love fully physical and fertile whose psychic
sting has been vitiated by his being part of a total image of natural
fertility within the framework of Spenser's contemplative ceremony
of innocence. This is brought out as well by the perpetual, steadfast
union of Cupid and Psyche, by whom he fathers an equally innocent
Pleasure (st. 50). Relieved of the psychic torments Cupid's weapons
rain on the minds of lovers in the dark world of ordinary experience
– a world we will explore in the second half of the book – sexual
pleasure, born of the union of eros and the soul, is both eternally
happy and constant. This pastoral of erotic fulfillment will come
back into focus in the more worldly Hellenore cantos. Meanwhile,
it is under the aegis of this chastened eroticism that Amoret grows
into "perfect ripenesse," the paragon and exemplar of "true love
alone, / And Lodestarre of all chaste affectione, / To all faire
Ladies, that doe live on ground" (st. 52). Along with Belphoebe, she
epitomizes the total chastity that Britomart will demonstrate in her
actions.

Throughout Book 3 Spenser tests his ideal of chastity in the
essentially courtly ambience of Britomart's performances with
Malecasta at Castle Joyeous, Marinell on the Rich Strond, and
Busyrane in his castle. But in addition to Britomart's adventures, in
the second half of the book our attention shifts from epiphanies of
virginity and chaste love to the mock-idyll of free love involving
Hellenore among the satyrs, those ancient avatars of erotic
pastoral.[42] Moreover, the rhetorical content of the sequence, i.e. the
corresponding action in the mind of the reader, deals with the
rational control of the dream of erotic perfection needed to reconcile
the pastoral ideal of eros with its destructive effects in the fallen
psyche.

Both cantos 7–8, where the focus is on Florimell, and 9–10, where
it is on Hellenore, oscillate between pastoral themes and images and
those of courtly love. The former interweave scenes depicting
Florimell's immersion in the erotic with others introducing male
characters who share the courtly ethos and thus pave the way for the

story of Hellenore that follows. As in canto 1, where she is pursued by both the "griesly Foster" and the virtuous Arthur and Guyon, Florimell's flight has the proportions of myth, though the emphasis now is on her feelings rather than those of her pursuers (7.1).[43] As she plunges deeper into a forest whose every shade or rustle conceals some unknown threat, Florimell's beauty fills the minds of those she meets with "terrour and with aw" (st. 13). Transmuted to an irresistible erotic attraction, this dread is shown to be the source of the protean nightmare she is caught up in. The connection becomes increasingly clear as her flight takes her from Witch and Churl and devouring Hyena to the pastoral seascape with its lecherous Fisherman and finally to Proteus himself in all his "dreadfull shapes" (8. 41), the presiding deity of this panerotic world. At each of these stops, Florimell is cast as the hapless mistress in a pastoral of erotic fulfillment, a passive love-object imprisoned and courted in an isolated *locus amoenus*. It is as though the universal erotic fear emanating from this vision of feminine beauty must be subdued to the bloodless convention of the pretty, docile sexual slave. In the grip of this dream of a denatured and domesticated eros, Florimell's "lovers" constitute for her a perpetual current of undifferentiated aggressive libido.[44]

In contrast to Florimell's pathos is the group of knights who counterpoint her story in cantos 7–8. These masculine figures gradually mediate between the pastoral settings, the erotic woods and sea, of Florimell and the main courtly locus, Malbecco's castle.[45] The relation of this male camaraderie to Florimell's story, muted through most of the sequence, becomes explicit on the arrival of Paridell, an event narrated immediately following Florimell's capture by Proteus. Here the chorus of laments and pledges of "service" to "faire *Florimell*" by these worldly knights (8.46–7) seems almost a reification of Proteus himself, whose many shapes represent the erotic as it impinges on Florimell. The coin has been reversed. Just as earlier Arthur's noble effort to rescue her from the "foster" is indistinguishable to her mind from the latter's lust – "Yet she no lesse the knight feard, then that villein rude" (4.50) – so now we recognize in these knights' solicitous concern the protean face of desire as Florimell has suffered it in the preceding adventures. As the narrative focuses, at the transition from canto 8 to 9, on the courtly-love material that will culminate in Malbecco's metamorphosis, we are being prepared to accept the story of Paridell and

Hellenore as an elaboration and inversion of that of Florimell. Not only are the plots similar, each arriving at its catastrophe in a *locus amoenus* of free love, but together they clarify the true function and the limits of the pastoral of erotic fulfillment. Moreover, the fluctuations of the narrative voice in this sequence, varying from naïve detachment to warm sympathy with Florimell to a surprising courtly sophistication, serve to distinguish the terrors of Florimell's polymorphous erotic world from the cosmic and comic urge, radiating from her own beauty, that underlies it. As we enter into the courtly comedy of Paridell and Hellenore and the quasi-tragedy of Malbecco, with the universal pastoral of protean sex still fresh in our minds, we are guided by this newly emergent narrator into the familiar courtly-love game of Hellenore and the erotic idyll that evolves from it.[46] Under his tutelage the naïve pastoral of the ultimate erotic dream in which we are about to be immersed is assured of a sophisticated literary control.[47]

In the climactic cantos 9 and 10 Spenser traverses a very broad terrain indeed. A frothy fabliau with tinctures of courtly romance and New Comedy farce is pushed near to tragedy (*The Merchant's Tale* supplies the obvious model) before dissolving in a grim parody of Ovidian metamorphosis. More important, a corresponding transformation takes place in the reader's understanding, revealing an unexpected and largely unprecedented psychological dimension to Spenser's erotic pastoral. Again, as previously with Florimell, it is with the phenomenology of the erotic and not its theory that Spenser is concerned. But exploring the dream that underlies the conventional view of eros, he creates in his reader a heightened awareness of the dream's social limits. In this journey our destination is the vision of Malbecco and Hellenore among the satyrs – Hellenore in total erotic abandon, Malbecco wode in a wood.

As the generally Ovidian portrayal of Hellenore's seduction unfolds, the focus settles slowly on Malbecco.[48] While we are never allowed to forget the "donghill mind" (10.15) that justifies his abuse, at the height of his victimization he becomes the chief object of our attention and even of our sympathies. Dismissing the lovers once they have brought off their plot, Spenser follows Malbecco as he seeks to rescue his wife from her paramour. Once his tormentors have been stripped of their dignity as nature's minions and reduced to crude personifications of appetite, Malbecco's relative humanity shows progressively through his comic sterotypes. If he loves gold, it is still love of a sort, just as his "foule gealosy" itself springs from "loves extremitie" (st. 22). It is the latter that draws him into the heart of the forest to the Bacchanale.

The horror with which the "bagpipes shrill, / And shrieking Hububs" fill the woods may remind us of Florimell in Proteus' cave. There Spenser's increasingly comic view of the scene, and the reassuring cosmological myth that governs the episode, serve to allay our own, though not Florimell's, sense of the terrors of unbridled eros. To put it another way, the forbidding landscape, which is a mirror of Florimell's mind, only partially masks the pastoral of erotic fulfillment that the reader, perhaps remembering the Garden of Adonis, intuits beyond it. Now, at the climax of cantos 9–10, the same point is reached from the opposite direction. Although the nightmare this time is the man's as he encounters the image of free feminine sexuality, we have in a sense returned to that terror and awe that seemed to motivate the various masculine efforts to dominate Florimell earlier. But also, where the causes of Florimell's terror were kept apart from her story and presented to us through the mildly libertine chatter of the Squire of Dames and his cohorts, here the erotic nightmare of Malbecco is made to reveal its ultimate source directly: the pastoral dream of uninhibited libido, stripped even of the condoning Garden of Adonis myth of generation. In short, the climactic scene becomes an anatomy of Malbecco's "wounded mind" (10.55).

Spenser's orchestration of the crucial stanzas is dictated by this central motive. As the action proceeds, Spenser dissociates Malbecco's fright from the purely idyllic, amoral image of the satyrs when they appear:

> The jolly *Satyres* full of fresh delight,
> Came dauncing forth, and with them nimbly led
> Faire *Hellenore*, with girlonds all bespred,
> Whom their May-lady they had newly made:
> She proud of that new honour, which they red,
> And of their lovely fellowship full glade,
> Daunst lively, and her face did with a Lawrell shade.   (st. 44)

Of course we realize the absurdity of the conceit that these mythic creatures of our own collective imagination mimic our rites of May-queen and laurel crown.[49] But at the same time we can appreciate the ideal freedom at the heart of the ritual: the freedom from sexual bondage, whether in marriage or in *amour courtois*, imposed on women throughout the European tradition. Malbecco's nightmare is also Hellenore's "dreame" (st. 49), from which she will never awaken, or rather by which Spenser allows her to be consumed, much as her husband will be consumed by his jealousy. Accepting the power of this dream, Spenser drives home the point that from her liberation "emongst the jolly Satyres" she will "by no meanes" be won back to Malbecco's "will" (st. 51).

While Hellenore is thus permanently assimilated to her archetype, the focus remains Malbecco, in whose purview it is taking place. At this juncture it becomes impossible for us any longer to share Malbecco's responses fully. When the May-lady stanza is followed immediately by a cut back to the "silly man" grovelling in the thicket and watching, like Milton's Satan in Paradise, "all this goodly sport" (st. 45), our attraction to the dream of pleasure collides with our sympathy for the tormented psyche that must suffer that dream. As disinterested readers we are on the side of "nature"; it is Malbecco, we remind ourselves, who has injected the bestial note, reptilian and goatish, into the idyll. An involuntary voyeur and a cuckold, his response is antithetical to the cosmic/comic one that the narration has all along been nurturing in us. Still, working against this detachment is the common humanity we share with Malbecco. Spenser has strained his reader's sympathies to the breaking point.

These warring perspectives are conflated in stanza 48, significantly the most "Ovidian" passage in the sequence:

> At night, when all they went to sleepe, he vewd,
>   Whereas his lovely wife emongst them lay,
>   Embraced of a *Satyre* rough and rude,
>   Who all the night did minde his joyous play:
>   Nine times he heard him come aloft ere day,
>   That all his hart with gealosie did swell;
>   But yet that nights ensample did bewray,
>   That not for nought his wife them loved so well,
> When one so oft a night did ring his matins bell.

As we approach this nocturnal – what: idyll or debauch? – we are with Malbecco still, yet kept apart in spirit by the commenting narrator. The first four lines maintain Malbecco's point of view ("his lovely wife," "a *Satyre* rough and rude"), yet allow the "natural," pastoral response to the love-making ("his joyous play").

Then the Ovidian motif ("Nine times"), which for us recalls the erotic élan of the *Amores*, in Malbecco triggers the eruption of "gealosie" that will eventually madden and transfigure him. The last three lines, though, are entirely Spenser's – and ours. For if the vision of pure animality in Hellenore and the satyrs has been refracted by the solitary and impassioned "fallen" perspective of Malbecco, we are saved from the latter's fantasies by the worldly, sanative twist of the final couplet, which retrieves the pastoral image and locates it once more within the controlling comic perspective of the book.

It is notable that Spenser chooses not to specify the beneficiary of "that nights ensample." In the context we might suppose it to be Malbecco himself; but his subsequent behavior suggests anything but enlightenment concerning his wife's motives, and Spenser's didactic theory of poetry dictates that his "ensamples" be directed at the reader. It is we who are reminded that concupiscence is an inescapable fact of the human condition. What is innocent for the no longer quite human Hellenore, and for those idealized projections of our erotic drives, the satyrs, can only by a willful and at best temporary suspension of our normal censors be innocent in the same way for us. Yet the truth of the dream and the need to acknowledge our erotic impulses, whether in May-games or love-elegy, is also part of our normal apprehension of life.

Rather than reading us a Chaucerian lecture on giving wives free rein, I believe that Spenser here is getting at the essence of the erotic imagination and exploring its consequences for the fallen mind. In Malbecco we experience the "selfe-murdring thought" (st. 57) that sexuality can produce and that is mythologized in his metamorphosis:[50]

> Griefe, and despight, and gealosie, and scorne
> Did all the way him follow hard behind,
> And he himselfe himselfe loath'd so forlorne,
> So shamefully forlorne of womankind;
> That as a Snake, still lurked in his wounded mind.   (st. 55)

But in the poetry of the episode as a whole, and particularly in the management of these climactic stanzas in the panic night, we also experience – there is created in us as we read – the balanced mind that is the product of poetry and of culture in general. The Spenserian voice in Book 3 emerges as a mediating agent between the undifferentiated eros of our dreams and the ego-threatening defenses of the "wounded mind." By reclaiming the pastoral dream and incorporating it into his reader's consciousness, Spenser fashions a broader understanding of love. This reclamation in turn lends to sexuality a new and less vulnerable innocence by delimiting its licit expressions (as well as elucidating its vicarious ones) in a fully civilized context where it is sanctioned by larger communal ends. Hence the Malbecco episode constitutes the most complete absorption of pastoral into the dominant heroic ethos that we will find in *The Faerie Queene*.

The narrative strategy of these cantos epitomizes Spenser's use of pastoral in the 1590 *Faerie Queene*. Although the first and last books of the installment enact the approach differently in both content and structure, both display the poet's intention to incorporate into his vision of the individual's personal and social roles facts of human life normally obscured from view. Poetry for Spenser therefore takes on a double function. On the one hand, the epic form carries its traditional obligation to encode those official values that bind readers into a cultural community. This is accomplished by celebrating ideal personages who translate the values into heroic action. Thus the Red Cross Knight ideally enacts the humanist pattern exemplified by Filelfo's reading of the *Aeneid* as an allegory of *sapientia* and *prudentia*. According to this view, it will be recalled, Aeneas seeks a "civil felicity" of valorous service to others grounded in an understanding of his own weaknesses and vulnerabilities. In much the same way, Spenser has Guyon undergo an array of temptations and threats to his rational self-control, manifesting in the process the inadequacy of classical *sophrosyne* in the face of the gross attractions of pleasure or power. In female form, Britomart realizes similar vulnerabilities, in this case not so much to delusions of heroic grandeur as to the biological need for a conjugal partner, as well as the providential purposes that govern it.[51] But because her perception of a sustaining providence is granted at the beginning of her journey instead of coming, like Redcrosse's, as its consummation, Britomart is a more static character than is the knight of Holiness. This feature of the struggle for Chastity is parcelled out variously among the lesser heroines (and, in Marinell's case, heroes) of Book 3, who furnish diverse insights into the nature of the moral victory Britomart achieves.

Complementing this epic function – which, in conformity with the "Vergilian" pattern, has already pre-empted the association of pastoral with contemplation – is Spenser's use of pastoral *tout court*. In keeping with the contemplative association, pastoral scenes and images in the 1590 installment serve, as I have tried to show, to keep the reader in mind of those universal impulses of the human spirit that the active heroes of the poem often unwittingly act out. In Book 1, the essential beneficence of the order of nature, including his own psychic and biological urges, is often obscure to the earnest, adolescent Redcrosse. Part of his earning the dents in his armor, i.e. living up to the hard-won knowledge of his precursors, lies in his suffering that knowledge in his maiden adventures. Meanwhile, in counterpoint with Redcrosse's struggle to know himself, the reader is afforded glimpses of this order through the pastoral scenes involving Una in primal concord with the simpler, less tormented creatures of the natural world. These moments of illumination are then gathered up into the two great pastoral–contemplative epiphanies that crown Redcrosse's education: the revelation of his personal destination in the vision of the New Jerusalem and the way-station of a restored earthly paradise of sensual innocence in his betrothal to Una. In Book 2, with the exception of our introduction to Belphoebe, pastoral images seem largely to adorn that destructive world of rest, idleness, and pleasure that challenge heroic activity. In Book 3 the epiphanies of chastity come early, whereas the existential struggles to realize it in action fill the second half of the book. The crux of the process is a two-fold movement of recovering and assimilating the radical motions of the mind within a socially determined artifice. The Stoic and Epicurean authorization of with-drawal, already implicit in Theocritean bucolic, is explicitly located by Vergil in his Eclogues within a problematic contemporary political setting. Spenser already seems to be aware of this revision in *The Shepheardes Calender*. In his heroic poem this motive is fully thematized within a narrative structure and assimilated to a larger poetic strategy whose rhythm includes a return from the nostalgic image of our heart's desire to a larger view of human existence in which the paradisal vision can be properly anchored. This vision of pastoral is the vehicle by which Spenser links the role of spokesman and prophetic educator adumbrated in the Moral eclogues of *The Shepheardes Calender* and now enthusiastically adopted in the apparatus and narrative stance of *The Faerie Queene*, with the more contemplative, private aspects of poetry enshrouded in the *Calender*'s Recreative core.

For even at the peak of his optimism about the possibilities of the public role he embraces in the proem to Book 1 and in the self-characterization in the first and last stanzas of canto 12, Spenser holds on to his intuition that the source of even the most public poetry is the private illumination bestowed on the poet as exemplar of the *vita contemplativa*. The pattern of retrieval and domestication in the sylvan pastoral of Una's satyrs, or the pastoral of erotic fulfillment of Hellenore's, is thus an important hallmark of Spenser's purposes as a pastoral poet writing in epic form – or perhaps better as a Vergilian poet moving from pastoral through georgic to epic without losing the pastoralist's basic insight. The ceremonies of innocence enacted by early Spenserian pastoral have to do precisely with this weaving of the radical impulses in nature and man into a workable and harmonious social fabric. If an understanding of the forces ruling psychic experience is necessary for the righteousness, self-mastery, and constancy of human communality, that communality itself looks to such illumination – for Spenser the special gift to and of the contemplative poet – as the cultural guarantor of its collective endeavor. When in 1590 he launched his projected masterpiece in London, it was through this uniquely personal version of pastoral that Spenser gave voice to the ultimate direction of his work.

4

Colin Clout

As is well known, sometime in 1589 Spenser returned to London after a decade's "exile" in Ireland to oversee the publication of the major fruit of his literary labors, the first three books of *The Faerie Queene*.[1] This event took place probably in January of that year (i.e. of 1590, New Style) and was of course attended by the famous Letter to Raleigh, who had played a major role in the event itself.[2] This role in turn forms the pretext, if not the chief burden, of *Colin Clouts Come Home Againe*, not published until 1595 but dated from Kilcolman, December 1591, and almost certainly written soon after the events it represents, in the long-discarded pastoral cipher of *The Shepheardes Calender*. Whereas *The Faerie Queene* had made sporadic use of the pastoral associations of certain well-established topoi – satyrs, the *locus amoenus* – and of shepherd-similes, while exploiting such meta-pastoral motifs as visionary epiphanies, the innocence of nature, and the appropriation of "natural" virtues to social life, *Colin Clout* returns once more to the central pastoral genre, the eclogue.

Yet it is also very much a court poem. True to the pastoral's associations with the court and courtly themes, this attenuated eclogue reflects the poet's journey to present his heroic poem at court, his experience there, his eventual judgment on that milieu, and his return "home." While *Colin Clout* is a pastoral of the court, therefore, it is far from being a courtly pastoral. Nor, on the other hand, does the poem's title imply Spenser's nostalgia for his adoptive Ireland so much as his reaffirmation of his pastoral persona and of pastoral itself as his definitive literary mode. This return to pastoral, however, does not necessarily imply a reversion to the pastoral *stance* of the *Calender*. It is the argument of this chapter that *Colin Clout* represents the consummation of a period of reflection by Spenser on his literary career, to be loosely identified with the years 1589–91, in which he retrospectively examines his own relation to the court and to political power in general.[3] This revaluation of his role takes the form, in part, of a critique of his own earlier versions of pastoral.

Colin Clout is not the only poem of this crucial period in Spenser's life. Also brought out by Ponsonby, who was evidently riding the crest of Spenser's popularity following his recent "setting forth of the *Faerie Queene*," and likewise dated 1591 was the motley volume of *Complaints*, containing poems that span the decade, and in some instances the two decades, prior to its publication.[4] There is little unanimity among scholars as to the dates of composition of many of these poems, let alone the intention of the volume itself. It has even been suggested that the book was improvised with the careless haste implied by his address to the reader: "gathered togeather" against the swarms of literary pirates seeking to capitalize on the stock of the "new Poet...since his departure over Sea."

Contrary to this view, I will be arguing for a more deliberate involvement by the poet himself in the publication of the *Complaints*. In fact, I believe that the seemingly shapeless composition of the book conceals a retrospective bias closely related to that of *Colin Clout*: along with aspects of the two pastoral elegies also dating from these years, *Daphnaïda* (1591) and *Astrophel* (published 1595, with *Colin Clout*), these minor products of Spenser's art from the late 1560s to 1590–1 suggest a pivotal, revisionary moment in the poet's career. Though in a less focused and consistent way than *Colin Clout*, the retrospection of these poems relies on versions of pastoral, as well as allusions to its major propagator Vergil, as a way of reviewing and redefining Spenser's understanding of his function as a poet. Together these works form a bridge from the more optimistic and conventional pastoral of his youth – a "pastoral of power" in which the poet, occupying a central place in the implied community, articulates its dominant social and ethical values – to his later conception of a more personal, detached, and contemplative pastoral whose sources transcend the political community altogether.[5]

Of all these productions, by far the most important is *Colin Clout*. From its dedication to Raleigh to its closing echo of the *Bucolics*, the poem reads like a self-conscious comment on the Vergilian pastoral tradition. The dedicatee is asked to excuse "the meannesse of the stile" of "this simple pastorall" and artfully begged to ward off any malicious constructions of "my simple meaning." In this way the poet announces the presence of a hidden message while denying its existence, offering his poem as simple sooth "agreeing with the truth in circumstance and matter" (p. 536). The poem's Vergilian associations are especially prominent at the beginning and end. Once again Colin is introduced as "The shepheards boy... / That after *Tityrus* first sung his lay" and is pictured in the basic pastoral posture of sitting and "Charming his oaten pipe unto his peres," who surround him in protective admiration (ll. 1–9). This recollection of Vergil's first eclogue ("Tityre, tu patulae recubans... ") is glossed by Hobbinoll's opening speech characterizing Colin as the Orphic *genius loci* whose return has revived the flagging spirits of the pastoral community (ll. 16–35). Moreover, Colin's return is from a visit to the seat of that divine "Angel" who protects the pastoral community. Like Augustus, "erit ille mihi semper deus" (That one will always be a god for me), a line Colin will echo at the turning-point of the poem, where it becomes clear that Spenser's strategy is to divorce praise of the Queen from criticism of her court. Equally conventional is the poem's ending: under the "glooming skies" (Vergil's *umbrae*) the shepherds "draw their bleating flocks to rest." The lines recall those that conclude the tenth Eclogue, which continue, "ite, domum saturae...capellae" (Go home, you well-fed sheep); like Tityrus and his friends, Colin has come home.

By so insistently couching his poem in the Vergilian idiom Spenser signals his revisionary intention. But if *Colin Clout* contains a statement on the Vergilian tradition, what kind of statement is more difficult to discern. Though lacking the *Calender*'s calendrical structure, which dictates a certain disjunction among the work's several parts, *Colin Clout* too is somewhat fragmentary. Partly under the pressure of the chorus of naïve shepherds who repeatedly interrupt the narrator, the story seems to meander like a classical eclogue book, at times almost desultorily touching the major themes of Spenserian pastoral: patronage, poetry, contemplation, love.[6] Within this typically pastoral narrative mode, however, one unmistakable pattern emerges: the displacement of Colin's royal mistress–Muse, Elisa – or, as she will be known throughout the poem, "Cynthia" – by his personal and platonic one, "Rosalind." As it wanders through its rehearsal of Colin's meeting with the Shepherd of the Ocean, his presentation at court, his awestruck recital of its glories, his very different subsequent account of its corruptions, and finally his return to discipleship to Cupid and Rosalind as a priest of Love, *Colin Clout* comes to organize itself in the reader's mind around two equally powerful but mutually exclusive allegiances: to Cynthia–Elisa and to Rosalind.

Viewed in this light, *Colin Clout* appears to be about the re-education of Colin as a pastoral poet, in effect displacing the pastoral's focus from the public to the private realm. Most of the structural features of the poem support this view. Most notorious, of course, is Colin's sudden reversal, two-thirds of the way through the poem, from praise of the court and Cynthia to sharp criticism of the former and silence about the latter. This reversal is accompanied in turn by a revision of the pastoral ratio of England and Ireland. In the first part of the poem England is cast as a pastoral paradise of security and abundance, with Ireland as its conventional Vergilian outlands, its simple virtues protected and eclipsed by the grandeur of the City. But when Thestylis poignantly asks why Colin left "that happie place, / In which such wealth might unto thee accrew," in order to return to "this barrein soyle, / Where cold and care and penury do dwell" (ll. 654–7), Colin launches into a reconstruction of the simple pastoral place sharply opposed to the corrupt, non-pastoral court. A third structural element concerns the roles of Raleigh and Spenser (in their pastoral guises) as lovers. Although the bulk of the poem focuses on Colin's pastoral identity with regard to the Queen and court, the finale insists on the central thematic function of love. In this connection the role of the Shepherd of the Ocean is to indoctrinate Colin into love-service of Cynthia as the focus of courtship. Yet the Shepherd, like his mistress Cynthia, disappears from the last major section of the poem.[7] Taking his place is the cult of Love practiced within the pastoral community. It is hard, therefore, not to read the poem as a critique of one kind of love and courtship – epitomized in the Shepherd's languishing worship of his cruel Petrarchan Cynthia – in the light of another kind centering on Rosalind and defended by Colin in his new role as Cupid's priest.

This last suggestion is supported by Raleigh's function within the poem's texture of Vergilian allusion. Though Colin in the beginning of the poem recalls Tityrus returned from Rome, there is no Meliboeus in the scene. When the Shepherd of the Ocean appears, it is at first without a hint of that exiled victim of arbitrary power:

> One day...I sat...
> Under the foote of *Mole*...
> There a straunge shepheard chaunst to find me out,
> Whether allured with my pipes delight,
> Whose pleasing sound yshrilled far about,
> Or thither led by chaunce, I know not right:
> Whom when I asked from what place he came,
> And how he hight, himselfe he did ycleepe,
> The shepheard of the Ocean by name,
> And said he came far from the main-sea deepe.   (ll. 56–67)

Yet Spenser's reader could hardly have forgotten that in 1589 Raleigh was in some disfavor at court and had come to Ireland partly to avoid the embarrassment of his temporary replacement by Essex as the Queen's favorite.[8] And this friction at Cynthia's court is soon revealed in the Shepherd's plaint as he and Colin exchange songs:

> His song was all a lamentable lay,
> Of great unkindnesse, and of usage hard,
> Of *Cynthia*, the Ladie of the sea,
> Which from her presence faultlesse him debard.   (ll. 164–7)

If this lament injects a Meliboean discord into the initial pastoral encounter, the end of the poem recalls by his absence yet another Vergilian presence: the lamented Gallus, estranged by love from the pastoral scene. Is it too much to see Raleigh's disappearance from *Colin Clout*'s pastoral allegory as a tacit result of *his* fatal commitment to a destructive "love"?[9]

I will return to this question and its implications below. I raise it here, along with the other structural paradigms, only to frame the argument of this chapter: namely, that Colin's shift of personal loyalty in the poem from Cynthia to Rosalind signifies Spenser's rejection of the pastoral of courtly service to Gloriana in favor of one centering on love and personal devotion to a transcendent source of moral and poetic values. Accompanied by the revaluations of his pastoral myth implied in the other poetry of 1589–91, this revision looks ahead to the central affirmations of Spenser's final decade, founded on the primacy of transcendent truths apprehended by the pastoral poet as practitioner of the contemplative life.

I

In order to clarify the intention of *Colin Clout* with regard to Spenser's pastoral myth, I wish to examine some of the other poetry from this period in Spenser's life. Here too there is evidence, I believe, of the poet's deliberate revision of pastoral as a vehicle for conveying his relation to courtly society. The *Complaints* of 1591 provide in many ways the most interesting gloss on Spenser's program. Although the printer pointedly alludes to Spenser's "departure over Sea" and his own hasty gathering of the poems (p. 470), scholars have long since doubted this fiction.[10] Nevertheless, as I hope to show, the trope of absence bears an integral relation to the book's contents. I believe that Spenser did indeed oversee the *Complaints*, though its publication was no doubt delayed till after his return to Ireland.[11] Since the poems in *Complaints* range from as early as the 1569 *Theatre for Worldlings* to as late as 1590, it is reasonable to assume some sort of retrospective intention. After all, beyond the mere occasion to capitalize on the success of *The Faerie Queene* that Ponsonby implies, the publication also provided Spenser with an opportunity to review his career to date by organizing a selection of his work to reflect his recent experience in London. In the absence of conclusive historical documentation, the burden of proof of this hypothesis must rest with an analysis of its contents, including their arrangements as well as the individual poems themselves.

Spenser's own purposes are suggested, in the first place, by the ordering of most of the poems around a few forms – visions, complaints, and political allegories – and, within each of these groupings, by a dialectic between earlier translations and original productions. Though not an exhaustive principle of selection and organization, this strategy does provide an initial understanding of Spenser's intentions in the book as a whole. It is notable that the most archaic poems in the collection, the sonnet-sequence in the form of "visions," appear at the end. As they are printed, the triad of *Visions of the Worlds Vanitie*, *Visions of Bellay*, and *Visions of Petrarch* constitute a retrogression both chronologically and from original composition to translation (in the last case, a double translation). The thematics of the sequences confirms the chronological and generic pattern. Placed first, Spenser's original vision-poem *Vanitie* is a programmatic theoretical commentary on a political theme dear to pastoral: the ambiguous relation of the socially "low" to the high and mighty. Each of the sonnets between the first and the last two presents an instance of injury done by a small, insignificant creature to his "better." Next in order, the *Bellay* sonnets, appended originally by du Bellay to his *Antiquitez de Rome*, attack the same theme on more historical grounds, localizing the fall of the great in the single but decisive instance of Rome. Finally, Petrarch's canzone, as mediated by Marot in his "Epigrams" and then translated by Spenser in *Petrarch*, abstracts from all historical cases to the basic medieval philosophical theme that "on earth…nothing doth endure" (*Petrarch* l. 81).[12] In thus reversing the logical and chronological order of the three poems, Spenser also implicitly inverts the personal and Renaissance historicist perspectives evolved in the series in their likely order of composition. From a personal and political cautionary sequence on the potential power of the "low degree," the *Complaints* visions proceed finally back to the timeless truth that all that rise must fall. In this process retrospection may be deliberate revision.

Yet this progressive abstraction from the actualities of power, as well as of history, conceals a deeper implication in the fact of Spenser's bringing out these poems at all as well as his placing them at the end of the collection. The immediate suggestion of this arrangement is that the poet is recanting his own, and his age's, increasing sophistication about the sources and contexts of poetry; everything builds up to the volume's valedictory admonition to "loath this base world, and thinke of heavens blis" (*Petrarch* l. 96). This suggestion is called into question, however, in Spenser's original contribution to the vision genre, *Vanitie*. Here the poet reminds us of the implicit power even of the most lowly to bring about the traditional Fall of Princes. His exempla of weak creatures' harming great and mighty ones include the venomous spider who "privilie" slips poison in the dragon's drink like any Machiavellian courtier (sonnet 6). (We will meet this spider again in *Muiopotmos*.) By thus "pastoralizing" the conventional visions-theme, imposing on it the pastoral allegory of socially high and low, Spenser ties this concluding and most archaic genre of *Complaints* to other, more transparently political items in the volume. Yet even here he maintains his pose of being innocent of any political intention. Of this act of perfidy the dreamer notes only that the victim "did so much in his owne greatnesse trust" and draws the standard moral:

> O how great vainnesse is it then to scorne
> The weake, that hath the strong so oft forlorne.   (ll. 83–4)

Moreover this and the other eight similar threats are mitigated in sonnet 11, where the lowly goose saves, rather than destroys or vexes, great Rome, forming a link with the Bellay series. Whatever threat or delusion of power is veiled in the other exempla is here balanced by a corresponding promise or offer of service.

This disclaimer is reinforced in the final sonnet, where the poet–visionary tempers his own implicit political message by generalizing it to fit the more "generic" theme of Petrarch and others:

> Thenceforth I gan in my engrieved brest
> To scorne all difference of great and small,
> Sith that the greatest often are opprest,
> And unawares doe into daunger fall.   (ll. 159–62)

The mock-naïveté of the passive "are opprest," which makes a series of hostile acts seem like an impersonal Fate, is re-enforced by the subsequent application of the moral to the reader. The latter is urged to "Learne by their losse to love the low degree" – an inference that comfortably suits the official late-Elizabethan abhorrence of the "aspiring mind" – and "if that fortune chaunce you up to call," to "forget not what you be." This conclusion blithely exorcizes the sonnets' pervasive hints of violence against the great, attributing men's rise to power to the blind, mysterious workings of "fortune." If the superimposition of the high–low schema on the visions-form instances Spenser's retrospective pastoralizing of the series, his disingenuous failure to acknowledge his own meaning further alerts us to the informing intention of a Colin Clout-like persona.

A similarly complex attitude towards his materials old and new informs Spenser's adaptation of the complaint genre that lends the volume its title. This time the earlier translation, Bellay's *Ruines of Rome*, introduces the second half of the collection, while Spenser's own more recent production, *The Ruines of Time*, is placed at the very beginning. Here too the retrospective intention is revealed by the original poem, where the poet grafts on to the genre's conventional lament for a fallen civilization a more engaged and specifically political attack on contemporary England under the putatively anti-intellectual dominance of Burghley.[13] Moreover, the dedication of the poem to Sidney's sister, and implicitly to the memory of Sidney himself, and its long eulogy of the Dudley and Bedford families place an undeniably political construction on the poet's confession of silence (ll. 222–5), an innuendo the more suggestive for its coming immediately after the well-known allusion to Burghley as "the Foxe [who] is crept / Into the hole, the which the Badger [Leicester?] swept" (ll. 216–7). The Leicester legacy of patronage, which he will accuse Burghley of abandoning in the second half of the poem, is moreover explicitly associated with pastoral: it is "carelesse *Colin Cloute*" who has refused to raise his "idle bagpipe... / Ne tell his sorrow to the listening rout / Of shepherd groomes" awaiting his song. "Wake shepheards boy, at length awake for shame," scolds Verulam, whose voice then merges with Colin's own in the necrology that follows. Influenced by this prelude, the reader is likely enough to attribute the scathing attack on Burghley that fills the second half of the poem, and that may indeed have resulted in the "calling in" of *Complaints* by the authorities, to Colin Clout, Spenser's long-time and hence transparent persona.[14]

Yet this same persona becomes the instrument of the poem's ostensible failure of purpose. The pastoral mask of simplicity is always a convenient protection against being called to account for one's utterances. But in *The Ruines of Time* Spenser wields this device so transparently as to invite precisely the opposite response, as later events confirmed. He practically flaunts his official readers with the political implications of his pastoral guise, in effect signalling a rejection of his earlier pastoral mode. The naïve speaker, now virtually identified with Colin Clout, comes across as one too obtuse to grasp the blatant meaning of Verulam's lament. At one point he finds himself "deepelie muzing" at a "doubtfull speach" (l. 485) that has just ended with the resounding challenge to Burghley or "who so els that sits in highest seate / Of this worlds glorie, worshipped of all" to be "warned" lest he too repeat Verulam's fall (ll. 463–9). There is little that is "doubtfull" about this message; yet it remains "above [the] slender reasons reach" of the speaker (l. 487). As a result of his incomprehension, he is granted by the anonymous powers of fate a "demonstration" in the form of the archaic "tragicke Pageants" that fill the last part of the poem. Readers have often felt this sequence of Spenserian sonnets, in which the demise of Leicester and Sidney is recapitulated in the emblem mode of the Visions, to be out of place in the poem.[15] But in the context of *Complaints* it consorts well enough with other examples of Spenser's retrospective program. Primarily, it brings into critical focus the pastoral device of the naïve or clownish persona.

This strategy in turn explains the unsatisfactory ending of the poem. Despite the special dispensation of his "demonstration," the speaker remains as evidently befuddled as he was by Verulam's lament. The envoy (appropriately archaicized as "L'Envoy") is evenly divided between an elegiac valediction to "Philisides" (Sidney) and an invitation to Sidney's sister to "unto heaven let your high minde aspire, / And loath this drosse of sinfull worlds desire" (ll. 685–6). Under cover of this apolitical finale we are prompted to forget, as the speaker himself has never even fully registered, the satiric assault on Burghley's administration that occupies the bulk of the poem. Verulam and her theme have been banished from the pastoralizing persona's world, wished away with a flicker of guilelessness. This pattern in *The Ruines of Time* nicely foreshadows the one in *Complaints* as a whole, which, as we have seen, culminates in a similar gesture of *contemptus mundi* at the end of the *Visions of Petrarch*. The pastoral device of a naïve speaker prepares the reader for the play throughout the volume between archaic and contemporary modes, in which the latter advertise the poet's dedication of his art to political realities implicitly denied by the former. The envoy's announced capitulation to the mood of *contemptus mundi* barely veils the poem's pervasive criticism of the court – "spurting the froth upon courtiers' noses," says Middleton in 1604 – which is Spenser's intention in the book from beginning to end.[16] In the self-exposure of his earlier pastoral mask Spenser implies an emerging new personal version of pastoral.

II

Ambiguities about Spenser's public posture in *Complaints* are rendered clearer by considering the trilogy of political allegories that form the substantive core of the volume. It is possible, as we saw, to read the valedictory verses concluding the collection, like the similar ones inaugurating it, as a renunciation of Spenser's activist stance in the 1580s. But an examination of *Mother Hubberds Tale*, *Virgils Gnat*, and *Muiopotmos* confirms the suspicion that the publication of the book was in fact intended to question openly the possibility of patronage and to advertise the more independent stance to be adopted in the years ahead.[17] In sharp contrast to the elaborate parade of endorsements with which Spenser surrounded the 1590 *Faerie Queene* – gestures of appeal for recognition that parallel the mood of innocent hope and credulity of his pastoral persona at the beginning of *Colin Clout* – the more complex signals of these central texts in *Complaints* suggest a decisive break with his earlier literary premises.

Without over-burdening the ordering of these poems, one might well conjecture that the yoking of *Gnat* and *Mother Hubberd* points once again to Spenser's retrospective agenda, whereas the evidently more recent composition, *Muiopotmos*, separated from these in the book by *The Ruines of Rome*, constitutes a revisionary comment on the earlier poems. In any case, the trilogy as it appears can be taken as a direct statement by Spenser in *c.* 1590 on the nature of politically oriented poetry and on his own status as a poet with respect to the bearers of power. Read as a group, they review the poet's activities over the past decade, reveal a new sophistication in expressing controversial views, extend the basically naïve pastoral persona, and present Spenser's verdict on the consequences of putting the dissimulative rhetoric of poetry at the service of those in power. By choosing to include the older generically related poems in the 1591 anthology, Spenser criticizes his previous attitudes toward the writing of courtly poetry and offers an example of the new poetry that might follow from his current, revised assumptions.

The earliest, longest, and most archaic of the three political poems is *Mother Hubberd*.[18] While it is impossible to identify the exact targets of this satire on the abuses of power by the new men of the Elizabethan court, the candor of the satire bespeaks the optimistic "New Poet" of *The Shepheardes Calender*, whose outspoken advocacy of the views of Leicester and his circle on matters social, political, and ecclesiastical comports easily with his self-proclaimed role of praiser of "Elisa" as the guarantor of his own freedom and of learning in general. A fairly uncomplicated allusion to this freedom is the pastoral episode in *Mother Hubberd* (ll. 223–342).

Here, as in Piers' tale in "May," the story of a predatory fox who devours his own charges has the social urgency of one who uses the pastoral allegory of the Christian–"Mantuanesque" eclogue form to convey open criticism of dangerous elements within Elisa's benign realm. That Spenser's confidence in the protected nature of such a vehicle was evidently misplaced, his promising future as a court poet shattered possibly within months of *Hubberd*'s writing (and certainly of the *Calender*'s publication), and the poet himself consigned to virtual exile in Ireland seem to us now the inevitable measure of his naïveté in *c.* 1579–80.

Spenser himself seems to have arrived at something like this judgment during the intervening decade, even while he was exploiting the Vergilian premises of *The Faerie Queene* Books 1–3. I have shown how the groups of visions and complaints in the 1591 anthology imply the poet's growing skepticism about the viability of various poetic conventions in the political climate of these years. The political allegories in the same volume confirm this revisionary outlook. This is especially evident in the critical relation of *Virgils Gnat*, "long since dedicated to...the Earle of Leicester, late deceased," as Spenser affirmed in 1590, to his later composition in the same mode, *Muiopotmos*. Here again we have a reversion to Vergil as the normative model of a poetic career, as well as the yoking of translation and original composition to make an evaluative "statement" on the Vergilian paradigm.

In *Virgils Gnat* there seems little doubt that Spenser is defending controversial acts like writing *Mother Hubberd* and dedicating it to Leicester.[19] The provocative sonnet to the latter gives us a revealing perspective on the ingenuous young poet's self-congratulatory role in the earlier events to which it alludes.[20] "Wrong'd, yet not daring to expresse my pain," the plaintiff explicitly names Leicester as "the causer of my care" and directs the reader to the *Gnat* for the cause of his complaint. Rarely, even in an age of obliquities and indirections, has a *poème à clef* been so ceremoniously introduced as a transparent dissimulation. Hence it is not surprising that *Gnat* turns on a pastoral fable adapted to convey the need for alertness to the perils inherent in public life. The innocent shepherd of the pseudo-Vergilian *Culex* enjoys an otium free of the greed and violent striving of the court. Yet the threatening serpent is there, and only the gnat's intervention stings the shepherd into awareness of his mortal danger. The inadequacy of the shepherd's personal idyll is brought out in the gnat's sarcastic admonition when his ghost returns to vindicate himself to the ungrateful shepherd:

> But doo thou haunt the soft downe rolling river,
> And wilde greene woods, and fruitful pastures minde,
> And let the flitting aire my vaine words sever. (ll. 636–8)

The disarming abundance of the pastoral *locus amoenus* is qualified by the gnat's ironic advice to commit political suicide by ignoring the realities of life as he had once lolled in blissful ignorance of the serpent in his garden. Implicitly, the poet's role is to inoculate his virtuous patron, content in the "happie life" of "idle leisour," against such self-deception.[21] As befits an occasional piece, the poem leaves it up in the air whether the gnat's advice will be heeded.

Muiopotmos replays the theme of the poet as moral instructor in an even more oblique mode. A certain airy quality has always been the source of this poem's charm, but the same quality has also recently been perceived as the key to its political message. According to Robert Brinkley, by modifying Ovid's criticism of Vergil in the Arachne episode of *Metamorphoses* 6, Spenser re-evaluates both his precursors' stances on the question of the poet's status in society.[22] Spenser suppresses Ovid's implicit condemnation of the weaver's victimization by Pallas, portraying the human contender as overcome by the goddess's superior art instead of brutalized, as in Ovid, by her physical force. Moreover, by emphasizing the motif of aesthetic compensation, Spenser also apparently justifies the injustice done to Astery which has created the butterfly's lovely wings. By these modifications of the critical Ovidian tone, Spenser seems to negate his precursor's resentment toward the powers that alone authorize all texts, as Pallas authorizes the butterfly by weaving her into the "text" of her tapestry.

Brinkley goes on to argue that by distancing himself equally from both victim and victimizer in the fall of Clarion, i.e. by refusing the perspective of insects and Olympians alike and typically presenting himself as a "stranger" in Elizabeth's England, Spenser tacitly urges political detachment as a way of survival:

the reader–narrator...by understanding the fate of the butterfly, absents himself from that fate...Rather than become a sign in the text of the poem, the narrator who reads what he envisions and relates what he reads, makes of his poem an index of his freedom to read...Unlike Arachne or the butterfly, Spenser is not a figure in Pallas' text. Having become its narrator, he evades the politics which has silenced them.   (674–5)

While one might question this inference, it seems certain that in *Muiopotmos* Spenser reassesses the Vergilian norm itself, which Brinkley identifies with the Augustan "spectacles of glory" parodied in the figures Ovid's Pallas weaves into the border of her text. Just as Ovid revises these spectacles from the *Georgics* and thus "demonstrates...that his audience can read the imperial order in a way that it does not authorize" (671), Spenser in turn applies the Ovidian revision to his own situation. Brinkley's conclusion bears out the revisionary implications of the other *Complaints* poems and of *Colin Clout*.

The relation of Spenser's position on this issue in *Muiopotmos* to that in *Virgils Gnat* seems to me decisive. The vulnerable innocence of the shepherd in the earlier poem allows the poet to identify his function with the Vergilian norm by locating his own acuity at the center of the poem's system of values. It is the shrewd poet who can save his naïve patron. The continuity of the courtly world figured as a pastoral community thus depends centrally on the poet as conservator through his exercise of the conventional duplicity of the mode, the concealment/revelation of the dedicatory sonnet functioning synecdochically in this regard. In *Muiopotmos*, whatever historical assignments of personae may be possible, the lovely butterfly with his illusion of security as the rightful heir of the kingdom clearly represents the complacency of the traditional pastoral persona. This is most evident in Clarion's two definitive postures: his contemplative soaring above the kingdom "To view the workmanship of heavens hight" (l. 45) and his dilettantish dipping into each delight in the "gay gardins," where he tastes with innocent excess all that nature provides for the delectation of the senses and fancy, much as the Spenserian persona had done in the gardens of Adonis in *The Faerie Queene*, Book 3.[23] This traditional prerogative of pastoral poetry to gourmandize on nature re-enforces the Edenic detachment Clarion enjoys before his fall:

> What more felicitie can fall to creature,
> Than to enjoy delight with libertie,
> And to be Lord of all the workes of Nature...
> To take what ever thing doth please the eie?   (ll. 209–14)

Like Adam before the fall, Clarion exercises his God-given lordship over the creatures.

Like the shepherd's naïveté in *Gnat*, however, the idyllic otium of the butterfly, mistranslated into a postlapsarian world, collapses because it fails to account for evil. From his illusory freedom at the center of the courtly world, he will fall victim to the reality of that world signified by his counterpart's imprisonment in Pallas' woven celebration of her own imperial power. He too will be entangled in a web. But unlike the shepherd's, Clarion's false security and freedom rest on a triple injustice of the gods. First of all he owes his beautiful wings to the arbitrary (and pseudo-Ovidian) metamorphosis of Astery into a butterfly "for memorie / Of pretended crime, though crime none were" (ll. 142–3). Then this same beauty, appended by Minerva to her tapestry as the crowning seal of her artistic superiority to Arachne, becomes the explicit cause of the girl's defeat and spur to her son Aragnol's revenge. Whereas Ovid's Arachne had been bludgeoned by a jealous Pallas and then transformed into a spider to save her from her attempted self-destruction by hanging, Spenser's undergoes instant metamorphosis on seeing the enmeshed butterfly added as the *coup de grâce* to the goddess's victorious weaving. By sharing emblematic pride of place with the olive trees, among which she "wantonly" flutters in the tapestry like Clarion in his garden, the woven butterfly also evokes the Vergilian identification of the poet with the dominant source of power in his civilization. By accepting the goddess's "authority" and becoming her "creature" he finds a place in a hierarchical scheme of things. This Vergilian conception of the poet's privileged status in the chambers of power falls along with Clarion, whose entanglement is unredeemedly mortal. Hence the central irony of the poem is the apparent third injustice of the gods, Jove's deliberate working of the butterfly's fate (ll. 233–40). Another weaver like Minerva – Clarion's "cruell fate is woven even now / Of *Joves* owne hand" (ll. 235–6) – the Homeric plotter of the hero's fall, as mediated by the bitter ironies of Vergil's more history- and dynasty-minded Jove, sanctions this injustice to rectify the former one of Pallas to Arachne. Clarion is sacrificed to the principle that the poet cannot innocently benefit from arbitrary abuses of power. Appropriately, the agent of *his* downfall is himself the descendant of a fellow-"poet" and earlier victim of the divine powers.

In this light it is hard to see how Spenser can be said to ground his function, as Brinkley suggests, on a "freedom to read" events independently of his political "author," by which act he "evades the politics which [have] silenced" the characters in the poem. It is precisely the freedom to read the imperial myth in her own terms, by weaving stories of the gods' violations of human integrity, that brings down the arbitrary wrath of the goddess on Arachne in Ovid's parable of the Vergilian poet. Rather than revising Ovid by disguising *his* message from the eye of authority, it seems to me that in Clarion's fate Spenser implies that any such effort at self-effacement is delusory. Furthermore, by publishing *Mother Hubberd* and *Gnat* long after the events they describe and even after the death of the patron by whom he had been "Wrong'd," and by further appending a sonnet to *Gnat* that invites a personal reading of an otherwise innocuous translation of the *Culex*, Spenser retrospectively announces the futility of his former dissemblings. By the addition of *Muiopotmos*, an original poem superficially in the mode of *Virgils Gnat* in which the Vergilian conception of the poet is criticized by way of Ovid, he further discredits the pose of detachment that glosses over the question of the poet's vicarious participation in acts of official injustice. The emblematic butterfly who exhibits the classical detachment of the poet is woven into the texture of authority in the poem. Spenser thus signals his own uneasiness with the Vergilian model and his desire to discard it in favor of a more acceptable one. He also implies the beginning of a search for a version of pastoral free from the Eclogues' associations with the Vergilian celebration of power.

In their different ways, the three major constellations of generically related poems in *Complaints* that I have been discussing all point to a radical revision of the operative pastoral myth in Spenser's earlier poetry. We have seen that according to that myth the poet's role is consonant with that of the good courtier in *Mother Hubberd*. Unlike his corrupted counterpart, this ideal courtier serves his prince "Not so much for to gaine, or for to raise / Himselfe to high degree" as to "winne worthie place" in his master's "liking" (*Mother Hubberd* ll. 773–6).[24] The instruments of his service include the full Machiavellian panoply of a Renaissance humanist-courtier:

> For he is practiz'd well in policie,
> And thereto doth his Courting most applie:
> To learne the enterdeale of Princes strange,

> To marke th'intent of Counsells, and the change
> Of states, and eke of private men somewhile,
> Supplanted by fine falshood and faire guile.   (ll. 783–8)

To this shrewd perceptiveness the "rightfull Courtier" adds the power of rhetoric necessary to make effective delivery of his skill in "policie."[25] Like the gnat in the fable, this courtier-rhetor-poet practices "Courting" by putting his linguistic skills at the service of his patron, by whose success he himself will deservedly rise.

If the sequence of *Gnat* and *Muiopotmos* effectively undermines Spenser's former ideal of the poet's social function by exposing as naïve his view of the poet–patron relation, the visions and complaints counterpoise a superficial medieval mood of *contemptus mundi* against an array of worldly explanations of the fall of men and states. This balancing of opposed accounts of evil is illuminated by the testimony of Urania in *The Teares of the Muses*, probably written around 1580.[26] Like her sister Muses, the wisdom-inspiring Urania has been banished by the very enemies of learning who could most benefit from her offices. Her remedy recalls the pastoral poet's in "June": she can outscorn her banishers "And please my selfe with mine owne selfe-delight, / In contemplation of things heavenlie wrought" (ll. 525–6). In 1589–90 this Clarion-like escape is no longer possible. Yet the volume pointedly ends with an even more extreme exhortation to its dedicatee to *respicere finem*, ignoring both the volatile contents of the volume and the aggressive act of publishing it. Such a delicate balance of concealment and revelation of his real motives shows Spenser in 1591 on the threshold of discovering a new alternative to the earlier pastoral of power. It also helps clarify the strategy of *Colin Clout*.

III

Before returning to *Colin Clout*, Spenser's major declaration of a new pastoral persona and program, it may be worth a moment to consider two works of the same period, *Astrophel* and *Daphnaïda*. Only the first of these is explicitly pastoral, but in a way that very fact bears on the argument of this chapter. *Astrophel*, Spenser's belated commemoration of Sidney's death in 1586, was not published till 1595, when it was, significantly, attached to *Colin Clout*.[27] Conventional to the point of tedium, at least for most modern readers, it is labelled "A Pastorall Elegie" and conducted within the familiar boundaries of that genre.[28] *Daphnaïda*, on the other hand, dated from London 1 January 1591 and necessarily written after the death of Douglas Howard in August of 1590, is distinctly *un*conventional, despite its regular use of pastoral motifs and conventions as well as its flagrant allusion to Colin Clout (ll. 225–31). Viewed in juxtaposition, the two elegies tell us something more about the direction Spenser is taking in these years.

It is not my intention to argue for any intrinsic poetic excellence in the often-derogated *Astrophel*: the poem is indeed a cold pastoral. But this fact seems to imply Spenser's deliberate return to the anonymity of the pastoral genres. He is willing to let the form itself convey the feeling, the medium be the message. This intention is announced in the three stanzas that introduce the formal praise of Astrophel and the mythologizing account (another choice of convention over realistic or personal narrative) of Sidney's death. In the latter the gruesome wound suffered at Zutphen is pastoralized into another death of Adonis, a unique and irregular life universalized as myth. Spenser himself appears at the outset only as the anonymous singer of Astrophel's death, "rehears[ing]" the formal lament sung by Clorinda, Astrophel's sister, in the lament/ reconciliation format of Vergil's fifth eclogue and "November." Presumably, he is satisfied to confine his role to the conventional, anonymous spokesman of the pastoral community. Only the gesture of commemoration itself – Spenser restoring his first literary patron to a pastoral England and a pastoralized eternal union with "Stella" – lends symbolic resonance to this act nearly anonymous. In a different sense from that of the sister-poem, Colin has come home.

By contrast *Daphnaïda*, a more interesting and varied work than *Astrophel*, is also more troubled. It may even be viewed as a pastoral elegy *manqué*, a poem that fails to fulfill its convention. Its departures from any expected mode of elegiac commemoration imply a gloss on Spenser's evolving pastoral myth and a critique of the earlier myth he is in the process of discarding. On the face of it, it may seem tendentious to treat *Daphnaïda* as a failed pastoral elegy. Spenser's use of the convention of the dream-vision after Chaucer's *Boke of the Duchesse* dictates a method wholly different from that of "November" or *Astrophel*. But within its vision structure the poet employs a number of pastoral motifs. Alcyon, despite his un-pastoral name, is a "jollie Shepheard swaine" wrenched from his pastoral paradise by the death of his white lioness.[29] And even the heraldic emblem–allegory is discarded, in pastoral fashion, midway through the poem as a result of the speaker's naïve inability to fathom this non-pastoral convention. The lioness becomes merely "Daphne," a shepherdess.

Rather surprisingly, in the end *Daphnaïda* evolves into another fairly overt version of Vergilian pastoral. Following Alcyon's prolonged and extreme lament, to which I will return in a moment, the speaker lamely offers him lodging:

> I him desirde, sith daie was overcast,
> And darke night fast approched, to be pleased
> To turne aside unto my Cabinet,
> And staie with me, till he were better eased
> Of that strong stownd, which him so sore beset.[30] (ll. 556–60)

This echo of the end of Eclogue 1, along with the customary Vergilian allusion to nightfall, imparts at the last possible moment a conventional pastoral touch to the elegy. The mysterious Chaucerian Man in Black, heretofore in the poem cast in the mould of the Wandering Jew doomed forever restlessly to mourn his isolation from normal human activities, is now assimilated to another exile, Meliboeus, and asked to resign himself to his fate. It is an invitation he cannot accept; instead, his Gallus-like isolation from the pastoral world is emphasized in the end, as he staggers out of the poem, leaving a benumbed would-be Tityrus to conclude, "But what of him became I cannot weene" (l. 567).

It would be tempting to read this move as simply a comment by Spenser on the extremity of Alcyon's grief. And certainly it is extreme: the seven seven-stanza complaints that fill his lament (each stanza comprising seven lines) constitute an insupportable litany on the theme of *contemptus mundi*.[31] But in fact the poem makes clear that its failure to achieve any consolation results not from the excesses of the bereaved Alcyon, but from the lack of authority in his would-be consoler. This intention is first indicated early in the poem, even before we meet the Man in Black. It is a "gloomie evening," and the speaker seeks fresh air in fields "whose flowring pride opprest / With early frosts, had lost their beautie faire" (ll. 26–8). Far from foreshadowing Alcyon and his story, however, this setting reflects the speaker's own "meditation / Of this worlds vainnesse and lifes wretchednesse" (ll. 33–4). Like the man he is about to meet, the speaker feels himself to be "of many most, / Most miserable man" (ll. 37–8). No reason is given for this profound self-pity, but in its light it is hard to see his later inability to provide consolation as merely a tactful gesture of sympathy to Arthur Gorges, the widower of "Daphne." He is from the outset implicated in the deep mood of pessimism and contempt for all pleasures radiating from Alcyon.

One further aspect of this encounter may suggest the relevance of *Daphnaïda* to Spenser's evolution as a pastoral poet. In the Dedication to the aunt of the deceased, and throughout the poem, Spenser hints at the strong opposition of the noble Howards, and especially Douglas/Daphne's father, to her marriage to Gorges.[32] This quasi-political motive is re-enforced by the poem's one allusion to Colin Clout. In a familiar gesture of formal respect that Spenser will repeat in his praise of Rosalind in *The Faerie Queene* 6.10, Alcyon interrupts his praise of Daphne to apologize to "*Elisa* royall Shepheardesse" for praising someone else – an apology one might have thought even Gloriana would find unnecessary under the circumstances. But Elisa doesn't need Alcyon's praise,

> For she hath praises in all plenteousnesse
> Powr'd upon her like showers of *Castaly*
> By her own Shepheard, *Colin* her owne Shepherd,
> That her with heavenly hymnes doth deifie.   (ll. 227–30)[33]

This seemingly gratuitous tarring of Colin with the brush of flattery reinforces the speaker's failure to achieve the usual consolation and reconciliation of the elegy, despite its pervasive pastoral motifs. The convention, Spenser implies, is outmoded, debased. Sterile praise of the Queen has pre-empted the poet's attention and rendered him and his pastoral persona incapable of fulfilling their normal functions. The spectre of power that haunts the poem in its dedication, the lion allegory, and elsewhere infects Spenser's use of the pastoral forms and conventions too, and encourages his surrender of conventional consolation to a mood of deep despair.

It is thus possible to see the relative conventionality of *Astrophel* as a reaffirmation of pastoral, in contrast to the invalidity of the myth implied in *Daphnaïda*.[34] In *Daphnaïda* the speaker shares the despair of the bereaved and his contempt for earthly joys, while Colin Clout is associated with an empty official pastoral myth. In *Astrophel*, the pastoral convention serves to set apart the Countess of Pembroke and her late brother, the shepherd-patron-hero of the

Sidney–Leicester circle, from Burghley and his fellow debasers of cultural norms. *Astrophel* does not go beyond the formal gesture of reasserting this pastoral standard. As a public statement it does not share with the *Complaints* poems or *Daphnaïda* the complex retrospective outlook I have been examining. Rather, it should be viewed as the complement of the work with which it shared publication, *Colin Clout*, the major expression of Spenser's new pastoral stance in which Spenser gathers together the strains of criticism and discontent of the other poems of 1589–91 and fashions them into a single comment on his break with the Vergilian persona and myth of his earlier poems.

IV

As I suggested earlier, one focus of *Colin Clout* revealed by its careful (though seemingly haphazard) structure is the poet's address to Raleigh, who in the late 1580s supplanted the deceased Sidney as Spenser's highly placed literary friend and oversaw his re-emergence in England with the first publication of *The Faerie Queene*. Not only is Raleigh the dedicatee of the poem, but as the Shepherd of the Ocean he is also a major figure in it, sponsoring as he does Spenser's earlier pastoral myth of service to Gloriana. In this capacity he introduces his country cousin to the City, center of that larger world which, according to Vergil, authorizes the poet's freedom in his private Arcadia. But in *Colin Clout* it is the rejection of this courtly version of pastoral around which Spenser constructs his poem. By the end of the poem the center of values shifts from England to Ireland, from Elisa to Rosalind, and from the Shepherd of the Ocean to Colin himself as the legitimate spokesman specifically on the question of love. Despite its dedication, then, *Colin Clout* must have had the effect of a friendly warning to Raleigh to examine the cultural premises underlying his own career, the Elizabethan myth of the *vita activa*, or life of aspiration. Hence the conjunction in the poem of two contending versions of pastoral: the Elizabethan pastoral of power and a contemplative pastoral transcending politics.[35] Hence too the implicit confrontation in the poem of two sources of authority, Elisa–Cynthia and Rosalind.

For all that, it is not primarily Raleigh whom Spenser addresses in *Colin Clout*, but himself. Perhaps out of tact, the implicit target of the poet's criticism is Spenser's own established pastoral persona,

Colin Clout. The Shepherd is at best the occasion and instigator of Colin's education. Throughout the poem, and not just in its final section on Colin's homecoming, the operative myth of the poet's function in the Elizabethan power structure, and particularly the element of self-deception in that myth, is subjected to continuous scrutiny. The apparently sudden reversal of outlook triggered by Thestylis' pointed question, Why did you return?, has in fact been thoroughly prepared for in the first two-thirds of the poem. In keeping with the poem's pastoral mode, this preparation is for the most part oblique. Its focus is the re-education of Spenser's pastoral persona.

Much of the poem concerns the exercise of power. As the conventional naïf of Vergilian pastoral, it is Colin's prerogative not to see beyond the surface of things. Spenser uses this ingenuousness to his satirical advantage in describing the passage overseas to England, by having Colin himself question the Shepherd of the Ocean's "pastoral of the sea," in which the pastoral myth is superimposed on an imperialist reality.[36] Colin's naïveté in these lines ranges from open-mouthed awe at the mariners' power to master the fearful element, to wonderment that the apparent chaos of the sea can be in fact "the Regiment / Of a great shepheardesse, that *Cynthia* hight," the surging waves her hills, the "fishes" her herds, and of course the courtiers her shepherds and nymphs (ll. 232–69). "Thereat I wondred much," says Colin, and we can hardly help but share his amazement at this blatant travesty of the pastoral of power.

But earlier in the poem, as well as later, Colin is subject to the constant queries of his admiring audience of shepherds. This chorus of listeners begins innocently enough as the usual yes-men to the shepherd-hero's recitation: their questions at first merely lend variety to Colin's discourse, frequently causing him to digress from his narrative. The first such interruption results in Colin's rehearsing the song he had sung to the Shepherd of the Ocean upon the latter's visit. In the exchange of songs we not only learn of the "faultlesse" Shepherd's banishment by, and yet unswerving loyalty to, Cynthia but are treated to an epitome of Spenser's strategy throughout the poem in Colin's innocent, seemingly unmotivated tale of Bregog and Mulla. Like the Shepherd's plaint, Colin's song is also about star-crossed lovers. Its moral obliquely glances at Spenser's message to Raleigh in *Colin Clout*: "So deare his love he bought" (l. 155).

Unlike the Shepherd, however, Bregog is not quite guiltless in this tale of thwarted love. Though no villain by nature, the crafty suitor is compelled to resort to underhanded trickery; "So secretly did he his love enjoy" (l. 145).[37] The lovers are introduced as mutually faithful and sincere: "Full faine she lov'd, and was belov'd full faine" (l. 116). It is the possessiveness of old Mole, who, "sitting still on hie, / ...from far observ'd with jealous eie" (ll. 132–4), that brings about the deception and its painful retribution. In the end Bregog sacrifices his very name to the father's prerogative to determine his child's marital destiny. Aspiring lovers beware.

What is most revealing about the story, though, is Colin's construction of it. For despite the basic innocence and truth of the lovers and the palpably contractual attitude toward marriage betrayed by Mole and the official suitor, Allo, Colin condones the tyrannization of love, masking it in the fiction of the "carefull" father's reasonable efforts to secure a good match for his child.[38] Spenser will return to this sort of conflict between affection and the prerogatives of power in Book 6, both in the Aladine–Priscilla episode (canto 3) and in the story of Bellamour and Claribell (canto 12). But even there, under the gentler aegis of Courtesy, no possible reconciliation of these conflicting claims will be ventured, except the timely death of Claribell's father. In the story of Mulla and Bregog, however, he allows two irreconcilable constructions to be simultaneously inferred: the frustration of genuine love by a tyrant, and a loving father's just annihilation of a social-climbing rake. Although Spenser leaves little doubt in the reader's mind that the former reading is the correct one, he simultaneously establishes Colin as a naïve defender of hierarchical privilege:

> So of a River, which he was of old,
> He none was made, but scattred all to nought,
> And lost emong those rocks into him rold,
> Did lose his name: so deare his love he bought.[39] (ll. 152–5)

This implication of over-credulity, or political obtuseness, in Colin's song is borne out by his narration of his stay at court. Here the hitherto innocuous questions of his audience bring out the underlying flaws and contradictions in Colin's posture. The poet's own location in the power structure has not been entirely ignored in the poem. Not only Raleigh's temporary exile, but also Spenser's prolonged one, is touched on in the two shepherds' conversation following their exchange of songs, and the comments lead to the Shepherd of the Ocean's taking Colin back to court. Characteristically, Colin's relation of this brief conversation masks the role of positive authority in the poet's banishment. Like those who mysteriously "chaunce" to rise to power at the end of *Vanitie* or the Shepherd himself, who "chaunst" to find Colin earlier in *Colin Clout*, Spenser's fall from grace is metamorphosed into Colin's

> luckelesse lot:
> That banisht had my selfe, like wight forlore,
> Into that waste, where I was quite forgot.   (ll. 181–3)

In the typically Spenserian syntax of the lines we may choose to understand either his vague "lot" or Colin himself as the cause of his banishment. In fact, the very ambiguity underscores the point that in exorcizing from the story any trace of external authority – no responsible individual and no collectivity has *authored* the action – Colin indeed embraces his fate and thus becomes in effect the agent of his own undoing.

It is precisely this kind of rhetorical strategy, by which the Vergilian pastoral poet derives his sense of authority from a participation in the true repositories of power, that Spenser ultimately exposes in *Colin Clout*. In the account of his visit to Cynthia's court this theme gradually emerges through the extended counterpoint between Colin's ingenuous narration on the one hand and the questions and comments of his rustic auditors on the other. These interruptions are aimed at bringing into critical focus the myth of Cynthia's realm as a pastoral paradise. Cuddie's question about other places (ll. 290f.), for example, triggers Colin's description of a pastoral England that ends in his pointed criticism of the "gracelesse men" that mar this idyllic state (l. 327). This criticism, however, leaves the pastoral of power intact; it is the questioning of Colin's effusions on his own place at court that brings into relief the personal myth Spenser is querying in the poem. And this myth rests precisely on the notion that poets are a necessary and independent source of positive values in the courtly ambience.

The most important interpolations are those of Alexis and later Cuddy regarding Colin's praise of Cynthia, at just the point where Colin is about to tell how the Shepherd of the Ocean "advanced" his cause (l. 357). First Alexis points out that by praising the Queen Colin "doe[th him]selfe upraise" (l. 355). This comment reminds us that the pastoral is often a ploy whereby the court poet disingenuously arrogates power and status to himself by humbly flattering his betters. Alexis follows up this observation a bit later by asking Colin why, given all the good poets he found at Court, Cynthia needs *his* song. From one point of view, the implied answer is that she doesn't, that the illusion of the exceptional poet's indispensable function goes along with that of an intrinsic authority independent of his flattery of the great. But Colin manages to evade this inference by describing at length the excellent singers surrounding Cynthia. Only his action in forswearing the court will really address this question.

Meanwhile, Alexis' first question is echoed by Cuddy following Colin's soaring praise of Cynthia near the end of this section of the poem. Once again it is the latter's high style, inappropriate to a shepherd, that is called into question. Colin is accused of having forgotten "Thy selfe...to mount so hie: / Such loftie flight, base shepheard seemeth not, / From flocks and fields, to Angels and to skie" (ll. 615–19). This time Colin counters with an aggressive apology for his epideictic style: it is Cynthia's own virtue that miraculously commands his tongue, as well as guaranteeing his song's immortality. Spenser is here touching on a tender spot in the mythology of court poetry: the fact that the fate of a poet's work hinges on the fashions and personal whims of patronage.[40] Yet Colin's defense of his fault, which ties his own eternal fame decisively to the Queen's, cannot explain away the element of self-aggrandizement implied in the pastoral myth of vicarious power. This myth is grounded in the poet's *raptio* from himself, his sacrifice (like Bregog's) of his own identity as a result of his contiguity with power. Cynthia's excellence

> Lifts me above the measure of my might:
> That being fild with furious insolence,
> I feele my selfe like one yrapt in spright. (ll. 621–3)

As "insolence" implies, that state is a self-deluding one that rests on the self-praise implicit in praise of the great.

Colin further justifies this myth by attributing to Cynthia an intrinsic spiritual value that matches her external, political power. Her force is claimed to derive not from her position as head of state but from her privileged perspective on reality.[41] Her mounting thoughts rise to the "vauted skies" (l. 611):

> There she beholds with high aspiring thought,
> The cradle of her owne creation:
> Emongst the seats of Angels heavenly wrought,
> Much like an Angell in all forme and fashion.   (ll. 612–15)

As in the Proem to *The Faerie Queene* Book 3, Spenser implies here that Elizabeth's true claim to adulation is her unique capacity for contemplation. According to the official Platonism of the time, her imperial status reflects and is justified by her metaphysically "aspiring mind," which in turn implicitly denies the same aspiration to any lesser personage than herself.[42] Only by derivation, Colin insists, can the lowly shepherd thus aspire. By the end of the poem Colin will have reversed this ratio by exposing its confusion of political with spiritual power and divorcing contemplation from social status. Only then can the poet, like his Augustan prototypes, make available to those with the capacity to benefit by it the full value of his unique access to the truth. To do this, however, requires a revaluation of the pastoral myth.

Primarily, such a revaluation is negotiated by way of Colin's purported decision to leave court because of the wicked courtiers. Thestylis' skepticism about this explanation – he accuses Colin of "spight" in speaking out against the very "felicitee" he had been praising – calls forth a shower of abuse on the evil ways of courtiers.[43] But Colin's pose of "simple honestye" takes on conviction only when he turns in the last hundred lines of the poem to the subject of love. Love has been an issue in the poem from the outset. The Shepherd of the Ocean's hopeless love for Cynthia picks up on Colin's own amatory difficulties – "lasse" becomes "losse" in his reply to a question of Cuddy's (ll. 80–9) – and the story of Mulla and Bregog provides a paradigm of courtly love-intrigue and patriarchal marriage rites, as we have seen. But it is his vindication of pastoral, as opposed to courtly, love that wins over Colin's audience of erstwhile skeptics and is presumably intended to win over the reader as well. Here Colin articulates a pastoral myth that both allows the dignity of the shepherd-poet and establishes a basis for that dignity which is not derived from a vicarious aspiration to political power disguised as pastoral humility. On the Senecan dictum of a legitimate withdrawal from civic activity under circumstances of political corruption, Spenser here begins to forge an erotically grounded contemplative pastoral.

The details of Spenser's version of Platonic love are too familiar to bear repeating here.[44] The nub of his doctrine in the present context is the spiritual and transcendent source of eroticism, derived from the "gardens of *Adonis*" (l. 804) and underwriting all harmony in nature and the human world, in contradistinction to the predatory "courting vaine" of would-be seducers (ll. 786–90). More important to the dialectic of *Colin Clout*, this Lucretian–Boethian Love is a truly universal "Lord of all the world by right" (l. 883). His *imperium* is immutable, though he presides over a mutable world; and Colin, in becoming his servant here as he was Cynthia's before, implicitly grounds his own poetic authority in an order whose power transcends that of any merely secular ruler.[45]

This inference is supported, I believe, by the new shape of Spenser's platonic myth. Whereas in the earlier passage the lowly poet could derive his contemplative powers only through the mediation of the Queen, now he has himself implicitly supplanted her authority. As Love's priest, Colin is praised for his eloquence where he had been explicitly criticized before. By deriving his power directly and solely from the god, he grounds his freedom on a shared creatureliness: Love "rules the creatures by his powrfull saw: / All being made the vassalls of his might" (ll. 884–5). Here at last is a figure of authority more potent even than the "great shepheardesse" and "Ladie of the sea." Similarly Rosalind, as a personal figura mediating between Colin and the divine power of love, is distinguished from the other "shepherds daughters" solely by her "divine regard and heavenly hew" (ll. 932–3). Like Cynthia before, her thoughts are as high as herself (l. 937); yet this spiritual superiority has no reference to any social status:

> For she is not like as the other crew
> Of shepheards daughters which emongst you bee,
> But of divine regard and heavenly hew,
> Excelling all that ever ye did see.
> Not then to her that scorned thing so base,
> But to my selfe the blame that lookt so hie:
> So hie her thoughts as she her selfe have place,
> And loath each lowly thing with loftie eie.[46]   (ll. 931–8)

With respect to her, as to her Lord, "each lowly thing" is equally worthy of preferment – or scorn (l. 938). The passage resonates with the rhetoric of power; and Rosalind, like Cupid, is as arbitrary as any Renaissance prince or tyrant. But the pastoral myth of the lowly subject now has a poetic rather than a political basis. As Petrarch had adumbrated in his Laura (= *lauro*, the symbol of his own poetic originality) the "secularization" or immanental grounding of the figura in the "free play" of the poetic imagination, so Spenser now grasps at a further metamorphosis of Rosalind into a surrogate for Cynthia, his pastoralized version of the Queen. Power or authority, at least in the mystical Tudor sense of deriving from a transcendent reality, is implicitly denied the Queen and arrogated to the contemplative poet himself. As the priest of love and humble suitor to Rosalind, Colin has attained an authority independent of his status at court. In thus rejecting the courtly pastoral of power Spenser lays the Platonic–contemplative foundation for a new pastoral myth.

As the closing echoes of the tenth eclogue imply, this reassessment of the operative pastoral myth also entails a revaluation of its Vergilian model. Colin's praise of Cynthia, which in turn is praise and exaltation of himself, recalls the imperial myth of *Georgics* 3. 1–45. Poised there between the simple pastoral ideal of his youth and the ambitious epic calling he anticipates, the Vergilian persona announces his intention to participate vicariously in Caesar's triumphs:[47]

No, I must venture a theme [that] will exalt me
From earth and give me wings and a triumph on every tongue...
Caesar's image shall stand there in the midst, commanding my temple,
While I, like a victor, conspicuous in crimson robes, shall drive
A hundred four-horse chariots up and down by the river. (ll. 8–9, 17–18)

At this juncture of his career, Spenser seems to return to that watershed in the Vergilian itinerary. Halfway (as it will turn out) through his own epic–imperial celebration of a regime, he looks not ahead but back to the pastoral point of departure he has shared with his major precursor.[48]

All Spenser's retrospective verse of 1589–91, as I have tried to show, seems to return to this critical juncture in order to redefine his own underlying pastoral myth. From the Augustan age onward, poets have looked upon Vergil as the uniquely blessed poet, whose official patrons rewarded his merits while granting free rein to his genius. This paradigm in turn inspired many poets in the Renaissance to apply the Vergilian model to themselves and their careers. For Spenser as for others, the progression from pastoral to georgic to epic enshrines that happy expectation. By the time of *Colin Clout*, however, this hope is perceived to be in vain. Though Gloriana may still be divorced from her flatterers and praised as the Muse of a national poetry, Spenser can no longer entertain the illusion of an independent moral authority granted by an indulgent secular power. When Colin rises at the end of *Colin Clout* to withdraw from impending night, we have no doubt that he will remain, despite his still unrequited love, spiritually within the newly discovered pastoral world with its own indigenous sources of values. It is there, perhaps more than in any literal milieu, that Colin has come home.

5

Exit Colin Clout

Colin Clouts Come Home Againe was written in 1591. How much of the three books that would be published in the second, and last, installment of *The Faerie Queene* five years later was already written at the time we do not know. But by the time of Spenser's courtship in 1594, as fictionalized in the *Amoretti* (published in 1595), all six books had been completed.[1] It seems likely, therefore, that Spenser began work on Books 4–6 shortly after his return to Ireland and finished them within three years of his fruitless bid for preferment at court in 1589–91.[2]

Certainly, as recent criticism has widely recognized, these later books reflect the same mood of disillusionment in this period as *Colin Clout*.[3] The plot of Book 4 resolves few of its central issues and leaves the main couples with whose fortunes we have been concerned since Book 3 still un-reunited. Only at the end of the book is Florimell released from Proteus' cave by the intervention of Neptune (4.12.29–33), but her wedding with Marinell is delayed until Book 5 (canto 3). Scudamour and Amoret, reunited in the original ending of Book 3, in the 1596 edition are not. Their story in Book 4 has an unsettling retrospective air as a succession of mishaps and misapprehensions culminates not in their marriage but in Scudamour's narration of his first finding her at the Temple of Venus (4.10). Neither character is heard of again in *The Faerie Queene*. The same is true of Britomart and Artegall, principal heroes of Books 3 and 4 respectively, whose union has been a major goal of the poem since early in Book 3. They meet in combat not once but twice in Book 4, and though they are eventually reconciled (4.6.40–1), they are separated again until Britomart has to rescue him from Radigund (5.7). But even this brief reunion, like Artegall's larger quest, ends ambiguously: they are separated once more, and Britomart disappears from the poem she has virtually dominated for three books.[4] Book 5 ends in a distinctly minor key, when Artegall's rescue of Irena is followed by his assault at the hands of Detraction, Envy, and the Blatant Beast.[5] When we last see him greeting Calidore as the latter sets out on his adventure, Artegall is still "halfe sad / From his late conquest" of Grantorto (6.1.4).

If the unconsummated marriages of these books testify to the difficulty of managing personal and dynastic relationships in a discordant world, Book 4 at least asserts an underlying concord in nature through its archetypal wedding of the Thames and Medway, the immediate context for Florimell's liberation from her bondage to Proteus and the adumbration of her eventual union with Marinell.[6] Similar archetypes of sexual and political harmony constitute the "allegorical cores" of these books – the Temple of Venus in Book 4 and Isis Church in Book 5 – against which their equivocal and increasingly problematical dénouements are played out. One might compare the tension in Book 3 between the theoretical exposition of a virtue and its difficulty of achievement in practice. As we have seen, Amoret and Florimell both have to struggle to fulfill their destinies in the face of personal anxieties about sexuality and male inconstancy. But offsetting these obstacles is Britomart's clarity about her own amatory and imperial fate, which renders her invincible in her encounters with the (male) heroic world. That role diminishes in importance in the second installment, as the emphasis shifts from problems of the heart, or self-mastery, to those of the world and social relationships. Now the almost automatic victory of Britomart over her antagonists takes on something of the Pyrrhic nature of Redcrosse's easy martial triumphs in the early cantos of Book 1. The values are reversed: it is now the external dynamics of the social structure that threaten to vitiate the personal triumphs of chastity. But we have the same sense of moving into areas of experience where the simpler expedients of valor or purity are no longer adequate to the challenges the heroes face.

This tendency is by no means overcome in Book 6. The book's apparent movement toward univocality and closure has often been noted.[7] The frustrations of an empirical realm in which the exercise of virtue turns out to be increasingly futile seem to dissipate with the book's sudden swerve in its last four cantos toward pastoral clarity, though this is in turn clouded by the violent disruption of the idyll and equivocal return to a more sombre heroic reality. The meaning of Calidore's "truancy" in the Pastorella episode initiated in canto 9, his fortuitous participation in Colin Clout's contemplative vision on Mt. Acidale in canto 10, the violent but successful rescue of his love in canto 11, and the ambiguous completion of his task in canto 12 have all proved highly controversial. The very courtesy of which he is the exemplary knight has been questioned, either as an ersatz virtue or because of its customary association with the court. He has been accused of heartlessly intruding on the intimacy of other lovers, or of using his social skills to manipulate others to serve his own ends, and has been blamed for both shattering Colin's poetic ecstasy and failing to learn from it when it is explained to him. Finally, the whole pastoral myth on which Calidore's adventure is built has been said to be exploded by the bloody dénouement of the episode, as his dereliction of his knightly duties brings down retribution on his own and the shepherds' heads.[8]

Yet while Calidore's drift into a quasi-contemplative pastoral existence seems at odds with public evils demanding renewed attention, the more private virtues come into focus throughout Book 6, culminating in Colin Clout's reappearance at the imaginative summit of the second installment. As Spenser's persona, Colin has been the main vehicle in his pastoral works for his assessments of his own career vis-à-vis a courtly society whose capacity for benefitting from his offices is repeatedly called into question. But Colin's final appearance in Spenser's work, near the climax of the last complete book of his heroic poem, is unique. Not only does it bring the poet into the poem as a character in direct relation to the hero Calidore, but it connects him intimately to the pastoral underside of his epic world. The completed portion of *The Faerie Queene* ends with a personal statement by Spenser, by means of his favorite pastoral convention, on the poem's central argument about the active and contemplative lives.

I

In general, the direction of Books 4–5 is away from the private and toward the public world. From the outset, even familiar character and plot elements are skewed toward the situations of individuals in a social context. Amoret, for example, whose imprisonment by Busyrane in Book 3 implies her psychological vulnerability as a virgin on the threshold of marriage, in 4.1 is depicted as almost obsessively concerned with preserving her "honor" (4.1.5, 6, 8) from "spot of blame" (4.1.4). Her prissiness with her still unrevealed rescuer, Britomart, anticipates that of Serena with Calepine in 6.8.

By the same token, the opening sequence in the anonymous castle (4.1.9–16) replays the comic night-scene in 3.1. But though the two episodes share the common motif of gender confusion, the focus shifts from the misdirected erotic desire of Malecasta, the incarnation of unchastity, to the social complications of courtly mating. The Ariostan "custome" of the castle poses a potentially destructive threat to sociability which Britomart's canny use of both her martial prowess and her feminine identity easily "salve[s]" (11.7). After such innocent beginnings, the true scope of the forces leading to social chaos is at once unveiled with the appearance of Ate (1.17–30). Wrecker of civilizations, hideously double of tongue, ear, and hand,

> So much her malice did her might surpas,
> That even th'Almightie selfe she did maligne,
> Because to man so mercifull he was,
> And unto all his creatures so benigne,
> Sith she her selfe was of his grace indigne:
> For all this worlds faire workmanship she tride,
> Unto his last confusion to bring,
> And that great golden chaine quite to divide,
> With which it blessed Concord hath together tide. (st. 30)

Between this apparition and the Blatant Beast turns the action of Books 4–6.

In this context the pastoral plays a declining role. Although the poet's primary function as reconciler of discordant societal forces is prominent in these books, it is in allusions to his Orphic attributes as "godlike man" more than in full-blown pastoral scenes or images that this function is conveyed.[9] On the other hand, typical figures of reconciliation such as Agape (see, e.g., 4.2.44) retain their associations with nature as the "privie place" where virtues naturally flourish. Like Sir Satyrane in Book 1, the three sons of Agape are conceived "in the salvage wood," their mother having been "oppressed" by a "noble...knight" as she sat combing her hair beside a stream (2.45; cf. 1.6.22). Again like Satyrane, as they grow to maturity their "fathers blood" shows through in their desire to practice arms (4.2.46; cf. 1.6.29). This connection of virtue with a *locus amoenus* will be exploited fully in Book 6, but even in 4 and 5 Florimell's chastity, for example, has had its nurture among the Graces on Mt. Acidale (4.5.5), while Artegall, the knight of Justice, first appears in *The Faerie Queene* as a "stranger knight" in "savage weed" bearing on his shield the motto "*Salvagesse sans finesse*" (4.4.39) in anticipation of several notable characters in Book 6.[10]

On the other hand, as in earlier books the same woods that nurture the chivalry of Satyrane or the brothers -*mond*, and the chastity of Belphoebe, are also the domain of the lustful, cannibalistic "Carle" who abducts Amoret in 4.7. This scene too, a transparent parody of the rape of Persephone–Amoret is strolling "through the wood, for pleasure, or for need" when she is seized (4.7.4) and the villain is said to be "of hellish kind" (st. 18) – recalls Florimell with her "Chorle" in 3.7. But it also looks forward to Book 6, not only in the Carle's foreshadowing of the cannibalism of the Salvage Nation, but in the curious insert-story of Aemylia, whose disobedience to her father in her choice of a mate brings her to the grove where instead of her lover she finds this incarnation of lust.[11] Both the isolated grove motif and that of parental "disaccord" (6.3) will be repeated in the story of Priscilla. In these same woods, finally, Timias, lamenting the jealousy he has caused in Belphoebe by his solacing of Amoret, learns the valuable political lesson "That the displeasure of the mightie is / Then death it selfe more dread and desperate" (4.8.1); while Belphoebe herself, as the narrator has exhorted his royal patroness (4.Pr.5), is led by the amorous dove to soften her haughty heart and pardon her squire's unwitting offense.

Overarching these scattered pastoral touches is Spenser's myth of the Golden Age, an *illud tempus* whose perfection is a foil, but also implicitly a paradigm, for quotidian action in the world. During the Sclaunder episode in Book 4, for example, the narrator – himself already fearful lest his "rimes be red / With misregard," for Sclaunder's house is a way-station on the road that leads from Ate to the Blatant Beast – contrasts the "simple truth and blamelesse chastitie" of the "antique age" with his own day's greedy lust:

> Then loyall love had royall regiment,
> And each unto his lust did make a lawe,
> From all forbidden things his liking to withdraw.

> The Lyon there did with the Lambe consort,
> And eke the Dove sate by the Faulcons side,
> Ne each of other feared fraud or tort,
> But did in safe securitie abide,
> Withouten perill of the stronger pride.   (4.8.30–1)

The same golden "image of the antique world," though without the echoes of Isaiah and the *Aeneid*, is conjured up in relation to Justice in the Proem to Book 5. Here Elizabeth is cast as that same Astraea who was Artegall's tutor (5.1.5), and who had fled, leaving Talus behind to deal with the sterner exigencies of Spenser's own iron age (1.11–12).

From time to time vestiges of this antique world mark the texture of these books. Thus Venus' Temple, despite its ambiguous evocation of erotic love, is characterized as a "second paradise" compounded of nature and art, a kind of landscaped Garden of Adonis in which the great lovers of history and mythology "sport / Their spotlesse pleasures, and sweet loves content" while others "on chast vertue grounded their desire" (4.10.23–6). Mercilla's court exhibits a similarly ideal peace and order. The lion under her feet (5.9.33), like the crocodile under Isis' earlier in the same book (7.22), suggests a reconstructed paradise achieved through a proper harmonizing of natural and civil agencies. For all the existential flaws and ethical murkiness displayed in these books, distancing the contemporary scene from these images of perfection *in illo tempore*, Spenser periodically strives to reaffirm a theoretical clarity diffused through the mutable world.

While maintaining this tension between the real and the ideal, Book 6 moves into largely uncharted terrain. It explores the interior sources of human conduct realized in areas of individual experience that are fairly impervious to social suasion. In Books 4 and 5 the difficulties encountered arise from the friction among individuals created as they struggle to realize communally their diverse personal and political ends. The obstacles raised by discord or injustice are formidable, and total success in overcoming them becomes less and less conceivable as the books unfold. Yet various kinds of success do occur; even more important, the poet finds a rationale for his own efforts as an educator and moralist after the Orphic model of healer and reconciler. In Book 6, however, we seem to be dealing with virtues and vices beyond any easy cure. From the outset, courtesy is portrayed as a gift of grace so serendipitous that it is hard to see how it can be inculcated or learned.[12] Like other virtues, it is said to be occulted from the empirical world in a way almost unprecedented in the poem. Hence the poet assumes a stance appropriately more private, his back figuratively half-turned from his audience as if to convey his ambivalence toward the public basis of his own vocation. In Book 6 the self-delighting, Recreative impulse of pastoral re-emerges in considerable tension with the ethical foundation of Spenser's art.

This change of focus is signalled in the book's proem. Spenser's proems always return to the central situation of the poet writing his poem. In the 1596 installment he typically situates himself between a flawed social reality and the idealism of the antique world, through whose recovery he proposes to furnish examples of better conduct. In the proem to Book 4 the specious austerity of his "Stoicke censours" is said to threaten the poet's proper reception and bar him from performing his self-appointed educative task. Taking his stand with Socrates, "the father of philosophie," against his stoical critics, the narrator attempts to neutralize those who fail to see that the "kindly flame" of "naturall affection" is the true basis of all honor and virtue.[13] The proem to Book 5 is less audacious and more apologetic precisely because in writing of justice Spenser is boldly poaching on his royal patroness' private preserve. Here Spenser's world, like Hamlet's, is portrayed as being out of joint; like Donne's, it is skewed by the new philosophy that calls all in doubt. The poem views this dismal scene from the prophetic vantage point of the "golden age" of justice, whose secret instruction he summons up the "boldnesse" to transmit even to his "Dread Soverayne Goddesse," the ultimate dispenser of justice to the poet's actual world.

In the proem to Book 6 the image of mediation is rendered with a difference. In contrast to both the ironic defensiveness of Book 4 – "The rugged forhead, that with grave foresight / Welds kingdomes causes" – and the quasi-prophetic musing of Book 5 – "So oft as I with state of present time, / The image of the antique world compare" – the opening note of Book 6 is almost sublimely private and self-referential:

> The waies, through which my weary steps I guyde,
>> In this delightfull land of Faery,
>> Are so exceeding spacious and wyde,
>> And sprinckled with such sweet variety,
>> Of all that pleasant is to eare or eye,
>> That I nigh ravisht with rare thoughts delight,
>> My tedious travell doe forget thereby;
>> And when I gin to feele decay of might,
> It strength to me supplies, and chears my dulled spright. (Pr.1)

The posture here suggests neither the existential situation of the poet with respect to his censorious elders, nor the formal function of the contemplative man mediating between an ideal golden age and the present stony one. Rather, we hear the voice of Colin in "June," though less plaintive and sullen, punfully acknowledging the travails of his travels, immersed in the contemplative delights of his own creativity, and only minimally mindful of any companions on his personal imaginative odyssey.

This posture is elaborated in the rest of the proem, where the narrator tries to link this intimate personal stance to the service of public ends. With some syntactical straining, he acknowledges that the "sacred imps" or Muses "well" and "infuse" the pleasures evoked in the opening stanzas into the "mindes of mortall men." But it remains principally his own mind that is to be so informed, his own "footing" that he prays the Muses to guide "In these strange waies, where never foote did use, / Ne none can find, but who was taught them by the Muse" (Pr. 2). And the "sacred noursery / Of vertue" is pointedly located in that same holy precinct of the Muses on Parnassus, "Where it in silver bowre does hidden ly / From view of men, and wicked worlds disdaine" (Pr.3). This sense of a division between the hidden source of virtue and a disdainful world will reach a climax on Mt. Acidale, where the far from disdainful knight of Courtesy will approach the nursery of his particular virtue. In the proem it is sharpened in the following stanzas, where we learn that courtesy, though apparently flourishing and branching out freely "through all civilitie," in fact grows "on a lowly stalke" and bears little resemblance to the "fayned showes" and "colours faire" that pass for courtesy in the poet's own time.[14]

The distinction between these ersatz displays of courtesy and the thing itself is made quite explicit:

> But in the triall of true curtesie,
>   Its now so farre from that, which then it was,
>   That it indeed is nought but forgerie,
>   Fashion'd to please the eies of them, that pas,
>   Which see not perfect things but in a glas:
>   Yet is that glasse so gay, that it can blynd
>   The wisest sight, to thinke gold that is bras.
>   But vertues seat is deepe within the mynd,
> And not in outward shows, but inward thoughts defynd.   (Pr.5)

It is precisely "deep within the mind" that true courtesy resides; its flower is as rare and delicate as Belphoebe's Rose of virginity in Book 3, or the fragile beauty in Shakespeare's sixty-fifth sonnet.[15] The narrator figuratively girds his loins to overcome these negative implications of his last book's titular virtue. It is in his sovereign's "pure mind" that he will seek the pattern of all courtesy, and he will return it to her and her admiring throngs of "Lords and Ladies, which ... adorne your Court, where courtesies excell" (st. 7).[16] But the futility of such a strategy becomes clear in the first stanza of canto 1: "Of Court it *seemes*, men Courtesie doe call" (emphasis added). As we quickly learn, Sir Calidore's courteous manners "were planted naturall" (st. 2), and much of Book 6 explores the mysterious serendipity of courtesy, which can distinguish a Salvage Man from a nation of cannibals, or an inhospitable but educable Crudor from an unregenerate, treacherous Turpine.[17] Along with this ambiguity about the nature and teachability of courtesy, Spenser will explore the deeper issue of the effect of this problematic on himself as a poet.[18] The first question is developed chiefly in terms of the several episodes of the first eight cantos; the second, in the pastoral episode that fills the last four.

While the details of the earlier episodes need not concern us here, a few observations about their general design may be helpful.[19] Like Book 3, the action of Book 6 begins and ends with its titular hero, in whose prolonged (and in this case total) absence from the central cantos its themes are developed with reference to other characters. Thus Calidore is supplanted by the similarly named Calepine, whose adventures in turn frame a core of action involving Arthur.[20] Like Britomart's in Book 3 or Artegall's in Book 5, Calidore's easy initial victories in Book 6 establish a minimal foundation for the meaning of his virtue. With Maleffort, Crudor, and Briana, and again with Priscilla and Aladine, he exercises the accepted significations of courtesy that align it with the poem's antecedent virtues.

But once he has moved off this relatively level ground, on which his own innate worldliness dictates easy solutions to social problems, Calidore's role in the book is quickly exhausted, at least until his pastoral holiday. By the time Calidore surprises Calepine and Serena dallying in their grove, Spenser is already dealing with a kind of experience that challenges the efficacy of any merely social skill.[21] Similarly, Serena's wound by the Blatant Beast signifies a susceptibility to slander or detraction whose psychic cost is only hinted at in the excessive shame she displays later, when her lover sees her naked (6.8.50–1). How they get over this "disgrace" is never shown. But we sense that Serena's problem is not remediable by the simple expedient of tactful persuasion that Calidore has used, for example, with Priscilla. The same may be said of Timias, whose fortunes in Book 6 parallel those of his fellow-victim of the Blatant Beast. Both he and Serena are vulnerable to the Beast's venom for reasons that have less to do with character than with circumstance: the squire's complicated courtship (perhaps in both senses of the word) of the unapproachable Belphoebe; the girl's compromising dalliance with her noble lover. Both are "cured" of their injuries by the wise Hermit; yet both fall subsequently into messes from which they must be extricated by others.[22] Finally, like the relationship of Calepine and Serena, that of Timias and Belphoebe is never resolved.

Spenser's pessimism about the enemies of courtesy is brought out in the scene with the Hermit, which occurs very near the center of the book. Like his prototypes in chivalric romance, the Hermit is a contemplative solitary, whose hermitage and abutting chapel stand "Far from all neighbourhood, the which annoy it may" (6.5.34).[23] A retired knight, he has in effect fulfilled in a more timely fashion the Red Cross Knight's premature desire to withdraw from the world:

> But being now attacht with timely age,
> And weary of this worlds unquiet waies,
> He took him selfe unto this Hermitage,
> In which he liv'd alone, like carelesse bird in cage.   (6.6.4)

Blending the classical and Christian–chivalric understandings of retirement and private contemplation as the crowning rewards of an active struggle with evil, he can now when called upon place at others' disposal the fruits of his hard-won worldly knowledge.[24] And so he does: gently probing the young people's wounds, he "Give[s] salves to every sore, but counsell to the minde" (st. 5). This ambiguously physical and spiritual treatment recalls Redcrosse's discipline at the House of Holiness.[25] But despite the similar confusion of literal and figurative cures, at the end of his stay Redcrosse is cured and proceeds from his hermit's instruction to his ultimate triumph. Moreover, the spiritual discipline of Redcrosse's instruction in faith and good works, sustained by his initiation into the contemplative life, renders him ready and able to withstand his last ordeal and receive the combined rewards of the active, contemplative, and pleasureable lives.

By contrast, whatever help Serena and Timias achieve with their Hermit is short-lived. There is evidently no permanent cure for their condition analogous in its efficacy to the spiritual solace of an ultimate contemplative reprieve tendered to Redcrosse in Book I. This is the case despite the living example of the Hermit himself, who to a degree embodies the promise made to Redcrosse by Contemplation.[26] Partly, this difference has to do with the kinds of advice given by the respective hermits. As contrasted with the encouragement to Redcrosse to fulfill the active life heroically on the assurance that it will be crowned at last with the satisfactions of the contemplative, Timias and Serena's Hermit is solely concerned with the modest possibility of survival in the world of courtly intrigue. In this respect he reflects *both* conditions of withdrawal from the active life authorized by Seneca. His counsel is reasonable but general:

> The best (sayd he) that I can you advize,
> Is to avoide the occasion of the ill:
> For when the cause, whence evill doth arize,
> Removed is, th'effect surceaseth still.
> Abstaine from pleasure, and restraine your will,
> Subdue desire, and bridle loose delight,
> Use scanted diet, and forbeare your fill,
> Shun secresie, and talke in open sight:
> So shall you soone repaire your present evill plight.   (st. 14)

This advice miraculously works, and a stanza later they are whole and hearty – and about to fall into the clutches of more hideous tormentors.

The point of all this seems clear enough. The Hermit is truly wise: if one is living in the world, and not free and "alone, like carelesse bird in cage," then what is required for immunity to the Blatant Beast is an austere and uncivil ascesis worthy of the stoic critics of *The Faerie Queene*. On the other hand, these consoling words, spoken out of a withdrawal from the active world to those who must return to it shortly, have obvious limitations. Placed as they are in a Legend of Courtesy, they are especially poignant. Is such a regimen as the hermit prescribes at all consonant with the possibility of healthy social intercourse warmed by the "kindly flame" of human love? Spenser doesn't answer this question directly, but even at this point in Book 6 we recognize that the world of courtesy, a courtly world in which the speaker trusts in his hearer's willingness to decode his utterances correctly and with good will, is severely under scrutiny. A different kind of "answer," rooted in the most deep-seated values of love and a non-courtly courtesy, is given in the final cantos of the book.

II

The prevailing verdict on the pastoral episode in Book 6 remains negative. Despite the warnings of C. S. Lewis and others against the view that "Calidore's long delay among the shepherds is a pastoral truancy of Spenser's from his moral intention," many readers continue to believe that in this sojourn the hero of Courtesy deserts his avowed quest of the Blatant Beast in order to indulge a wayward personal whim.[27] Calidore has been introduced to us as almost the paragon of Spenserian knights (6.1.1–2). But he is not without his weaknesses, and the mixed appeal of Pastorella's beauty and Melibee's doctrine of "content" is enough to divert him from the rigorous prosecution of his quest. One of Calidore's more censorious recent critics has gone so far as to accuse him of entertaining a flattering "illusion of life suitable to a fairy tale," an illusion that only deepens when the knight wanders even further off from this escapist world into the wholly "imaginary" one of Mt. Acidale.[28] Only the havoc wreaked by the non-illusory band of Brigands and Merchants after the abduction of Pastorella can awaken Calidore from his idyllic slumber and restore him to his epic role, as symbolized by the armor he wears concealed under his cloak when he sets out to liberate her.

On the surface Spenser himself seems to provide the strongest support of this reading. Surveying the spectacle of his hero's surrender to the pastoral bait, the narrator laments, "Who now does follow the foule *Blatant Beast*," acknowledging that Calidore has become "Unmyndfull of his vow and high beheast, / ...entrapt of love, which him betrayd" (6.10.1). Yet no sooner has the narrator thus indicted the hero for his delay than he launches into an equally passionate defense (stt. 3–4): Blatant Beast or no, Calidore's desertion is not to be "greatly blamed," for it brings rewards far beyond his losses. I will return to this question of Spenser's attitude toward Calidore's delay shortly. For the moment, I would simply note that the poet's vindication of his hero hints at a deeper identification of the two than has generally been granted. To read Calidore as *l'homme moyen sensuel* of Spenser's courtly world is to miss a fundamental idea about the poet's relation to his audience in Book 6 – and perhaps in *The Faerie Queene* as a whole. To correct this distortion we must observe carefully Spenser's distribution of his sympathies between the two principals in this central encounter in the poem of a typical hero and his creator, Calidore and Colin Clout. When we do so, what we see is not only a temporary union of the epic and pastoral voices of the poem, but a deeper, perhaps permanent marriage between the heroic life and the pastoral vision.[29] As in a Giorgione landscape, knight and shepherd meet in a single imaginative perspective, that of the poet himself. (For a Giorgionesque parallel, see the illustration on p. 148.)

That something like this is going on is implicit in Spenser's conduct of his narration. The relative detachment with which he relates the exploits of Calidore, Calepine, and Arthur in the first eight cantos is radically altered as we approach the pastoral material of cantos 9–10. In the stanzas already cited that introduce the Acidale episode (10.1–4), the relationship of Spenser to his hero is further complicated and enriched. While endorsing Calidore's truancy the narrator closely echoes the knight's own previous speech to Melibee in praise of the contemplative life (9.27–8). Now it is the narrator who rhapsodizes on the "perfect pleasures" and "happy peace" of the shepherd's life, as opposed to the "painted show / Of such false blisse" as is offered by the court (10.3–4). All that is added to Calidore's own statement is the vaguely Platonic vocabulary adumbrating the true meaning of the vision to which Calidore is about to be exposed. From the outset the reader is prompted to accept Calidore's experience as valid by hints of a resonance that even Calidore cannot yet hear. As I will try to demonstrate in more detail below, Spenser is leading us gently into an initiation parallel to Calidore's but informed by his narrator's superior understanding.

Thus it should be no surprise that at the end of the episode, when the hero has won his love and is back on the trail of the Blatant Beast, Spenser makes explicit his deep personal identification with Calidore in his truancy. What is especially revealing, though, is the metaphor adopted for this purpose. Just as all that has kept Calidore

Detail from 'Mosè alla prova dei carboni' in the Uffizi, Florence
(reproduction courtesy of Ed. Alinari, Florence)

from his "first quest" has been "out of course, yet hath not bene missayd" (12.2), so too the errant path of the narration is like that of a ship which masters wind and tide by temporarily yielding to them: though devious, it "still winneth way" to its destination, "ne hath her compasse lost." The poet's course, like the knight's, though "often stayd, yet never is astray" (12.1).[30] Just as Calidore has justly digressed "To shew the courtesie, by him profest, / Even unto the lowest and the least," so too the teller of his story has been right to include in his heroic narrative the pastoral interlude: it is a necessary part of *his* path. The truancy, therefore, belongs equally to both, and both are equally vindicated. More important, that truancy, with its implied lack of purpose and control, is affirmed by the ship-metaphor to have been properly directed – on course, as it were – all along.

Hence throughout the pastoral episode Spenser is at the very least aware of the implications of Calidore's story for his own struggle to realize personal ends in a complex and troubled social context, an awareness that will be explored in the love-poetry of his last years. As the narration moves from Calepine's rescue of Serena from the cannibals in canto 8, with its ultimate failure to resolve a sensitive personal issue, to Calidore's ostensibly more truly serene courtship of Pastorella in canto 9, what strikes most readers at once is an almost arbitrary release from tension, a sense that vexing social issues which cloud even the simplest personal satisfactions have suddenly dissipated, so that something like the habitual courtesy Calidore displays in the opening cantos may again be sufficient. What has been progressively depicted as a battle against formidable adversaries becomes almost easy and painless in an Arcadian setting where the fundamental needs involved appear once more in all their clarity. Early in the episode Calidore asks the shepherds if they have seen the Blatant Beast:

> They answer'd him, that no such beast they saw,
> Nor any wicked feend, that mote offend
> Their happie flockes, nor daunger to them draw:
> But if that such there were (as none they kend)
> They prayd high God him farre from them to send. (9.6)

It is that kind of place. Even in the end when the idyll is shattered, it is not in the first instance by the insidious detractions of the Blatant Beast but by the more overtly violent greed of the Brigands.

This impression of a lightening of the atmosphere is re-enforced by a shift in the book's dominant spatial metaphor. From the prevailing images of a labyrinthine journey through mostly dark woods filled with unexpected quirks and surprises – one thinks of

Calepine and the Bear, Timias and the three *-etto* brothers, Serena and the Blatant Beast – we move now to static, circular ones like the wide clearing where Calidore first sees Pastorella on her hillock surrounded by shepherds, and later Mt. Acidale itself, with Colin and the dancing maidens at its even more emphatically visionary core.[31] Another indication of the changing mood is the "georgic" note sounded at the outset of the Pastorella cantos (9.1): the narrator is pictured as a farmer urging his plowman to turn back to the as yet unworked "furrow" of Calidore's adventures.[32] But georgic shades into pastoral at once. The laborer is but a "jolly swayne" after all; and the vocabulary of toil, notably absent from this stanza, is assigned in the next to the hero, who has endured great "travell" and is about to be granted some respite at last. The signal seems clear: Spenser is temporarily abandoning his anatomy of the active edifice of courtesy in order to examine its contemplative foundation.

To buttress the connection between public and private strivings, and between the realization and exposition of ideals, Spenser executes a series of transitions from Calidore's pastoral pause to his vision on Acidale and back again to his more mundane labors. Colin's Fourth Grace is adumbrated by the similarly engarlanded and admired Serena and Pastorella.[33] When the "sweating" Calidore pursues the Blatant Beast into the Arcadian precincts of the shepherds, what he first encounters is an idyllic version of his own courtesy. Though his "restlesse" energy is contrasted with their easy piping and carolling, the knight immediately sees his own virtues reflected in their natural good manners (9.5–6). This conjunction of high and low, which will be the prime justification of Calidore's truancy, is marked by his first glimpse of Pastorella on her little hill, a vignette that clearly establishes her as the focus of the values he is about to appropriate. In this way Spenser makes it clear at the outset that the whole adventure is one continuous unfolding of the hero's central virtue. A bit later, he characterizes the vision his hero is about to experience in terms reminiscent of the philosopher's vision of the Good in Plato's myth of the Cave:

> The glaunce whereof their dimmed eies would daze,
> That never more they should endure the shew
> Of that sunne-shine, that makes them looke askew.   (10.4)

In the fundamental formula of pastoral, by stooping low one reaches the heights.[34]

We are thus encouraged to read Calidore's truancy as a statement of Spenser's poetic faith in contemplation, in accord with which the pastoral digression entails a renewal of insight into the nature of courtesy as a social virtue. As elsewhere in *The Faerie Queene*, Spenser keeps us in mind of the underlying tension between the ideal values embodied in certain key images and characters and their necessarily qualified translation into action. I have mentioned the middle cantos, where the abstract advice of the Hermit to victims of the Blatant Beast is set off against the simultaneous action of Arthur. A similar intention governs the different strategy of the pastoral cantos, which reach their climax in Calidore's attempt to appropriate the truth revealed on Mt. Acidale. Here, as we will see, the poet relies on his management of perspective, and particularly on the temporary dissociation of the reader from his hero, to guide our understanding of events, and specifically of the disjunction between the ideal and the real.

This strategy is already evident in canto 9. Take the case of Melibee, often maligned and occasionally praised as the focus of anti-courtly, anti-heroic values in the book.[35] The rights and wrongs of this local argument have been strongly contested, but it is not at all clear that the two speakers in the scene are fundamentally at odds. Melibee is sometimes taxed with naïveté, as evidenced by his helplessness before the marauding Brigands. His assertion that "It is the mynd, that maketh good or ill" (9.30), if taken out of context seems the simplistic cliché of an unworldly shepherd, though one who has served his time in the world after leaving his native milieu. But that is precisely Melibee's point, or at least part of it. Himself a failed social climber, he argues not for universal retirement into Arcadian "content" but for each man's adapting his virtue to the gifts of fortune whatever they be:

> But fittest is, that all contented rest,
> With that they hold: each hath his fortune in his brest. (9.29)

Melibee is noncommittal about Calidore's choice. He criticizes the knight's discontentment with his own lot and urges the cultivation of "mind" to deal adequately with "fortune"; thus "each unto himselfe his life may fortunize" (st. 30).

If Melibee thus equivocates on "fortune," Calidore does the

same, more seriously, on "estate." Taking, or pretending to take, Melibee's doctrine that each man must "fashion his owne lyfes estate" to mean that one must choose and determine his own social status, rather than that he must adapt himself to the one that falls to his lot, the knight asks permission to remain in this peaceful haven to ponder whether he should return to his chivalric role. It must be granted that Calidore's obtuseness is governed by his determination to "worke his mind / And...insinuate his harts desire" (st. 27). He is buying time to gain the fair Pastorella – at least at this point. It is by no means certain that the hero has bought into the notion of seeking permanent contentment in a pastoral withdrawal from action. Indeed, at this inaugural moment of his adventure Calidore does not seem to understand *what* he is seeking. This he will presumably discover in his encounter with Colin: namely, the true function of contemplation in the heroic life. Spenser himself, on the other hand, never implies that Calidore's *raptio* at the vision of Pastorella's beauty entails his permanent capitulation to a misunderstood doctrine of "content" as an alternative course of life. Even if he allows the hero a temporary confusion of motives at the beginning of canto 10, he at least insists that *we* retain a sense of separation between the ideal and its potential realization; and Calidore himself shortly follows suit. Thus Calidore's wonder at Pastorella precedes even the appearance of Melibee (9.12). And if that wonder does come momentarily to include Melibee's eloquence along with Pastorella's beauty (st. 26), the knight soon realizes that in order to attain this felicity he must somehow translate his intuition of grace in her presence into purposeful action. No more with Melibee than with Colin can he rely on serendipity and passiveness alone. Contemplation must precede action if action is to have meaning; but action must follow contemplation if the contemplated truth is to bear fruit.

To this end Spenser's narration never lets us forget where his hero's truancy is pointing. Repeatedly, the reader is assured that Calidore's departure from his true path is temporary as well as worthwhile. At the very outset the narrator tells us, in the omniscient past tense of the recollecting story-teller, that his hero eventually "atchieved" his quest, "Reaping eternall glorie of his restlesse paines"(9.2). Both the proleptic verb and the trope implicit in the participle are operative here: we are embarking on an episode in a success story, and that success is closely associated with the narrator's own. Even "restlesse" serves to remind us that the values of retirement and repose will be assimilated to the dominant heroic tenor of the knight's active life. In the same way, Calidore's courtship of Pastorella is punctuated with reminders to the reader of its eventual outcome. Even before Calidore has succumbed to Pastorella's beauty (9.26), Spenser has shown us the lowly shepherds worshipping her "As if some miracle of heavenly hew/Were downe to them descended in that earthly vew" (st. 8). Similarly, the canto ends with the narrator informing us that the "seeds of perfect love" that Calidore implants in the shepherdess's mind "forth *brought* / The fruite of joy and blisse, though long time dearely bought" (9.45; emphasis added). Though Calidore will not comprehend the meaning of Pastorella until his encounter with Colin Clout, Spenser has already made it clear to us that she enfolds some supernatural grace.

III

The intention behind Spenser's exercise of his narrative privilege becomes clearer in the Acidale incident itself. Here the whole emphasis is on the hero's entry into a consciousness that the speaker and his audience already possess. The strategy recalls the one adopted in the Malbecco episode of Book 3.[36] But where the purpose there had been to distance the reader from the action in order to embed a pastoral of free love in a dominant social perspective, here it is rather to orchestrate a *rapprochement* between the pastoral and heroic aspects of the book. The difference measures the degree of strain that has entered into Spenser's use of pastoral. Whereas formerly an easy accommodation of the pastoral perspective to the ethical–social one could be taken for granted, the two modes are now felt to be sufficiently at odds to necessitate a deliberate reconciliation. Moreover, it is now the ethical perspective that must be reconciled to the pastoral–aesthetic one, and not vice versa.

Following the reassuring prologue, Spenser immediately adopts Calidore's point of view as he approaches the magical hill. But his neutrality is soon invaded by information beyond the observer's capacity:

> And at the foote thereof, a gentle flud
> His silver waves did softly tumble downe,
> Unmard with ragged mosse or filthy mud,
> Ne mote wylde beastes, ne mote the ruder clowne

> Therto approch, ne filth mote therein drowne:
> But Nymphes and Faeries by the bancks did sit,
> In the woods shade, which did the waters crowne,
> Keeping all noysome things away from it,
> And to the waters fall tuning their accents fit. (10.7)

The first three lines maintain the hero's perspective, inviting us to share his observations. But only the narrator can know that the "ruder clowne" cannot approach the river, or that the nymphs and fairies, who are surely not seen there now, tune to its fall accents that Calidore can hardly be hearing, and *either* dance *or* play games on the upper plain. Description blurs into generalization. This enlarged perspective is confirmed when the narrator tells us confidentially that all these features make the place "rightly cleeped...mount *Acidale*" (st. 8), casually adding that "they say" Venus herself prefers it to Cytheron for her sport (st. 9).

This pattern of informing the reader should temper our understanding of Calidore's intrusion into Colin's vision. While we can share his urgency to attain such felicity, we are also fully apprised of its nature in a way that Calidore himself is not, at least not yet. The description begins objectively enough. As the knight approaches the place, he hears the sounds of piping and dancing. Then, drawing near, he sees the "troupe of ladies" dancing around the piping shepherd (st. 10). In the following stanza the narrator informs us of Calidore's fear of being seen and the delight with which he spies the circle of naked maidens. This neutral perspective, however, begins to dissolve as the narrator interposes the tropes of garland and ring that prepare us for the famous stanza on Ariadne's crown. The two similes of stanza 12 are still neutral enough for us to imagine that they are part of the viewer's consciousness, still being interpreted to us by the relatively anonymous narrator:

> The whilest the rest them round about did hemme,
> And like a girlond did in compasse stemme:
> And in the middest of those same three, was placed
> Another Damzell, as a precious gemme.

But this ambiguous perspective is at once superseded by the outburst of stanza 13, containing another simile, this time of the fully developed epic variety, whose vehicle, Ariadne's crown, is elaborated with the garbled story of the Lapiths and centaurs and fills an entire stanza by itself before being applied – "Such was the beauty of this goodly band" – to the dancing maidens in stanza 14.[37]

The mythological allusion in stanza 13, so emphatically if inaccurately imposed on the visual scene revealed to Calidore, inevitably adds an intellectual dimension to the sensual experience share by knight and reader alike. After this revelation it is impossible for us to resume Calidore's innocent perspective, and we must be prepared to allow for our superior understanding of these phenomena if we are not to misjudge his subsequent actions, as is often done. We revert momentarily to that common experience in stanza 14, the reiterated tenor of Spenser's epic simile returning us to Calidore's merely visual point of view:

> Such was the beauty of this goodly band,
>   Whose sundry parts were here too long to tell:
>   But she that in the midst of them did stand.
>   Seem'd all the rest in beauty to excell,
>   Crownd with a rosie girlond, that right well
>   Did her beseeme...
> But most of all, those three did her with gifts endew.

Once again we are simply seeing a homely maid attended lovingly by three ministering ladies, the four encircled by a hundred other naked dancers. But our sensitivity to the extraordinariness of the event remains informed by the Ariadne stanza, with its intimate and emphatic "Looke."

Any remaining suspense is abruptly dispelled in the next stanza by the narrator's direct and even casual declaration of the scene's content. "Those were the Graces," he announces, reminding us of their traditional offices to Venus; and "Those three to men all gifts of grace do graunt" (st. 15). To which he adds, what even with all the help we have had from Spenser we might not have guessed, that the "faire one" in the middle "Was she to whome that shepheard pypt alone, / That made him pipe so merrily, as never none." Spenser executes this most personal of all revelations in *The Faerie Queene* with a coy teasing of his reader:

> She was to weete that jolly Shepheards lasse,
>   Which piped there unto that merry rout,
>   That jolly shepheard, which there piped, was
>   Poore *Colin Clout* (who knowes not *Colin Clout?*)

> He pypt apace, whilest they him daunst about.
> Pype jolly shepheard, pype thou now apace
> Unto thy love, that made thee low to lout:
> Thy love is present there with thee in place,
> Thy love is there advaunst to be another Grace. (st. 16).

I will have something more to say, as will Spenser, about this elevation of Colin's "love" to the rank of Fourth Grace. For now it is enough to note that this crucial identification of the principals of Colin's vision is negotiated entirely between the narrator and the reader, imposing on the material of the story a private allusion to the poet's own status as both poet and lover that is far removed from his narration of Calidore's adventures.

Spenser will resume the more limited perspective during Colin's exposition one more time. But at the critical moment when Calidore interrupts Colin's ecstasy he does not know what we know and so naturally does what we hope we would not do. Thus the poet can count on our at least partially discounting what he had told us of the real nature of the vision when he shifts his attention and ours back to Calidore's "rapt," almost somnambulistic intrusion:

> Much wondred *Calidore* at this straunge sight,
> Whose like before his eye had never seene,
> And standing long astonished in spright,
> And rapt with pleasaunce, wist not what to weene. (st. 17).

For the moment at least we are compelled to divorce our knowing from his doing, to become conscious, as we experience it, of the gulf separating Calidore's perception from our own. The complete rhetorical event, the intuition and the rational explanation of it, is ours alone.

It may be objected to this reading of Spenser's narrative strategy that throughout the episode Calidore is depicted as little more than a low voyeur intruding, as he had done with Calepine and Serena, on someone else's cherished privacy.[38] True, if in that earlier episode he confesses his action to be a "rash default" (3.21), in the same stanza he begs pardon on the grounds that "it was his fortune, not his fault." But in the later incident things look far worse for our hero. Though his initial encounter with Colin and the Graces simply "chaunst" to happen (10.5), much like the intrusion on Calepine and Serena, we are told (st. 11) that Calidore "durst not enter" their precinct for fear of "breaking of their daunce, if he were seene"; he knows that he must spy on them from "the covert of the wood … yet of them unespyde." Why then, only six stanzas later, does he abandon his cover and blunder into the midst of the dance? Understanding as we do that the "sacred noursery / Of vertue … does hidden ly / From view of men" (Pr. 3), surely the answer must be that "Calidore tactlessly betrays that understanding and thus betrays Courtesy when his resolution to know overcomes his better knowledge"? "Dressed down as Phrygian Paris," his true nature disguised in shepherd's weeds, like Pentheus and Actaeon he deliberately "betrays" his understanding to his baser curiosity.[39]

Attractive as this objection may seem, I do not think it accurately reflects Spenser's intentions. For one thing, it is a bit unfair to Calidore to accuse him in one breath of being too furtive, indeed a voyeur, and then in the next turn around and claim that he is too stupidly blatant. Moreover, this reading depends too heavily on extraneous mythological extrapolations, while disregarding the important rhetorical advantage we have as readers of the text. In the four stanzas immediately preceding Calidore's fateful act, Spenser has gone out of his way to furnish us with both facts and mythological associations that give us a distinct edge over Calidore in "reading" the scene before us both. Hence when we return to his perspective, we may forget that what he is reacting to is simply the scene itself, stripped of the interpretation with which Spenser has overlaid it:

> Much wondred *Calidore* at this straunge sight …
> And standing long astonished in spright,
> And rapt with pleasaunce, wist not what to weene …
> Therefore resolving, what it was, to know,
> Out of the wood he rose, and toward them did go.   (st. 17)

We should not be too quick to discount the narrator's claim that Calidore "wist not what to weene" nor to attribute his confusion to courtly obtuseness. The vocabulary of the stanza is that not of calculated discourtesy but of a Neoplatonic *raptio*, as "wondred," "astonished," and "rapt" declare. There is of course a movement of the will implied. But it is, in effect, the desire to gain the same degree of understanding that we have just been privileged to acquire by authorial digression, and we are meant to recognize in him the impulse that has been satisfied in us. If Spenser has been effective, his rhetorical and descriptive verve will have provoked us to the same admiration, the same powerful wonder at such a vision and desire to know what it means, as now moves Calidore to risk recognition and advance toward the scene.

The reading offered here is borne out by the sequel as well. When Calidore does shatter Colin's vision, to the latter's great dismay, his regret at that misfortune seems more insistent than his own curiosity to know "the truth of all" that he has seen (st. 18). If his tone with Colin at first is over-hearty, his apology a bit too correct and philosophically disinterested to do justice to the latter's feelings at this moment, one must remember that he does not know at this point the true nature of the injury he has done him. In the following stanzas (21–8) Colin explains the revelations he has experienced. Calidore learns at last that these are the Graces and that he has stumbled upon no less than the "sacred noursery" of his own peculiar virtue.[40] More important, he discovers that the vision is also of intense personal relevance to Colin, as he learns the identity of the crowned maiden – Colin's Pastorella in effect – at the center of the ring and hears the shepherd's apology to Gloriana, supposedly the presiding deity of both their worlds, for having paused in his normal celebration of her to elevate his love to the same heights. For as in *Colin Clouts Come Home Againe*, Colin again, though more obliquely, acknowledges a source of inspiration independent of the Queen's authority, the basis of his author's evolving pastoral of contemplation.[41] Though he can hardly be expected to grasp the full significance of the Spenserian *figura*, at this point Calidore does understand the nature of his blunder and is truly sorry for it:

> But gentle Shepheard pardon thou my shame,
> Who rashly sought that, which I mote not see.
> Thus did the courteous Knight excuse his blame,
> And to recomfort him, all comely meanes did frame.   (st. 29)

He admits that he has been wrong to seek such knowledge, that in a sense he has intervened in a contemplative ecstasy which it is the sole province of the poet to enjoy. And his former superficial regret at Colin's discomfort gives way, at least as I hear it, to genuine remorse.[42]

This final phase of the episode clinches the partial identification of Spenser's narrator with his pastoral persona. While Spenser has all along implied a deep commitment to the knight of courtesy, the narration in canto 10 has gradually broadened his sympathies to include Colin Clout. Twelve stanzas after the narrator's exhortation to the latter – "Pype jolly shepheard" – their voices merge in the apostrophe to Gloriana in stanza 28. When the speaker begs her to "Pardon thy shepheard, mongst so many layes," etc., we simply forget that it is Colin, not Spenser, who is speaking.[43] Such a fusion of voices epitomizes the collapsing of the epic and pastoral poles of the poem. By shifting the narrator's primary sympathy from Calidore to Colin, Spenser merges Calidore's earlier "wonder" with our own more enlightened understanding. The hero's indoctrination into the pastoral core of the book's meaning turns out to have been the reader's as well. This narrative strategy gives us the opportunity both to learn the source of courtesy and to observe Calidore in the process of discovering it. Through the close identity of roles among narrator, hero, and pastoral persona Spenser has invited us to share in that sense of life as an initiation into awareness that is a hallmark of his art in *The Faerie Queene*. He has thus implicitly defined the visionary *métier* of the contemplative pastoral as the real basis of our own public and private lives.

It is often suggested that the disruptive encounter of Calidore and Colin signifies the impossibility of any useful translation of Colin's vision into heroic action.[44] Yet Calidore clearly comes to a better understanding of the beauty he pursues; as Diotima would say, his vision of true beauty makes him momentarily forget the derivative beauty of Pastorella. Once again he "had no will away to fare, / But wisht, that with that shepheard he mote dwelling share" (10.30). But despite this harmony of vision and understanding the experience must mean something different to Calidore than it does to Colin. For Colin, Spenser's persona, the shepherd's song is the consummation of the poetic *vita contemplativa* now conceived under the Plotinian–Petrarchan aspect of a creative figuration or quasi-creation of the truth of things while the lower faculties wither away. Visionary poetry alone, or rather that ecstasy in which the contemplative poet achieves the vision, is the ultimate vindication of the literary shepherd's life.

For this reason the communion between Colin and Calidore can be only momentary. This fact, however, need not reflect entirely unfavorably on the hero. For as the voyage metaphors and the orchestration of the narrative imply, it is part of Spenser's strategy in Book 6 to underscore the continuities between his principal exemplars of the active and contemplative lives. Certainly these continuities have been worn, as have other threads binding the social fabric, in these last books of the poem. Throughout the second installment those forces of slander, envy, and detraction that embody the anti-*logos* in Spenser's social world have raised formidable barriers to the poet's Orphic task of reconciliation. The difficulties that Calidore and others experience in simply avoiding violations of privacy attest to Spenser's growing unease about the possibility of normal intercourse in an increasingly contentious public arena. Nevertheless, even in this problematical last book the poet makes a grudging effort, I believe, to reassert the communal ideal of earlier books, and to exercise the reconciling function implicit in pastoral from its inception (see above, p. 54). And it is still the poet himself who is the cynosure of this community; while love, in its full signification as the community-nourishing "kindly flame," remains the poet's central theme.

In this context it is significant that Spenser distributes his sympathies evenly between the shepherd and the knight. The moment of empathy on Mt. Acidale must perforce be brief. The vision of courtesy that undergirds Calidore's heroic activity must yield in due course to a resumption of that activity, and the pastoral sojourn itself can be only a temporary excursion into a larger contemplative space. In Book 6 Arcadia is suspended between Acidale and the everyday world. If Acidale is the site of love's epiphany mediated by the vision of the beloved as the true focus of contemplative song, Arcadia is the place where the hero who normally transacts that vision in the labyrinth of Faery land discovers that the soul of courtesy and chivalry is love.

Hence as Sidney had discovered, Arcadia projects a friction between the realms of ordinary existence and pure contemplation, fraught with pessimism about the fruitful conjunction of the two estates. But the differences between the hero and his pastoral mentor should not lead us to exaggerate that pessimism. For Calidore love can never be, as it is for Colin, merely the contemplative basis of the active life. It is precisely love's "envenimd sting" that puts an end to the knight's rapture and compels his return to the active pursuit of his love. No more than Redcrosse can Calidore as a chivalric lover rest in the contemplation of the source of his vocation. His love may strike the reader as less disinterested and even less intimate than Colin's – in terms of Renaissance Platonism, the desire of Venus

Pandemus instead of Venus Anadyomene.[45] If so, that is yet another of his hero's pardonable flaws. But even as late in his career as the early 1590s, Spenser retains his commitment to this world as at the very least a worthy battleground on which to test one's spiritual mettle, and throughout *The Faerie Queene* love-skirmishes provide ample challenges to his exemplary knights.

If Calidore, the chivalric lover and man of action, cannot remain permanently in the *templum* or sacred space of Acidale, can Colin Clout? The answer is yes, but only as one aspect of the author. In the act of poetic contemplation, pastoralized as arousing echoes of the invisible world with one's song, the shepherd sublimates his "love" to pure vision.[46] But Colin is not Spenser. In the *Amoretti*, as we will see, he too, like Calidore, will return to the active life, and even resort to guile, in the pursuit of his desire. For all his reservations about such a choice, Spenser still seems to feel that in his active role of protégé or lover he must break his pastoral pipe and enter into the painful arena of action. Though the poet alone can comprehend those forces that drive our desire and inform heroic conduct, the fulfillment of the vision will always be impure. Book 6 and the completed *Faerie Queene* end appropriately with Spenser himself as the latest victim of the Blatant Beast. This sober image challenges the continuing efficacy of uttering careful (or, as Spenser would say, *carefull*) words in the teeth of their corruption by others. Nevertheless it supports, not negates, the urgency of Spenser's call for a harmonizing of the two estates.

Calidore's truancy among the Arcadian shepherds is therefore, finally, a consummate comment on *The Faerie Queene* as a public poem.[47] Like his continental contemporaries, Spenser endorses implicitly the *vita contemplativa*. In the life of a community the poet's function is primary: without his unique vision of the "sacred nursery of virtue" the ethical significance of the aspiring mind would be lost. At the same time, he is acutely aware of the stringent demands and sparse rewards of the Elizabethan version of the active life, the real ardors and labors of serving Gloriana, a stingy and fickle mistress at best. Undermining the old community between the active and contemplative lives is an emerging consciousness that contemplation is the poet's province *par excellence*.

At the penultimate moment of his career, then, Spenser ventures one more paradigm of the poet's life framed in a public context. In the truancy of Calidore, wherein he apprehends the source and meaning of his quest, and in his victory over the Blatant Beast, by which he temporarily fulfills it, Spenser suggests an ideal if ambivalent posture for a civilized being in the mutable world – a much more defensive stance, to be sure, than that implied in the pastoral episode in Book 3. This posture combines a passive alertness to what the world offers as meaningful – the essence of that *templum* at the etymological heart of contemplation, what some of us today would call Presence – with the energy to translate that immanent order of things into ethical action by articulating it through a morally informed rhetoric. Even at so late a moment, the vestiges of humanist rhetorical culture are discernible in Spenser's final fable. As Filelfo had understood the *Aeneid* to be urging a rooting of *prudentia* in *sapientia*, of "civil felicity" in "vision," so the last complete book of Spenser's national epic betrays a lingering humanistic bias – with the additional accent on the unique function of the humanist as poet. In this sense Calidore and Colin present the active and contemplative dimensions of Spenser's image of himself as a cultural exemplar: his conception of the poet's function as both Platonic contemplator and heroic enactor of ethical values on the stage of courtly life. It is only in the love poetry of his last years that his doubts about a synthesis of the estates surface and Spenser returns to the pastoralist's native ground.

6

The pastoral of the self

Standard pastoral items play a negligible part in Spenser's works after the last published installment of *The Faerie Queene*. Though referred to once in the Mutability Cantos (7.6.40), Colin Clout does not reappear, nor are there any stock pastoral scenes either in the fragmentary "seventh book" or in the minor poems of 1595–6. Nevertheless, several of the crucial motifs of Spenserian pastoral do occur in these last poems, and in a sense it would do greater violence to the integrity of this book to ignore them than to risk "globalizing" the concept of pastoral beyond recognition.[1] Even more than the four preceding chapters, therefore, this final one will be dealing with themes and attitudes typically associated with the pastoral in Spenser's writings rather than with the obligatory shepherds, *loci amoeni*, or satyrs of the traditional pastoral genres.

The main tensions informing Spenser's pastoral poetry remain prominent in his latest poems. Most readers perceive an increasing disillusionment with public life, perhaps owing to the poet's failure to attain status at the Elizabethan court, as well as an intensified desire to celebrate private experience.[2] The perplexities of *Colin Clout* and, conversely, the strenuous effort in Book 6 of *The Faerie Queene* to promote an ideal balance between public and private concerns, or the active and contemplative lives, seem to indicate the demise of the courtly-ceremonial pastoral perfected by Spenser in his middle years, and to adumbrate the return to a self-delighting, recreative pastoral of contemplation. My own argument in the previous chapter concedes Spenser's growing pessimism about poetry's public usefulness and his inclination to withdraw from the active world into an inviolate and wholly private contemplative center.

This anticipated retreat from his earlier mode, however, is not totally realized in Spenser's latest poetry. One might speculate, of course, on the direction his work might have taken had he lived longer.[3] But the only solid evidence we have is the handful of poems – little more than 2,000 lines in all – probably composed after the completion of Books 4–6: the two Mutability Cantos, which were not published in Spenser's lifetime and appear to have been intended for one of the six remaining projected books of *The Faerie Queene*; the *Amoretti* and *Epithalamion* (1595), written during his courtship of Elizabeth Boyle, whom he married in 1594; the *Prothalamion*, written and published in 1596; and the *Fowre Hymnes*, published the same year, though Spenser claims (and there seems to be no reason to doubt him) that two of the four were composed "in the greener times of my youth" (Dedicatory Letter).

Of these works, the impulse toward a wholly private orientation is most discernible in the Mutability Cantos, the *Amoretti*, and the *Hymnes*. Indeed, one argument for dating the actual composition of the Mutability Cantos is their consonance with Books 4–6 in this regard. In Book 6 the presentation of Colin on Mt. Acidale and substitution of the anonymous beloved for Gloriana as the Fourth Grace bespeak a desire to exalt private vision as the source of the poet's creative gifts, to find an authorizing voice apart from the official authorities of Elizabethan society. In the Mutability Cantos, as in the Pastorella episode, the narrative structure betrays an urge to circumscribe time and change in the mythic and memorial dimension of the poet's contemplative vision. This impulse reaches its apogee in the *Amoretti*, where love itself, under the colors of pastoral, effects a breach in the poet's public role, turning him away from action and social aspiration toward pure contemplation. In the *Hymnes* the same tendency leads to a dualism that all but annihilates the world of empirical experience, and with it the possibility of a viable pastoral myth.

The central motive in these poems is the desire for rest, a motive that is anatomized in the theoretical conflict of *Mutability* and consummated in the love poetry. The search for erotic or spiritual release from aspiration dictates the familiar Spenserian motif of a haven of contemplative delight, a kind of pure recreative stillness in a sacred space free from labor and change. In the *Amoretti* such a refuge is located at the juncture of courtship and writing. Poetry itself becomes the medium in which action and contemplation achieve stasis. But the stasis is temporary: already in the *Epithalamion*, probably intended as a complement to the *Amoretti*, the thrust of world-transcendence is deflected toward a more modest reconciliation with time and change parallel to that in *Mutability*. Both of the latter works reaffirm Spenser's belief that poetry mediates between intellectual essences and palpable experience. This aesthetic ideal is again threatened by the personal malaise and civic misgivings of the *Prothalamion* and by the radical philosophical bifurcation of the *Hymnes*.

What I hope to show, then, in the following discussion of Spenser's last poems is that the effort to reconcile antithetical impulses that pervades the major pastoral poems and passages is still at work in his final productive years. The chief vehicles of this attenuated pastoralism – The Mutability Cantos, the *Amoretti*, and the *Epithalamion* – reveal, and the *Prothalamion* and *Hymnes* confirm, that Spenser never resolved his personal and social conflicts as a poet. Although the frustration attending this struggle is clearly displayed in these works, there is little in them to suggest that Spenser ever satisfactorily translated his basic reconciling impulse into a permanent poetic creed.

I

The salient feature of the Mutability Cantos is not their fragmentary nature but their unity. It is unlikely that we will ever know more than the accompanying editorial apparatus of the posthumous first edition tells us about their structural relation to the rest of *The Faerie Queene*, finished or projected.[4] To *whom* they "appear to be parcell of" a Legend of Constancy, for example, however intriguing a question it may be, is finally less germane to their overall place in Spenser's work than is their almost paradigmatic internal structure.[5] Similarly self-contained units are found in the six "perfect" books, though only a few – the House of Pride in 1 and the Pastorella episode in 6 come immediately to mind – approach the Mutability Cantos in length. Such units, while they gain additional significance from their placement in their respective books, exhibit a degree of autonomy that makes it possible, for instance, to lift them from their contexts and print them in anthologies.

In the case of *Mutability* this air of completeness is owing in large part to its character as a narrative. The reason one can easily imagine it as the "allegorical core" of a putative Legend of Constancy is that it reads like a sustained personal meditation by the narrator. Indeed, this feature is so marked that, at least as we have it, one might define the Cantos' subject as a conflict of motives in the narrator's mind. At first this conflict is presented impersonally:

> What man that sees the ever-whirling wheele
>> Of *Change*, the which all mortall things doth sway,
>> But that therby doth find, and plainly feele,
>> How MUTABILITY in them doth play
>> Her cruell sports, to many mens decay? (7.6.1)

Although the mode is prophetic, the prophetic experience is not claimed to be peculiar to the poet. His function, rather, is merely to aid in the collective process of seeing, finding, and feeling by reporting the hearsay about Mutability's rebellion so that the truth about her great sway in the world "may better yet appeare" to the rest of us (*ibid.*). What the narrator thinks and feels about Mutability is what we all must think and feel. From the outset the reader is invited to engage with the poet, through his story-teller, in a meditation on time and change and their common status in the modern world. The *vita contemplativa* is open to all.

This is not an unprecedented mode of presentation for Spenser. But the strategy of merging the "I" of an allegorical narrative with the collective consciousness of his readers bears special fruit in the Mutability Cantos. For the sequence, at least as we have it, displays unusual closure. The two stanzas of the "unperfite" eighth canto constitute an intensely personal response to the just-completed narrative:

> When I bethinke me on that speech whyleare,
>> Of *Mutability*, and well it way:
>> Me seemes, that though she all unworthy were
>> Of the Heav'ns Rule; yet very sooth to say,
>> In all things else she beares the greatest sway.
>> Which makes me loath this state of life so tickle,
>> And love of things so vaine to cast away...
>
> Then gin I thinke on that which Nature sayd,
>> Of that same time when no more *Change* shall be...
>> But thence-forth all shall rest eternally
>> With Him that is the God of Sabbaoth hight:
>> O that great Sabbaoth God, graunt me that Sabaoths sight.

> (7.8.1–2)

Reading these lines, we may of course feel that the narrator's seemingly spontaneous reaction to his story is merely a device to direct our own. But as the sequence stops just there – and one can more easily imagine that the next stanza would have abruptly returned to a major plot-strand than that it would have carried forward the "What man" of 7.6.1 – the net effect is that what began as a generalized meditation-cum-exemplum on change ends up as an act of sustained personal contemplation.

Here again the movement is from vision to meditation to affect. As the speaker says, the two stanzas answer precisely to the respective speeches of Mutability and Nature, which by virtue of this response come even more emphatically to stand as *moti spirituali* (as Dante would say) of the speaker's mind, competing assents to antithetical claims on his intellect.[6] But the narrator's reflection on Mutability's speech ("bethinke") leads not only to a logical if tentative conclusion ("me seemes...she beares the greatest sway") but to a strong emotional reaction ("which makes me loath...") as well. With respect to Nature's reply the pattern is the same, although it is rendered more dramatic by the speaker's recapitulating and elaborating her doctrine for seven lines (omitted here) prior to expressing his affective response in the famous outburst that concludes the fragment. This final alteration in mode confirms the shift from a collective to an individual contemplative act. What begins as a universal observation on the nature of change and its effect on all men ends as a spontaneous expression of one meditator's desire for permanency. That meditator may still be representative, but he no longer explicitly claims to be so.

This terminus, however, is itself articulated in terms of two consummatory states: "rest" and "sight." These words in fact sum up the dual *telos* towards which all of Spenser's reflective poetry moves. In effect, the Mutability Cantos epitomize the dynamic of Spenser's visionary mode. All desire, whether expressed in heroic action, love, or recreative contemplation, seeks an ultimate consummation in which all activity will permanently cease and all perception will be subsumed under one eternal vision, which Spenser calls "that Sabaoths sight." Spenser is fully aware of the gratuitousness of this desired consummation. But together the logical concession to Mutability's argument – hardly an argument, but the transparent factuality of things – and the prayer that grace will eventually complete nature and terminate change aptly conclude the episode described in the two "perfect" cantos. For the substance of these cantos is precisely Spenser's own effort to reconcile time and eternity, change and permanence, ephemeralcy and vision, labor and rest.

What the narrative framework of *Mutability* suggests is borne out by its interior structure. The basic action of the cantos is the Titaness's heroic aspiration to power. It is accompanied by Mutability's speeches to the gods and concluded by more speeches by Mutability, her adversaries, Jove, and finally Nature, following whose verdict the episode abruptly ends.[7] Physical activity and its attendant rhetoric together fill some seventy-one of the 116 stanzas of the fragment. The rest consists of utterances by the narrator in various non-narrative modes. Besides the meditative framework already discussed (6.1–3, 8.1–2), there is also the invocation to the "greater Muse" (= Calliope?) to inspire the speaker's rehearsal of the trial in canto 7:

> Doe thou my weaker wit with skill inspire,
> Fit for this turne; and in my feeble brest
> Kindle fresh sparks of that immortall fire,
> Which learned minds inflameth with desire
> Of heavenly things. (7.2)

The formal *occupatio* is a device familiar in Spenser's work from as early as *The Shepheardes Calender*. As we approach the climax of the episode, the epic muse is asked to raise the poet's "weaker wit" to the level of his unequal task. This poet is the Vergilian pastoralist ("Lo I the man...") of Spenser's major work, forcibly dragged from the more congenial "woods and pleasing forrests" and compelled to tune his spirit "in bigger noates to sing" of the great event. Hence the climactic event in the story is introduced in proper bucolic fashion (*paulo maiora cano*) as an unwonted and unwanted digression from the actual digression that has preceded it.

The earlier digression is the story of Arlo Hill and its fall, as well as Ireland's, into its present state of decline. Inserted as part of the background of the trial, it is a tale of metamorphosis framed as a homely pastoral mythopoeia and centering in the "foolish" wood-god Faunus' Actaeon-like attempt to see Diana naked. This tale occupies a full third of canto 6, and our attention is drawn to its arbitrary nature by the narrator himself:

> And, were it not ill fitting for this file,
> To sing of hilles and woods, mongst warres and Knights,
> I would abate the sternenesse of my stile,
> Mongst these sterne stounds to mingle soft delights.[8] (6.37)

The pastoral of the self

As implied in the invocation preceding the trial, though more intrusive in an epic context the pastoral tale *per se* is more congenial to its teller. A "Shepheards quill" has already "renowned" old Father Mole "with hymnes fit for a rurall skill" (st. 36). Indeed, "Shepherd *Colin*" himself has sung of Mulla, sister of Molanna (*Colin Clout*, ll. 104–55). Like that story, this of Molanna and Faunus is one of "soft delights," and we infer, even before we are told so in canto 7, that this sort of story better suits the singer's native talents.

The reason for this preference is not hard to divine. In the internal dialectic of the poet, which generates that of the narrated action, the pastoral digression is counterpoised to the main story of Mutability's aspiration. Like all such tales, the metamorphic–etiological myth of Faunus and Molanna has to do principally with imposing stasis on the processes of time. Characters in a story are stopped in time and frozen into trees or rivers or hills with the quasi-permanence of natural forms on one level, and on another as logical entities in the mind. So it is with Faunus and Molanna. Ostensibly a tale of violation, voyeurism (the real thing, versus Calidore's supposed variety), and retribution, its irrelevance as such is brought out by the relative success of the conspirators. Faunus escapes the vengeful nymphs and dogs, while Molanna is united with her lover, the Fanchin.

It is true that Diana has forever forsaken Arlo Hill, leaving behind her curse of wolves and thieves. But I think that this trade-off (besides being partly a topical joke) is part of Spenser's main point in the tale and in the episode as a whole. The Golden Age is gone – is, as Mutability's logic forces us to see, a fiction. We are to find permanence not in dreams of paradise nor assertions of the illusory nature of the phenomenal world. Rather, as Nature will announce, change is real, but it is part of a larger pattern viewed in and through change: the "being" of things, "dilated" (7.58) in the phenomena of growth, decay, and transformation, is contained in and remains an essential part of this change, until all change be permanently negated at the far-off end of time.[9] In the meantime, wolves and thieves notwithstanding, Molanna and Fanchin are united, their physical union enduring as a visible feature of the landscape and the meaning of their story given permanence in its mythic telling. In Spenser's modest resignation to time, erotic fulfillment compensates for Diana's lost inviolability; nature as process supplants Nature in stories.

This implicit moral of the pastoral digression does not, however, cancel out the contrary thrust of the Mutability episode as a whole. If Spenser accepts Mutability's logic, this does not negate his loathing for this world's palpable mutability. The impulse to deny time pervades the episode as a whole, though muted, one senses, by an Empsonian reluctance to admit the distasteful conditions of life. In any case, by accepting change, even as part of a larger, theoretically permanent pattern, Spenser also postpones that personal rest for which he longs. As a version of the *vita contemplativa* poetry can grasp this pattern fitfully. As in Books I and 6, the pastoral core of *Mutability* at best offers but glimpses of a permanence behind the phenomena of this world. What is different here, perhaps, from both Redcrosse's and Calidore's contemplative epiphanies – besides the absence of a Redcrosse or a Calidore – is the psychological chasm adumbrated in Spenser's fragmentary eighth canto. If the opposing impulses in the poet's mind are still barely contained in the episode's resolution, one feels the urgent centrifugality of loathing the world and longing for rest, motives that tug with a new intensity at a center that can hold now only with increasing difficulty.[10]

II

One should not make too much of the absence of heroic virtue in the Mutability Cantos. Knowing so little about their intended context, we might easily overrate the fact that the only image of heroic effort in the fragment is Mutability's challenge to the established pantheon. Nevertheless, it seems safe to say that the prominence given the meditating narrator in the episode betrays the poet's primary interest in the play of internal forces objectified in the allegory itself and in the rhythmic alternation of epic narration and pastoral digression, and formally articulated in the "unperfite" eighth canto. With respect to the *Amoretti* and *Epithalamion*, published together in 1595, there is no need for speculation.[11] This composite work gathers together heroic and pastoral features under the single aspect of amatory lyric. From beginning to end its "hero" is the singer himself, sometimes in the role of poet, sometimes as lover or bridegroom.[12] In lieu of any dramatic or allegorical dialectic the entire ideological conflict of the work is contained in a lyric meditation sustained through the eighty-nine sonnets and twenty-four strophes respectively of the two sequences.[13]

These poems consummate Spenser's pastoral of love.[14] In the *Amoretti* the contemplative havens alternately sought and shunned in earlier works are explicitly identified with erotic fulfillment. Here too poetry retains its function as ceremonial guarantor of innocence, now on a purely private and individual plane. In the *Epithalamion* eros is again affirmed as the source of the private virtues, but the transcendental thrust of Spenser's contemplative pastoral, though still fundamentally personal and affective, is reconciled with the realities of time.

I have already noted Spenser's periodic self-presentation in *The Faerie Queene* as a heroic agent yearning for respite from his own poetic labors. Just as the several heroes of the poem typically find refuge in a *locus amoenus* from the exercise of heroic virtue, so the narrator himself needs to rest occasionally in those visionary moments of calm that punctuate his struggle toward an ultimate sabbath. Within this paradigm the problem is to reconcile two aspects of pastoral, to connect the illusions of a seductive otium with the illuminations of visionary delight. In the *Amoretti* the rhythm of labor and relaxation underlies Spenser's use of the Petrarchan convention. Fundamentally a visionary instrument in the Platonic mode, the Petrarchan lady mirrors a transcendent ideal and may thus translate her lover beyond particulars to the pure truth of things.

Yet real communion in the *Amoretti* takes place in the phenomenal not the noumenal world. In sonnet 72 the lover's spirit, poised on the brink of flight, is weighed down "with thoght of earthly things." But the dualism of body and spirit, earth and "purest sky," is dissolved by Spenser's doctrine of divine resemblance. Tied to the earth, he finds in the beloved a "soverayne beauty... / resembling heavens glory in her light," and this simulacrum of the transcendent beauty is enough to compensate the would-be seeker for its loss. Lured back to earth "with sweet pleasures bayt," his "fraile fancy" finds "blisse" and "ease" in her earthly beauty, "ne thinks of other heaven" but her. The poem concludes without a hint of disapproval:

> Hart need not with none other happinesse,
> but here on earth to have such hevens blisse.[15]

The mirror of transcendent bliss becomes its surrogate. Elsewhere, the contemplated light of the "Idæa playne," while it feeds the mind, starves the body and blinds the eye (sonnet 88). Spiritual enlightenment must be ballasted with physical union. The sonnets already point to their consummation in the marriage hymn.[16]

The *telos* of the sequence is the consummation of desire under the protective warrant of matrimony. But if this consummation is to bring contentment, desire itself must be rendered innocent. For this reason a number of the *Amoretti* are aimed at fashioning the lady herself as a type of Edenic haven, a chastened image of felicity in which the poet can safely rest. This effort to purify the image of the lady in the poet's soul links the sequence closely with the epic struggles for clarity and innocence in *The Faerie Queene*.

Interestingly, both of the sonnets that refer to Spenser's masterpiece treat courtship as part of a conflict between otium and heroic effort. Sonnet 33, to Lodowick Bryskett, records the poet's "troublous fit" of distraction from his epic labors by a "proud love, that doth my spirite spoyle." Only when she has vouchsafed to "grawnt me rest" can he hope to complete his great task. In sonnet 80 the opposition of labor and repose remains, but now it is courtship itself and its poetry that figure as a release from the larger enterprise. The main contrast is between the burden of creative effort and the otium of love. Moreover, this refuge is no longer merely a distraction from heroic effort. It is true that the poem begins with a defensive plea for "leave to rest me... and gather to my selfe new breath awhile" before resuming the "race... / Through Faery land." But the "prison" of courtship, from which the poet promises to "breake anew" like a well-rested horse, is transformed in the sestet into something quite different:

> Till then give leave to me in pleasant mew,
>   to sport my muse and sing my loves sweet praise:
>   the contemplation of whose heavenly hew,
>   my spirit to an higher pitch will rayse.

Like the typical Spenserian hero engaged in heroic labors, the poet begins by viewing courtship as a pleasant diversion, a kind of *locus amoenus* that is also a cage and a refuge, from which in due course he will emerge refreshed. But once entered, like Calidore he finds it to be an oasis of contemplation, a place of illumination at whose center is his beloved and in which the spirit intuits the very reality he is trying to capture in his masterwork. In this "pleasant mew" he must "sport [his] Muse" if he is to perform his appointed role; his

172

love is both a respite and a recreation. The implications of this conceit go a long way toward elucidating the underlying meaning of the experience dramatized in the sonnets and given consummate expression in the marriage hymn.

Throughout the sequence love is thus conceived as a kind of haven from the storms of life. Often it is the lady herself who is the lover's port; in her the lover sees the promise of his own escape from "devouring tyme and changeful chance" (sonnet 58). In sonnet 63, "After long stormes and tempests sad assay," his "silly barke" is still afloat as he spots ahead the "happy shore" for which he is bound. Like Una's homeland it is a "fayre soyle...fraught with store / of all that deare and daynty is alyve." It offers the promise of repose:

> Most happy he that can at last atchyve
> the joyous safety of so sweet a rest:
> whose least delight sufficeth to deprive
> remembrance of all paines which him opprest.

These lines sum up the positive side of otium in Spenser's pastoral of love. After long labors the lover achieves at last a haven of earthly joy. Offering both safety and rest, this Edenic state begins in sensual delight and ends in "eternall blisse." It redeems pain with pleasure and time with the hope of immortality.

The essence of this long-sought refuge is spiritual freedom. If his release is to be acceptable, it must offer "safety" as well as "delight." In the *Amoretti*, as in *The Faerie Queene*, this warranty is a function of love's willing bondage.[17] Sonnet 65, for example, celebrates the liberation achieved by the lovers' mutual forfeit of their separate liberties in the interest of a greater freedom:

> Sweet be the bands, the which true love doth tye,
> without constraynt or dread of any ill:
> the gentle birde feeles no captivity
> within her cage, but singes and feeds her fill.

The nourishing prison of sonnet 80 is now enlarged to include lady and lover alike. This "mutual render," as Shakespeare will call it in his sonnet 125, has the virtue of banishing all danger from the private enclosure of their love:

> There pride dare not approch, nor discord spill
>   the league twixt them, that loyal love hath bound:
> but simple truth and mutuall good will,
>   seekes with sweet peace to salve each others wound.

The last trope acknowledges the vulnerability, so fundamental to Spenser's philosophy, that all creatures share in their human separateness, a vulnerability that makes any union hazardous yet indispensable.[18] But the poem imagines a redemptive "salve" as well in the mutuality of giving comfort. Its effect is to encloister their union, physical and spiritual, and purge it of the demons that threaten it:

> There fayth doth fearlesse dwell in brazen towre,
>   and spotlesse pleasure builds her sacred bowre.

The cage in which a captive songbird expands its soul in freedom has become a tower of faith without fear and a prelapsarian bower of erotic pleasure without blemish.

Spenser's portrayal of love as mutual render comes to focus on the lady's apprehensions about her spiritual condition on the threshold of sexual fulfillment. In doing so it anticipates the *Epithalamion*'s depiction of Christian humility and liberty as warrants of the sensual bond. An example is Spenser's version of the Petrarch and Wyatt sonnets on the hunt, sonnet 67.[19] Here Spenser revives the original Petrarchan visionary ambience by implying a Christlike self-sacrifice in the deer's submission to captivity. The courtly conceit of Wyatt's hunter, forsaking the "weary chace ... after long pursuit and vaine assay," undergoes a curious twist when Spenser's "gentle deare" converts her capture to a self-transcending act of surrender:

> There she beholding me with mylder looke,
>   sought not to fly, but fearelesse still did bide:
> till I in hand her yet halfe trembling tooke,
>   and with her owne goodwill hir fyrmely tyde.
> Strange thing me seemd to see a beast so wyld,
>   so goodly wonne with her owne will beguyld.

The last word echoes the earlier trope of the hunting "hounds beguiled of their pray," thus reasserting the basic courtly ambience of the topos. But Spenser's captor–hunter is himself taken by the strangeness of his prey's submission, in which he senses an almost supernatural "goodwill." The hint of sacred pattern behind these events is strengthened by the following poem's definition of love as "the lesson which the Lord us taught": Christ's redemptive sacrifice is the specific and overarching model for the general admonition to love (sonnet 68).[20]

But as the sequence nears completion, there is an increased emphasis on the poet's own willing capture as well. The most intriguing example is sonnet 71, which employs the mythological trope of the spider and the bee. Having lurked in secret ambush, the lover once again claims to have "thralled" her to his love "in cunning snare." But Spenser embeds this conventional conceit, half serious at best, in the context of the lady's "drawen work," a sketch or embroidered design:

> I joy to see how in your drawen work,
>> your selfe unto the Bee ye doe compare;
>> and me unto the Spyder that doth lurke,
>> in close awayt to catch her unaware.

The speaker goes on to approve the analogy: she is so firmly "captived" in his bonds that she may never "remove." In the sestet, however, he adapts this motif to the underlying pastoral myth of the sequence:

> But as your worke is woven all above,
>> with woodbynd flowers and fragrant Eglantine:
>> so sweet your prison you in time shall prove
>> with many deare delights bedecked fyne.

One must recall that other spider captured by a different kind of weaver in *Muiopotmos* to appreciate the subtle compliment concealed behind this boasting. If the lady correctly depicts her own capture in the spider and the bee, she also represents her capturing of her lover by weaving the story into her "work."

It is not inappropriate, therefore, that these lines anticipate the tornata of the *Epithalamion*. The beloved is tacitly invited to share in the sport and play – the *art* – whereby lovers embellish their bondage, converting prisons to gardens. This is an attitude traditionally associated with pastoral. The notion of scenes of violence or ruin contained by artful décor goes back at least to Theocritus' first Idyll, in the famous pastoral ecphrasis of the graven cup, where it embodies the conception of a precious, momentary freedom gained by means of the reconciling imagination.[21] Spenser's application of the topos here does not deny the trope of his beloved's permanent captivity in his own "streight bands." Rather, it invokes the larger theme, implied in his own willing submission in *The Faerie Queene* sonnet (80) and in the allusion to Christian sacrifice in "Most glorious Lord of lyfe" (68), of a more spacious freedom attained in a sensual prison that has become a spotless bower through the artfully constructed innocence of love. Traditionally the spider and the bee are not so much actors in a predatory struggle as types (normally antithetical) of the artist.[22] And it is as such, collaborating in the fashioning of a paradise of harmless delights, that Spenser leaves them:

> And all thensforth eternall peace shall see,
> betweene the Spyder and the gentle Bee.

In what is a rather more even combat to begin with than that of the spider and the butterfly in *Muiopotmos*, if this spider has been denied its traditional venom, the bee has lost its sting. All is concord in the resulting emblem of prelapsarian joy.

Spenser's pastoral of love in the *Amoretti* may be characterized as the purification of eros in a pastoral oasis of contemplation. Since the sequence terminates in absence, the process it narrates is circumscribed by the solitary imagination of the poet. In a sense, therefore, the sequence itself constitutes a pastoral of contemplation, in which poetry serves as a kind of ecphrasis, casting a shade over erotic experience, certifying its innocence, and imparting to it an aura of ideality. Only the terminal hints of frustration and non-closure adumbrate a re-admission of the principle of time. Of course the *Epithalamion* too takes place in the projecting imagination of the solitary poet. As Richard Neuse has eloquently described, the poem begins and ends in darkness. The bride's progress from the virgin "bower" through the ceremonies of the wedding day to the consummation of the marriage chamber is sheer confabulation, the poet summoning and shaping her perfected image out of the absence registered at the end of the *Amoretti* and conducting her to the literal darkness of the wedding night.[23] At the outset the speaker's stance is not only solitary and private but implicitly pastoral. Evoking the power of the Vergilian *poésie à écho* to "teach the woods and waters to lament," he bids the Muses "lay those sorrowfull complaints aside" (ll. 10–12). Forsaking the plaintive mode of Colin in the

Calender, he casts himself as another Orpheus braving the "death" of unfulfillment to rescue his bride.

But this sequence of action clearly implies the poet's surrender of the idealizing mode of the pastoral of pure contemplation. Whereas the isolated contemplative lover of the *Amoretti* hymns his idealized beloved in solitude, the bridegroom of the *Epithalamion* locates his bride in a specific milieu. If he fails to take full account of the reality of married love, he will not escape his solitude and his bride will remain unrecoverable. Spenser records this juncture in familiar pastoral terms: if he does succeed in breaking out of the plaintive mood of self-enclosure, his song will find echoes and an "answer" from without (ll. 17–18). The recreative joy that Spenser proffers his muse in lieu of plaintive sorrows implies the recreation of a broader context for love than the pure erotic pastoral of the *Amoretti*.

This context is both public and ceremonial. Under the aegis of Hymen, the marriage rites center on the bride as a unifying emblem of public virtues. As the procession unfolds, she becomes the focus first of the private world of poetic imagination peculiar to the poet as poet, then of the social – but no longer courtly – world of onlookers lining the streets through which she passes. As in the nuptials of Redcrosse and Una, the wedding music forges a bond between private joy, social ceremony, and cosmic purpose:

> Hymen io Hymen, Hymen they do shout,
> That even to the heavens theyr shouting shrill
> Doth reach, and all the firmament doth fill,
> To which the people standing all about,
> As in approvance doe thereto applaud
> And loud advance her laud,
> And evermore they Hymen Hymen sing,
> That al the woods them answer and theyr eccho ring.
>
> (ll. 140–7)

Between the heavens and the echoing woods stand the applauding and consenting "people" who witness and participate in the ritual. From the initial personal evocation of the bride in the first seven strophes, in which the speaker awakens, dresses, and surrounds her with the creations of his own poetic fancy, the middle strophes, 8–16, situate the beloved in a communal setting where her beauty and virtue take on a public function much as those of the emblematic heroines of Book 3 of *The Faerie Queene*.

This public function of the bride as exemplar of womanly virtue is succeeded by the private rites of the wedding-chamber. The final strophes of the *Epithalamion* are Spenser's last great ceremony of innocence. The emphasis in the final third of the poem is on the bride's "proud humility" and heroic surrender in accepting her sexual destiny. Spenser pastoralizes the event by likening the bride in bed to Maia

> when as Jove her tooke,
> In Tempe, lying on the flowry gras,
> Twixt sleepe and wake, after she weary was,
> With bathing in the Acidalian brooke.   (ll. 307–10)

This simultaneous surrender to a divine lover and to repose in a pastoral pleasance implies a conjunction of the natural and the supernatural. The next strophe expands upon this suggestion by subtly diminishing the male superiority of "Jove." Praying to night to "Spread thy broad wing over my love and me, / ...And in thy sable mantle us enwrap, / From feare of perrill and foule horror free" (ll. 319–22), the poet concludes his exorcism of the demonic night with two mythological analogies:

> Lyke as when Jove with fayre Alcmena lay,
> When he begot the great Tirynthian groome:
> Or lyke as when he with thy selfe [i.e. night] did lie,
> And begot Majesty.   (ll. 328–31)

To the literal conception of the pagan god and demigod, Mercury and Hercules, is added the quasi-figurative generation of another offspring: Ovid's *maiestas*, the consummate externalization of the bride's intrinsic dignity and virtue.[24] Emulating Maia's and Alcmena's submission to the divine will, the bridegroom himself enters with the bride into the mysteries of creation.

In this section Spenser stresses the sanctity of the creative act.[25] The erotic darkness of the marriage bed at the moment of sexual consummation is illuminated by the redemptive light of "Cinthia" invoked as both Endymion's lover and patroness of childbirth, i.e. bringer of sexual "pleasures" and the "comfort" of procreation. As in the earlier allusion to the Holy Spirit as Comforter, Spenser's usual fear of the otium of night is tinged here with the memory of God's original act of creation, which their act will imitate. On this prayer, and the subsequent summoning of that "glad Genius" by whose hands the pleasures of the marriage bed are justified in the multiplication of "blessed Saints," Spenser rests his hope for a final release. And so the labors of the wedding night end together with those of the visionary poet's song.

The reliance on bodily issue supplants the "Sabaoths sight" of *Mutability*. The final vision of the heavens' "torches flaming bright" reminds the lover that he and his bride are but "wretched earthly clods, / [enshrouded] in dreadful darknesse" (ll. 410–12). But in place of the dualistic implications of the last "unperfite" Mutability canto, the speaker here – who of course is also the chief actor in the events – consoles himself with the thought of his posterity, whose "lasting happinesse" will be fulfilled among the "heavenly taber-nacles" of "the stars" (ll. 419, 422). By accepting their subjection to their own limited condition as well as to a larger providential plan, the married lovers find release from their mutual fears and the common terrors of the night.

To this divine warrant the tornata adds a purely human one, bringing the poem implicitly into relation with Spenser's earlier work. The speaker hints that his song exercises the same creative energy celebrated in his hymning of the bride. This claim is perhaps his ultimate justification of the pastoral otium acknowledged in the sonnets on *The Faerie Queene*. In a sense the bride's Phoebe-like progress as she arises "to run her mighty race" (l. 150) toward the hopeful "rest" of her wedding night becomes an analogue for the poet's own race through Fairyland, from whose rigors he was (as he thought) pausing to raise "[his] spirit to an higher pitch" in the contemplation of his love (*Amor.* 80). That contemplation now issues in a vision of fruitful sexual love as both the epitome of human dependency and a hope for redemptive innocence in a fallen world. When Arthur patiently explains to Redcrosse and Una that no soul may hope to escape being bound in beauty's chain, for love is a type of the bondage all flesh must suffer, he tempers his painful truth with the gift of a balm "that any wound could heal incontinent" (1.9.19). Similarly, the lovers of the *Amoretti* in banishing pride and discord seek the "sweet peace to salve each others wound" (*Amor.* 65). In the *Epithalamion* the poet's gift is his vision of sexual fulfillment as part of God's creative plan. The heroic rhythm of the creative life has been so woven into the texture of Spenser's erotic imagination that a temporary haven is transformed into a surrogate for the eschatological "Sabaoths sight."

In the wedding hymn Spenser has "decked" the beloved in an

illuminating vision of marriage that is the result of a purely contemplative act. But the nature of that vision is such as to confirm eroticism as the vehicle for a ritual surrender to "short time." For the moment, sexual experience has provided a resolution to the problem of time through Diotima's first mode of procreation, even as it reaffirms her second mode in offering itself as an "endlesse moniment." The moment was evidently brief. In Spenser's last published work, which appeared in London a year later, the old strains appear once more.

III

The poems of 1596 have little to add to our understanding of Spenserian pastoral, but suggest a great deal about its underlying dialectic. Coming so soon after the affirmations of the love poetry, in which Spenser is able to re-imagine the earthly paradise of his earlier pastorals, they figure chiefly as tokens of fatigue if not despair. The competing claims of the public and private realms, held in solution in the great pastoral works and scenes, in these final poems separate out again. The poetic contemplation of transcendent reality is divorced from both courtly service and the articulation of cultural norms. Poetry can still function on either of these planes. It can no longer claim to mediate between them, and hence effectively ceases to be a version of pastoral.

This apparently irreparable collapse of the Spenserian compromise is patent in the *Fowre Hymnes*. Without attempting to address questions of chronology or of the plausibility of the poet's "retraction" in the dedication, we can take the published version as a reliable index to Spenser's own conception of the work in the year of its publication.[26] The poet celebrates the progress of love from "earthly or naturall" to "heavenly and celestial," i.e. the two Eroses of Renaissance Platonism. But this abstraction acquires solidity once again through the self-characterization of the speaker. From Love's victim propitiating his tormentor with a hymn of praise (*Hymne of Love* ll. 8–14), or inspired by his "wontlesse fury" to praise his mother, the principle of beauty immanent in the creation, the speaker becomes the regenerate seeker of a trinitarian Love anterior to creation (*Heavenly Love* ll. 22–42), ravished by thought and lifted beyond the "base world" to the realm of pure contemplation (*Heavenly Beautie* ll. 1–28). From these heights he views the earlier, earthly hymns as "lewd layes" (*Heavenly Love* l. 8).

Of course the progression from physical to spiritual love is as old as Diotima's instruction to the young Socrates and as new as Pietro Bembo's to his fellow courtiers at Urbino. But as we saw in the *Epithalamion*, for Spenser there is no necessary contradiction between them. At the peak of his faith in poetry as mediation, Spenser can posit genesis in the flesh and in the soul as mutually re-enforcing. The poem itself in its monumental eternality – the famous phrase from the tornata encapsulates Spenser's essential paradox of poetic incarnation – complements the poet's commitment to a physical posterity. By the same token, Spenser views his vocation as not simply to ascend in fits of pure contemplation to a direct apprehension of eternal forms, but to retrieve and implant them in the minds of his audience as operative motives of human action.[27] Even in the more intimate love poems, erotic activity itself displays this mediating impulse: lovers repeat in their union the archetypal creative harmony of Venus and Adonis, matter and form, and are rewarded with an untainted pleasure.

Spenser acknowledges this earlier paradigm in the *Hymne in Honour of Beautie*:

> For Love is a celestiall harmonie,
> Of likely harts composd of starres concent,
> Which joyne together in sweete sympathie,
> To worke ech others joy and true content,
> Which they have harbourd since their first descent
> Out of their heavenly bowres, where they did see
> And know each other here belov'd to bee. (ll. 197–203)

In this hymn the "earthly or naturall" love is still at root "celestiall" even though it is fulfilled by limited creatures in their attraction to physical beauty. Hence the recurrent plea for "grace" in the first two hymns signifies this creaturely dependence of the poet–lover on another person to re-enact the primal creative experience. In the "later" hymns this delicate knot of flesh and spirit has been cut, and with it all Diotimesque continuity between the two geneses.

Although thoroughly Christian in diction these poems discard the incarnational and creaturely doctrine of Arthur's counsel to Redcrosse, or the "proud humility" of the bride's (or Britomart's) acceptance of her sexual destiny, in favor of a world-denying act of pure contemplation. In contrast to the physical imperatives of *Amoretti* 67, where "love is the lesson which the Lord us taught," the *Hymne of Heavenly Love* begins and ends with the Son himself: "Him first to love, great right and reason is" (l. 190). We must "lift up [our] mind" to him and "learne him to love" (ll. 256, 258). This love annihilates "all worlds desire" (l. 274). As in Aristotle, contemplation (*theoria*) is conceived as more than human. At its height one is "ravisht" out of his bodily limitations:

> Then shall thy ravisht soule inspired bee
> With heavenly thoughts, farre above humane skil,
> And thy bright radiant eyes shall plainely see
> Th'Idee of his pure glorie, present still
> Before thy face, that all thy spirits shall fill
> With sweete enragement of celestiall love,
> Kindled through sight of those faire things above.
>
> (*Heavenly Love* ll. 281–7)

But unlike Redcrosse on Contemplation's hill, the solitary contemplator of *Heavenly Love* has no hermit to redirect him to his own earthly origins; moreover, there is no earthly paradise to shadow the incarnation of perfection in a restored nature.[28]

The *Hymne of Heavenly Beautie* assesses the contemplative ascent from "th'easie vew / Of this base world... by order dew, / To contemplation of th'immortall sky" (ll. 22–5). Acknowledging its difficulty, the singer reduces the material world to its mere instrumentality as foundation for the ladder:

> Thence gathering plumes of perfect speculation,
> To impe the wings of thy high flying mynd,
> Mount up aloft through heavenly contemplation,
> From this darke world, whose damps the soul do blynd,
> And like the native brood of Eagles kynd,
> On that bright Sunne of glorie fixe thine eyes,
> Clear'd from grosse mists of fraile infirmities.[29]   (ll. 134–40)

In Book I (10.47) of *The Faerie Queene* the eagle, emblem of the contemplative evangelist, John, had symbolized the visionary penetration of Contemplation.[30] But there the aged hermit tempered his vision with the exhortation to the hero to fulfill the active life. Here the poet implicitly casts himself as Contemplation rather than the Red Cross Knight. Lacking the unifying figure of a Una, or her avatar the bride, to incarnate the heavenly beauty, the poet prays not for the grace of erotic union and release, but for a vision of Sapience.[31]

Hence in place of the "false beauties" of creatures he now seeks only the "perfect beauty"

> That kindleth love in every godly spright,
> Even the love of God, which loathing brings
> Of this vile world, and these gay seeming things;
> With whose sweete pleasures being so possest,
> Thy straying thoughts henceforth for ever rest. (ll. 297–301)

In such a rapturous visitation, earlier described as a quasi-Acidalian act of serendipity (ll. 253–5), the contemplative poet can expect to find "rest," that poignantly characteristic final word of the *Fowre Hymnes*. But this time repose is sought in a total release from world and flesh that no longer derives from active delight in the beauties of this world nor anticipates the bringing forth of an earthly posterity to repeat the heroic struggle for redemption. Rather, it resides in an act of spiritual transcendence in which the earthly paradise of Spenserian pastoral becomes again a loathed "vile world."

Paradoxically, the same world is implied in the *Prothalamion*. As a marriage hymn this broken public rite contains echoes of the old Spenserian ceremony of innocence:

> Let endlesse Peace your steadfast hearts accord,
> And blessed Plentie wait upon your bord,
> And let your bed with pleasures chast abound,
> That fruitfull issue may to you afford. (ll. 101–4)

Significantly, though, the poet here is not even the singer of the song, which is arbitrarily delegated to one of the "nymphs" attending the two swans. This displacement is a minor consequence of Spenser's overall self-characterization in the poem. The singer of the *Prothalamion* resembles the narrators of medieval dream-visions or of Spenser's own earlier *Daphnaïda*. Walking alongside an idealized Thames, he sees in a vaguely pastoralized landscape the swans emblematic of the two brides. But from the outset he is sentimentally cut off from the idyllic scene. And the reason now is not unreciprocated love, but a much more blatant malaise:

> When I whom sullein care,
> Through discontent of my long fruitlesse stay
> In Princes Court, and expectation vayne
> Of idle hopes, which still doe fly away,
> Like empty shaddowes, did aflict my brayne,
> Walkt forth...
>
> (ll. 5–10)

This clash of an idyllic literary landscape with the continuing frustration of an aspiring courtier dooms the poem to failure as a conventional vehicle in the ceremonial public mode. In moving perfunctorily toward its consummation in the wedding ceremony – "at th'appointed tyde, / Each one did make his Bryde" (ll. 177–8) – the swans' procession comes to "mery *London*." At this point the poet's personal circumstances once more intrude upon the public rite, burdening it beyond tolerance. *This* London is "my most kyndly Nurse," the source of the speaker's earliest nurture, "Though from another place I take my name, / An house of auncient fame" (ll. 129–31); and the speaker himself is for once transparently Edmund Spenser.[32] Moreover, the towers of the Temple, "where now the studious Lawyers have their bowers" – the last word seems a flagrant piece of mock-pastoral – are also where "whylome wont the Templer Knights to byde, / Till they decayd through pride" (ll. 134–6). Ironically, following this allusion to pride is the observation that standing next to the Temple is Essex House, home of Spenser's latest patron, the rising nobleman whose praise fills the penultimate strophe of this supposed marriage hymn.

But the same palace also once housed Spenser's earliest patron, Leicester, now viewed through the tinted lenses of nostalgia:

> a stately place,
> Where oft I gayned giftes and goodly grace
> Of that great Lord, which therein wont to dwell,
> Whose want too well now feeles my freendles case:
> But Ah here fits not well
> Olde woes but joyes to tell.
>
> (ll. 137–42)

The sense of exclusion from a happiness dependent on patronage and aristocratic favor are scarcely at all disguised, and they devastate the lame semi-allegorical account of the union of knights and swan-brides.[33] Spenser may be sincere in his proclaimed faith in Essex to restore "great *Elisaes* glorious name" to its former lustre throughout the world (ll. 157–60). But the prominence of his personal grievance effectively undermines his attempt to use the marriage-hymn as the conventional vehicle for mediating private delights and public forms. Spenser's doubts in the last years of his life concerning his own and perhaps any poet's continuing performance of the ceremonial role central to his former conception effectively prevent proper closure. The wedding ceremony comes across as a hollow ritual in which the poet's own discontent and his transparent bid for Essex's favor upstage the wedding itself and rend the thin fabric of its allegorical mode.[34]

7

Conclusion

Taken together, the *Fowre Hymnes* and *Prothalamion* amply demonstrate the ultimate failure of the myth of the poet in courtly society that underlies Spenserian pastoral. According to that myth the courtier class itself is the repository of ethical values, which it best expresses in an aspiring yet communal active life. These values and that life are in turn continually refreshed and articulated by the courtly poet, who forgoes the self-delighting ecstasies of contemplation in favor of his heroic labors as a public personage.

The pastoral is a principal instrument in the conveyance of this myth. Drawing upon a long-established tradition in European thought and letters, Spenserian pastoral centers on the *vita contemplativa*, the commitment to which enables the poet to apprehend the permanent truths that inform the active life. It is by fulfilling the necessary precondition of otium ideally provided by his patron in the courtly setting that the poet confirms a tradition devolving ultimately from classical Greek speculations on the *paideia* of a gentleman but displaced in post-Hellenic culture to quasi-specialists in dialectic or rhetoric, philosophers or poets. The indispensable attribute of peace or leisure, and the release from obligations of trivial services and blandishments, encourage the linking of this myth of the poet with its generic or modal counterpart, the pastoral. The simplicity and hence authenticity of the conventional literary shepherd becomes an apt vehicle for the superior spirituality that justifies the central place claimed by poets in courtly cultures.

Whatever the realities that lie behind this myth and its attendant version of pastoral, Spenser can legitimately claim to be their chief perpetrator in Elizabethan England. His formal public début as a poet in *The Shepheardes Calender* endorses the Vergilian pastoral viewed by Renaissance literati as paradigmatic of the function of the courtly poet, including its associations in the exegetical tradition with the *vita contemplativa*. While carefully articulating his anonymous bid for useful employment on the larger stage of Elizabethan public life, Spenser in these eclogues grounds his claims to merit such employment on the traditional social humility but moral superiority of the typical pastoral persona, along with the model career embodied in the Vergilian generic paradigm. Though Colin himself has been banished from his simplistic prelapsarian paradise by the wounds of unhappy erotic love, as a poet he transplants into the heroic arena – or offers to do so if the ethical tenor of his potential audience warrants a positive response – the pristine communal values of the Vergilian Arcadia. This promise is realized in the first installment of *The Faerie Queene*, which embodies the fullest and boldest expression of Spenser's ceremonies of innocence: his conception of public poetry as an instrument for the sublimation and ordering of nature in culture. Here the pastoral elements focus reflexively on the process whereby contemplation is translated into action and spiritual values recovered by poetry inform the heroic virtues of men and women struggling to fulfill themselves in the toils of the world, the flesh, and the devil.

Spenser's failure to secure the high status at court merited by his services as a heroic poet is reflected in the revisionist pastoral of the *Complaints* and *Colin Clouts Come Home Againe*, twin products of his return to London in 1589–91. Complementing each other in the public revaluation of his pastoral myth of the courtly poet, the retrospective reconstruction of his career to date in the one, and revision of the nature and provenance of pastoralism itself in the other, effectively foreshadow the more private orientation of Spenser's poetry in the 1590s. This mood of retrenchment permeates the second installment of *The Faerie Queene*, though the pessimistic account of late-Elizabethan society recorded there is counterbalanced still by the idealistic and hopeful version of pastoral with which it ends. In the final appearance of Colin Clout, Spenser once again affirms the necessary and intimate bond between the visionary poet who epitomizes the contemplative life and the courtly audience who must be inspired by his poetry to fulfill his vision in ethical action. Although the personal bias of Colin Clout is strong in the feminine figura of Colin's Acidalian vision and in Calidore's heroic translation of it in the Pastorella episode, the connection of the private source of virtue to its public utility, though severely strained, is nonetheless reaffirmed.

The same effort to maintain a fundamental faith in poetry as reconciler and restorer is manifest in the Mutability Cantos and the love poetry of 1594–5. However slanted toward the intimate joys of lovers, the latter still succeeds in bridging the ideal world of forms and the immediate arena of experience, while the former accepts the reality of that experience and defers release to a Sabbath at the end of long labors. Almost to the end of his career Spenser retains, if not the conviction, at least the desire to affirm his lifelong view of poetry as a ceremony of innocence and the poet as the articulator of permanence. In the end national policy, personal disappointment, and perhaps a premature old age conspired to shatter Spenser's pastoral myth. The published poems of 1596 display a wide divorce between public and private values, and between transcendent and immanent orders of being, that makes it impossible any longer to construct poetic models of the earthly paradise. Both the blighted idyll of the *Prothalamion*, violated by the poet's sense of failure in his public role, and the transcendence of the *Fowre Hymnes*, obviating any notion of a redeemable nature, put a quietus to Spenser's search for a permanent realization of those versions of pastoral he had done so much to promote.

In tracing the fortunes of the pastoral trope in Spenser's poetry, I have tried to let the poet's several voices speak for themselves, to the extent that this is possible across the linguistic and sociohistorical gap dividing us from Elizabethan England. At the same time I have allowed Spenser the indulgence of his posture as a free subject inserting himself into his culture on his own terms. At some point, however, the question arises whether the poet has not all along been confirming Puttenham's evidently scandalous observation in the *Arte of English Poesie* that courtiers "seeme idle when they be earnestly occupied…and…busily negotiat by colour of otiation" (3.25). Doubtless he has, at times, and I hope that this study has suggested how Puttenham's view of pastoral as the dissimulative genre ("under the vaile of homely persons, and in rude speeches to insinuate and glaunce at greater matters," 1.18) informs the sustained literary "negotiating with Princes" of Spenser's *œuvre*. For all the play of signifiers across the surface of texts that contemporary theory has brought into focus, in the final analysis poetry's play is, as Louis Montrose and others have pointed out, doing the cultural work of its place and time. And whether the effort of a specific text is principally to certify or to contest prevailing social norms, there is an implicit dissembling of that labor in the concept of *theoria* that I have tried to show underlies the European pastoral myth.

I believe that, like Puttenham himself, Spenser is aware of these cultural issues as he rings his changes on this myth over the twenty years of production by which he negotiated his personal version of the Elizabethan social contract. Nor does it seem likely, writing as he was in an intensely rhetorical age, that he ever thought he was negotiating it on precisely his own terms. Given our own post-modern disillusionment, it would be bizarre if we were to be scandalized by Puttenham's punning observation. As a child of his age, Spenser takes it for granted that linguistically as well as politically he has been dealt a limited hand and has to cut the best deal he can. Nevertheless, I have tried to argue that among Spenser's few cards was the philosophical topos of contemplation as it had historically lent added resonance to the pastoral mode. Para-doxically – but it is the kind of Renaissance paradox with which we are beginning to feel comfortable – in the rhetorically saturated culture in which Spenser lived and wrote, negotiating the dialectic of the active and contemplative lives, far from being a "theoretical" activity in Aristotle's sense, was precisely an action or, as we would say, a *praxis* or social practice.

Given these inevitable contextual constraints, however, it is possible – and I have tried as best I can – to sketch the evolution of one particular negotiation of the theoretical conflict of *otium* and *negotium*. Viewed as a set of absolute options, of course, these categories are the mere shadow of a dream. But I don't think Spenser ever mistook them for such absolutes. Rather, within the literary and social codes he inherited, and in which he had no choice but to inscribe himself, he played out his variations on the familiar theme. In doing so, I believe that he not only enacted one part of the story of his time, but contributed his share to the writing of that story. To tell his story, history – and her story too, "Eliza's," the master-mistress of his passion – is, after all, to do the traditional work of the courtly poet even if it is done on the margins of the greater text. I believe that Spenser's pastoralism, once we get it right, will have made it a bit easier for us to read that story.

Notes

Introduction

1 On the question of "contextualism" in current historiography, philosophy, and literary theory, see Dominick La Capra, *Rethinking Intellectual History* (Ithaca: Cornell University Press, 1983), esp. pp. 1–71.

2 Jonathan Goldberg, *James I and the Politics of Literature* (Baltimore: Johns Hopkins University Press, 1983), pp. 1–17. See also Goldberg, *Endlesse Worke* (Baltimore and London: Johns Hopkins University Press, 1981); Louis A. Montrose, "'Eliza, Queene of Shepheardes,' and the Pastoral of Power," *ELR* 10 (1980), 153–82; Richard Helgerson, "The New Poet Presents Himself: Spenser and the Idea of a Literary Career," *PMLA* 93 (1978), 893–901; Stephen Greenblatt, *Renaissance Self-Fashioning* (Chicago: University of Chicago Press, 1980), pp. 157–92; and Stephen Orgel, "Making Greatness Familiar," in *The Power of Forms in the English Renaissance*, ed. Stephen Greenblatt (Norman, Oklahoma: Pilgrim Books, 1982), p. 43.

3 For an excellent review of "new historical" criticism of the Renaissance, see Jean E. Howard, "The New Historicism in Renaissance Studies," *ELR* 16 (1986), 13–43. For more recent, and more critical, discussions see Edward Pechter, "The New Historicism and Its Discontents," *PMLA* 102 (1987), 292–303; A. Leigh DeNeef, "Of Dialogues and Historicisms," *SAQ* 86 (1987), 497–517.

4 William Empson, *Some Versions of Pastoral* (New York: New Directions, 1950).

5 Montrose, "Eliza, Queene of Shepheardes"; cf. Montrose's more recent article, "Of Gentlemen and Shepherds: The Politics of Elizabethan Pastoral Form," *ELH* 50 (1983), 415–59; and his remarks on a paper by Ronald Bond, "Interpreting Spenser's February Eclogue: Some Contexts and Implications," *SSt* 2 (1981), 67–73.

6 *Essai sur les moeurs et l'esprit des nations*, ed. R. Pomeau (Paris: Garnier, 1963), II. 169.

7 Roberto Weiss, *The Spread of Italian Humanism* (London: Hutchinson University Library, 1964), pp. 64f.

8 On the general tenor of humanist fiction around 1500, see Charles Mitchell, "Archaeology and Romance in Renaissance Italy," in *Italian Renaissance Studies*, ed. E. F. Jacob (London: Faber & Faber, 1960), pp. 455–83. See also Helen Cooper, *Pastoral: Medieval into Renaissance* (Ipswich: D. S. Brewer; and Totowa, NJ: Rowman and Littlefield, 1977).

9 Daniel Javitch, *Poetry and Courtliness in Renaissance England* (Princeton: Princeton University Press, 1978), pp. 55–8.

10 In addition to Javitch, see Lawrence L. Lipking, "The Dialectic of *Il Cortegiano*," *PMLA* 81 (1966), 355–62; Dain A. Trafton, "Structure and Meaning in *The Courtier*," *ELR* 2 (1972), 283–97; and Wayne Rebhorn, *Courtly Performances* (Detroit: Wayne State University Press, 1978).

11 Montrose, "Of Gentlemen and Shepherds," 451f. See also Goldberg, *James I*, p. 12: "The *Faerie Queene* speaks the language of power, hedging itself round with disclaimers, denying the poet's voice in order to proclaim the truth, a truth that is not its own." Having no independent source of authority, Goldberg argues, Spenser's voice and verse are "authorized" only by those with real authority, primarily his royal mistress. Goldberg accuses Stephen Greenblatt of a similar reductivism in "The Politics of Renaissance Literature," *ELH* 49 (1982), 533.

12 While acknowledging the poet's powerlessness, Montrose denies any "dispraise of power": pastoral in fact enacts "the symbolic mediation of social relationships" ("Eliza, Queene of Shepheardes," 153); cf. Javitch, *Poetry and Courtliness*, pp. 79–82 and 154f.

13 Javitch, *Poetry and Courtliness*, especially pp. 18–49.

14 For a recent application of the didactic theory of Renaissance poetry to *The Faerie Queene*, see Robin Headlam Wells, *Spenser's "Faerie Queene" and the Cult of Elizabeth* (Totowa, NJ: Barnes and Noble, 1983).

15 "Renaissance Literary Studies and the Subject of History," *ELR* 16 (1986), 9f. See also Louis A. Montrose, "The Elizabethan Subject and the Spenserian Text," in *Literary Theory/Renaissance Texts*, ed. Patricia Parker and David Quint (Baltimore: Johns Hopkins University Press, 1986), pp. 317f.: "At a fundamental level, all Elizabethan subjects may be said to have participated in a ceaseless and casual process of producing and reproducing 'the Queen' in their daily practices." This is especially true of poets and others "specifically engaged in production of texts" representing the Queen to the people: "such fashioning and such manipulation were reciprocal." Hence, "the ruler and the ruled, the queen and the poet, are construable as subjects differentially shaped within a shared conjuncture of language and social relations, and jointly

reshaping the conjuncture in the very process of living it." One might observe that Montrose's self-revision reverses that of his mentor, Greenblatt, during the very course of writing *Renaissance Self-Fashioning*; see the latter, p. 256.

16 Howard points out that Greenblatt too has recently begun to deny that "in Elizabethan culture subversion is inevitably contained" ("The New Historicism," 41).

17 James E. Congleton, *Theories of Pastoral in England, 1684–1798* (New York: Haskell House, 1968 [1952]), pp. 45–9.

18 Quoted in Congleton, *Theories of Pastoral*, p. 46.

19 See Jack H. Hexter, *More's "Utopia": The Biography of an Idea* (Princeton: Princeton University Press, 1952).

20 C. G. Starr, "Virgil's Acceptance of Octavian," *AJP* 76 (1955), 34–46; see also Gary Miles and Archibald Allen, "Vergil and the Augustan Experience," in *Vergil at 2000: Commemorative Essays on the Poet and his Influence*, ed John D. Bernard (New York: AMS Press, 1986), pp. 14–21; and Matthew Santirocco, *Unity and Design in Horace's Odes* (Chapel Hill: University of North Carolina Press, 1986).

21 To be sure, the Renaissance humanist version tempers the element of freedom in Vergil's work. This may be seen in the ceremonial "conclusion" to the *Aeneid* appended in 1471 by Maffeus Vegius and reprinted in nearly every major edition and translation of the epic for the next 150 years. The thirteenth book of the *Aeneid*, replete with its marvellous woodcuts in Brant's 1501 edition, is a monument to the courtly allegorizing of a classic. The wedding of Aeneas and Lavinia, Aeneas' death and translation (a "pastoral" motif borrowed from the fifth eclogue) – these and other features make of Vergil's poem a humanist rite of imperial courtliness. See Anna Cox Brinton, *Mapheus Vegius and his Thirteenth Book of the Aeneid* (Stanford: Stanford University Press, 1930).

22 Cf. Ottaviano Fregoso in Castiglione's *The Book of the Courtier*, trans. Charles S. Singleton (New York: Anchor Books, 1959), p. 293 (4.8). The same issue is debated in Part I of More's *Utopia*, ed. Edward Surtz (New Haven: Yale University Press, 1964), pp. 48–50.

23 This is especially true so soon after Erasmus had demonstrated the unique power of the press. See Johan Huizinga, *Erasmus and the Age of Revolution* (New York: Harper, 1957), p. 65.

24 "Renaissance Literary Studies," 11. Cf. Howard, "The New Historicism," 25: literature is now conceived by the new historicists as "an agent in constructing a culture's sense of reality."

25 Angus Fletcher, *The Prophetic Moment* (Chicago: University of Chicago Press, 1971). See also Harry Berger, Jr., "The Prospect of Imagination," *SEL* 1 (1961), 93–120.

26 Michael O'Connell, *Mirror and Veil: The Historical Dimension of Spenser's Faerie Queene* (Chapel Hill: University of North Carolina Press, 1977), pp. 36f., 67f. O'Connell further states that Calidore discovers both the "pastoral pleasure" and the contemplative bias of Colin Clout (p. 173).

27 Cf. William Sessions' scheme of a pervasive Vergilian paradigm in Spenser's writing, in "Spenser's Georgics," *ELR* 10 (1980), 202–38. Sessions argues that Spenser offers the reader and the nation a redemptive model of labor in time which supports a Christian–imperial myth and invites the courtier to be a hero striving from lowly tasks now to an exalted consummation hereafter. See also Andrew Fichter, *Poets Historical: Dynastic Epic in the Renaissance* (New Haven: Yale University Press, 1982).

28 Kenelm Foster, *The Two Dantes and Other Studies* (London: Darton, Longman & Todd, 1977); see also David Thompson, *Dante's Epic Journeys* (Baltimore: Johns Hopkins Press, 1974).

29 Peter Dronke, *Medieval Latin and the Rise of the European Love-Lyric* (Oxford: Clarendon Press, 1965). Cf. Cooper, *Pastoral*, pp. 90–3.

30 For a similarly moderating view of the Marxist reading of Renaissance literature and ideology, see also David Quint, "Introduction," in *Literary Theory/Renaissance Texts*, ed. Patricia Parker and David Quint, (Baltimore: Johns Hopkins Press, 1986), pp. 1–19.

31 See Louis A. Montrose, "Celebration and Insinuation: Sir Philip Sidney and the Motives of Elizabethan Courtship," *RenD* n.s. 8 (1977), 3–35.

32 Louis Althusser, *Lenin and Philosophy*, trans. Ben Brewster (New York and London: Monthly Review Press, 1971), p. 165.

1 *Vita contemplativa* and the pastoral

1 The term is Francis Bacon's, *Advancement of Learning*, in *Works*, ed. J. Spedding *et al.* (Boston: Houghton, Mifflin & Co., 1900), VI. 138. For the Latin version, see *ibid.*, II. 146f. See below, pp. 36f.

2 *Mythologiae* 2.1, ed. R. Helm (Stuttgart: Teubner, 1970), p. 36; cf. *Nichomachean Ethics* [*NE*] 10.1177b26–31; Aquinas, *Quaestiones disputatae, De virtutibus cardinalibus*, 1.

3 "I have followed all the antique Poets historicall, first Homere...then Virgil...after him Ariosto...and lately Tasso...[who] formed both parts in two persons, namely that part which they in Philosophy call Ethice, or vertues of a private man...The other named Politice..." Letter to Raleigh, *Poetical Works*, ed. J. C. Smith and E. de Selincourt (London: Oxford University Press, 1970), p. 407. All citations of Spenser's text are to this edition.

4 Hannah Arendt, *The Human Condition: A Study of the Central Dilemmas Facing Modern Man* (Garden City, NY: Doubleday & Co., 1959), p. 16.

5 Franz J. Boll, *Vita Contemplativa* (Heidelberg: C. Winter, 1922), pp. 6f.; Josef Pieper, *Leisure: The Basis of Culture*, trans. Alexander Dru (New York: Pantheon Books, 1952), pp. 34–7. Pieper points out that the fundamental denotation of *templum* is of a sacred space demarcated on the earth or in the sky. The Latin word is cognate with Greek *temenos*, a sacral region (pp. 73f.).

6 See E. A. Havelock, *The Liberal Temper in Greek Politics* (New Haven: Yale University Press, 1957). The *Republic* in particular exhibits a deep ambiguity as to the desirability or even possibility of useful political action: see especially *Rep.* 9.592a5–b5. The question of whether to return to the Cave (*Rep.* 7.520) is resolved in the *Phaedrus*, where the intuition of the Forms is not the goal of human development, and the contemplator must create or encourage the good life in others; see John M. Rist, *Eros and Psyche* (Toronto: University of Toronto Press, 1964), p. 28.

7 *Eudemian Ethics* [*EE*] 1215a35; *NE* 1.1095b14–19. Although the *Eudemian Ethics* are probably not by Aristotle, they clearly reflect an Aristotelian provenance.

8 Robert Joly, *Le Thème philosophique des genres de vie dans l'antiquité classique* (Brussels: Académie des sciences de Belgique, 1956), p. 127, sees *theoria* as a "mystical" process in Aristotle, both mystical and dialectical in Plato. But even in Plato dialectic is probably an instrument to achieve *theoria* (*Rep.* 7.533a–4a), just as Aristotle divides "pure" thought into *theoria* and *dianoia* (*Politics* [*Pol.*] 7.1325b21).

9 That Aristotle resists drawing this conclusion is at least partly due to the semantics of the case. Since virtue is activity, happiness is "doing well" (*NE* 1.1095a19, and *Pol.* 7.9.1325a29, both echoing the end of Plato *Rep.* 10.621a). But can a man who does nothing do well? For Aristotle *theoria* is not only an "activity" (*energeia*), in the sense of the actualization of a potentiality (*dynamis*); it is also an "action" (*praxis*). (See, however, Alberto Grilli, *Il problema della vita contemplativa nel mondo greco-romano* [Milan: Bocca, 1953], p. 126, who treats *energeia* as "activity" in an unqualified sense, contrary to the usual limitation of the term to bringing a potentiality "into deed" [*en + ergon*].) Aristotle can thus argue that inaction is not better than action because "happiness is an activity" (1325a33); therefore the active life is the best (b17). But to save the active life Aristotle has stretched it in such a way as practically to demolish the distinction among the three *bioi*. For the "actions" included are not only actions taken with respect to other men, nor even the prudential thinking about external objects that concern such actions,

but also speculations and thoughts (*theorias kai dianoeseis*) that have their ends in themselves (*autoteleis*). "For the end," he concludes in a sublime tautology, "is to do well (*eupraxia telos*) and therefore is a certain form of action (*hoste kai praxis tis*)" (1325b22). The logic of language and the conviction of a hierarchical organization of the soul combine to force Aristotle, even when he is most passionately defending political involvement, to find a place among the activities of men for purely contemplative thinking.

10 On Chrysippus' life of reason, see Sen. *Ep.* 95.10, in Seneca, *Ad Lucilium Epistulae Morales*, trans. Richard M. Gummere (London: Heinemann, 1934), III.64.x. The Middle Stoa, and especially Posidonius, rejected the tendency to embrace philosophy, and the requisite conditions of peace or leisure, on the ground that they bar the proper fulfillment of man as much as does the opposite extreme of frenetic engagement in meaningless activity.

11 G. W. Bowersock, *Augustus and the Greek World* (Oxford: Clarendon Press, 1965), pp. 45f.; see also Jean-Marie André, *L'Otium dans la vie morale et intellectuelle romaine des origines à l'époque augustéenne* (Paris: Publications de la faculté des lettres et sciences humaines, 1956), pp. 39f. On philosophers in Hellenized Rome, see William V. Harris, *War and Imperialism in Republican Rome, 327–70 B.C.* (Oxford: Clarendon Press, 1979), p. 14.

12 See the famous passage in the *Hortensius* cited by St. Augustine, where Cicero says that once beyond earthly shows we would also be beyond the need for eloquence and the cardinal virtues; as well as *De trinitate* 14.9: "beati cognitione naturae et scientia qua sola etiam deorum est vita laudanda" (translated on p. 19); cf. *NE* 10.1177b26 and 10.1178b20. In his few recorded utterances on the rival estates Cicero apparently identifies *contemplatio* with mere cognition or even science. At one point he claims to be turning from Dicearchus, who favors "ton praktikon bion," to Theophrastus, with his preference for "ton theoretikon [bion]" (*Epistulae ad Atticum* [*Att.*] 2.16.1; cf. *Att.* 2.3, where Cicero asks Atticus for a copy of Theophrastus' book). But he never seems to have grasped the basic distinction between *contemplatio*, or Greek *theoria*, and *cognitio*, a more rational activity, akin to the Peripatetics' "vision of universal order" and perhaps tinged with Lucretius' Epicurean science (André, *L'Otium dans la vie morale*, p. 332); cf. *De finibus* 5.4.11, for example, where it is not clear whether *contemplatio* and *cognitio* are in opposition or apposition.

13 Translation from the Loeb edition: *Cicero, The Letters to his Friends*, trans. W. Glynn Williams (London: William Heinemann, Ltd., 1965), III. 265. See also *De officiis* [*Off.*] 1.21.69–70.

14 In similar fashion the transplanted Greek, Plutarch, reconciles his own

philosophical antipathy to Epicureanism with a profound attraction to solitude and quiet. In his formal exposition of the three *bioi–praktikos, theoretikos, apolaustikos* – Plutarch sounds like a Romanized Aristotle. The life of pleasure is bestial and mean; the contemplative life "falls short in the practical [realm]"; the purely practical is "without culture or taste." Thus one must emulate public men such as Pericles and Dion in combining politics and philosophy (*De liberis educandis* 8). But in the Panaetian *Peri euthymias* (= *Moralia* [*Mor.*] 464–77), after scolding the Epicureans for counselling idleness, Plutarch invokes the Delphic "know thyself" to justify the quiet life and leisure (*apragmosynes kai skholes*) as the proper setting for the study of rhetoric and mathematics, defining political activities, including friendship with kings, as "the thing done without leisure" (*to pragmaton askholion*). The fundamentally Stoic thrust of the essay comes out in its concluding section: in the face of the pains inflicted by Fortune, one can suppress the answering evil impulse in one's soul and create true tranquillity of mind. Hence it is finally not circumstances, but a rational equanimity cultivated in retirement and acquired by contemplation, that enables one to fashion his life into the Cynics' "feast" and meet the future cheerfully.

15 In addition to the works already cited by Joly, Grilli, and André, see Ernst Bernert, "Otium," *Wurzburger Jahrbücher für die Altertums-wissenschaft* 4 (1949–50), 76–80; Erich Burck, "Vom Sinn des Otium in alten Rom," in *Römische Wertbegriffe*, ed. Hans Oppermann (Darmstadt: Wissenschaftliche Buchgesellschaft, 1967), pp. 503–15; and *Les Loisirs des romains: textes latins et traductions, documents commentés*, ed. Suzanne Barthèlemy and Danielle Gourevitch (Paris: Société d'édition d'enseignement supérieur, 1975). I deliberately omit the poets in the present discussion because their role will be treated separately in my discussion of poetry and power in section II of this chapter.

16 Chaim Wirszubski, "Cicero's *Cum Dignitate Otium*: A Reconsideration," *JRS* 44 (1954), 12, cites *Brutus* 8 and *Off.* 2.2.4.42. See also André, *L'Otium dans la vie morale*, pp. 279–330, and P. Boyance, "*Otium cum dignitate*," *REA* 43 (1941), 172–91. Through all the nuances of the word in Cicero one senses the old Roman (or "new man" assuming conservative values) who resists Greek refinements, or the Stoic intellectual and practical man who denies the seductions of pleasure, preferring service to humanity even over a life free of the fear of pain. For a somewhat different attitude, see *Att.* 2.4, where Cicero is divided between *otium* as study and as sheer *inertia*. According to J. P. V. D. Balsdon, *Life and Leisure in Ancient Rome* (New York: McGraw-Hill, 1969), p. 136, otium is "always a second-best life" for the Romans.

17 The translation is from the Loeb edition, *Seneca, Moral Essays*, trans. John W. Basore (London: Heinemann, 1963).

18 Translations of Pliny are from *Letters*, with trans. by Betty Radice (Cambridge: Harvard University Press, 1975). On the concept of *aeternitas* in Pliny and the related one of *immortalitas*, see below, pp. 27f.

19 The *locus classicus* is *Enn.* 3.8.3, in Plotinus, *The Enneads*, trans. Stephen MacKenna (London: Faber and Faber Ltd., 1962), 3rd edn, pp. 240f.; on *katharsis*, see Joly, *Le Thème philosophique*, p. 190, and Grilli, *Il problema della vita contemplativa*, p. 286.

20 René Arnou, *ΠΡΑΞΙΣ et ΘΕΩΡΙΑ* [*Praxis et Theoria*] (Paris: Félix Alcan, 1921); Rist, *Eros and Psyche*, p. 170, claims that in this *homoiosis theo* Plotinus "fathers" the Aristotelian *theoria* on Plato.

21 Though Plotinan poetics has much in common with modern theories of creativity, it of course is distinguished, for example, from the Derridean "free play" of language by its "metaphysics of presence," or grounding of the individual mind in a transcendent Truth, the last vestiges of which Derrida deconstructs in Heidegger's revisionary critique of Nietzsche. See Jacques Derrida, *Spurs: Nietzsche's Styles*, trans. Barbara Harlow (Chicago: University of Chicago Press, 1979), especially p. 115.

22 This view also brings Plotinus into conformity with the Roman rhetorical tradition with which his thought is often fused by Renaissance humanists. See Ernesto Grassi, *Rhetoric as Philosophy: The Humanist Tradition* (University Park: Pennsylvania State University Press, 1980); Nancy Struever, *The Language of History in the Renaissance* (Princeton: Princeton University Press, 1970); and Jerrold E. Seigel, *Rhetoric and Philosophy in Renaissance Humanism* (Princeton: Princeton University Press, 1968).

23 Grilli, *Il problema della vita contemplativa*, pp. 290–306, also cites Augustine, *De beata vita* 4.34, 25, 32–3; and Jerome, *Adversus Jovinianum*. On monasticism and the *vita contemplativa*, see, for example, Francis D. S. Darwin, *The English Medieval Recluse* (London: Society for Promoting Christian Knowledge, n.d.); Rotha M. Clay, *The Hermits and Anchorites of England* (London: Methuen, 1964); and Charles P. Weaver, *The Hermit in English Literature* (Nashville: George Peabody College, 1924).

24 Robert J. O'Connell, *Art and the Christian Intelligence in St. Augustine* (Cambridge, Mass: Harvard University Press, 1978), p. 78; on p. 205 O'Connell cites *De musica* 5.18–29, viz., the hymn beginning "Procul negotio" with its Epicurean source in Horace, *Epodes* 2.1. In the *City of God* 8.4, Augustine acknowledges the two major *vitae* as equal "avenues" to wisdom, defining their ends respectively as the conduct of life and "natural causality, or truth as such," and adds a third life, namely the life of truth (versus error) pertaining to rational philosophy as against natural philosophy; see *M. Tulli Ciceronis Academica*, rev.

and ed. James S. Reid (London: Macmillan & Co., 1885), pp. 115–20. Augustine then telescopes this third life with contemplation on the grounds that the latter too attains a vision of truth. In this way he attempts to overcome the Ciceronian dichotomy of *cognitio* and *contemplatio* (see note 12, above) and intuitively recover the Platonic–Aristotelian unity of *theoria*. On the crucial concept of *sapientia* in Augustine, Fulgentius, and Isidore, see R. E. Kaske, "*Sapientia et Fortitudo* as the Controlling Theme of *Beowulf*," *SP* 55 (1958), 423–56.

25 *Scala Paradiso, liber unus*, in Migne, *Patrologiae Cursus, series Latina* [*PL*] 50, col. 997ff.

26 Appendix xiv to his *Opera, PL* 83.1243–8. Isidore adds that the active life can be valid without contemplation, but while we are alive the contemplative live "cannot show itself [*se explicare*] without the active" (37). Indeed, no one in this life can be so perfect in the contemplation of God that he is not sometimes compelled to descend to earthly action (38). The truly "perfect" therefore know both how to rise to contemplation and how to descend to action "per compassionem" (2).

27 Cited in Thomas Aquinas, *Summa Theologica* [*ST*] 2.2.179.2, 171.1,2. Bernard also identifies Leah: Rachel with Mary: Martha: *In assumptionem Mariae*, Serm. 3, cited Edward Moore, *Studies in Dante*, 3rd ser. (Oxford: Clarendon Press, 1968), p. 211n; and *In Cantica*, Serm. 46, *PL* 183.1004–6. Serm. 52 views contemplation as an excessive dampening of the fervent soul's zeal, a sentiment echoed by Dante in *Purgatorio* 19 in the sudden apparition of the zealous.

28 *In X libros Ethicorum ad Nichomachum* 10, lect. 12. Aquinas notes that moral virtue and prudence pertain to our "compound" nature whereas the "speculative life and felicity [of *intellectus*] are divine." On *ratio* and *intellectus*, see above, p. 23, and Pieper, *Leisure: The Basis of Culture*, pp. 34–7; see also Etienne H. Gilson, *Dante the Philosopher*, trans. David Moore (New York: Sheed and Ward, 1949), pp. 137f.

29 *Convito*, ed. V. Piccoli (Torino: Unione Tipografico-Editrice, 1927), 2.5 [4.10 in the Società Dantesca edition]. Dante concedes (2.4) that "he who contemplates does not govern, [and] he who governs does not contemplate."

30 According to Gilson, *Dante the Philosopher*, p. 140, the mutual independence of the "hierarchies" of dignity and authority in Dante constitutes a "breach of [their] classic relationship." But as we have seen, in Plato and Aristotle, as in virtually all their predecessors, power and science or knowledge have little rapport – witness the shocking "third wave of ridicule" with which Socrates in *Rep.* 5 introduces his radically utopian proposal that they be linked – and a good part of the post-Aristotelian debate on the *bioi* I have reviewed can be seen as

enshrining the recoil of the powerless from the "classic" effort to hold them together in the face of their obvious divorce in the actual world. It seems to me that Gilson (pp. 141f.) exaggerates the conflicting imperatives in the *Convivio* between the superiority of contemplation and the ethical preeminence resulting from Dante's exalting the *donna gentile*.

31 Dronke, *Medieval Latin, passim*; see also Ricardo Quinones, *The Renaissance Discovery of Time* (Cambridge, Mass.: Harvard University Press, 1972), pp. 124–6. For related examples of figuralism in Renaissance love poetry, see John D. Bernard, "To Constancie Confin'de': The Poetics of Shakespeare's Sonnets," *PMLA* 94 (1979), 77–90.

32 See Charles Trinkaus, *In Our Image and Likeness* (Chicago: University of Chicago Press, 1970), I.169f.; Eugene F. Rice, *The Renaissance Idea of Wisdom* (Cambridge, Mass.: Harvard University Press, 1958), especially pp. 43–56; and Erwin Panofsky, *Studies in Iconology* (New York: Harper & Row, 1962), pp. 129–69.

33 One might compare, e.g., *Il libro del cortegiano* 4.26. On Ficino see Edgar Wind, *Pagan Mysteries in the Renaissance* (New York: Norton, 1969), pp. 81–3; and Paul Oskar Kristeller, *Renaissance Thought, II: Papers on Humanism and the Arts* (New York: Harper & Row, 1965), p. 95.

34 Giovanni Pico della Mirandola, "Oration on the Dignity of Man," in *The Renaissance Philosophy of Man*, ed. Ernst Cassirer *et al.* (Chicago: University of Chicago Press, 1948), pp. 223–54; all translations of this text are by E. L. Forbes in this edition. Pico identifies the active life with the angelic order of the Thrones, the contemplative with that of the Cherubim, and the mystical or unitive with the Seraphim (pp. 227f.). Cf. Francis Bacon, *Advancement of Learning*, in *Francis Bacon: A Selection of His Works*, ed. Sidney Warhaft (Indianapolis: Bobbs Merrill, 1965), p. 237, where the Seraphim are equated with mercy or charity, the divine sanction of science, emblematized by the Cherubim; science in turn controls the political life, Pico's active life of power. See also Rice, *The Renaissance Idea of Wisdom*, pp. 61ff.; and Elizabeth Sewell, *The Orphic Voice: Poetry and Natural History* (New York: Harper & Row, 1971), pp. 64ff.

35 Cf. Bacon's "second causes," in *Works*, p. 205. The work of Elyot's referred to is "Of the knowledge of...a wise man," cited by Rice, *The Renaissance Idea of Wisdom*, pp. 85–7.

36 Calvin believes the intellect is capable of knowing God, though only aided and directed by God, provided that it begins with knowledge of one's own debased condition: Paul N. Siegel, "Spenser and the Calvinist View of Life," *SP* 41 (1944), 216–21; cf. Bacon, *Works*, p. 204.

37 Edward Morris, ed., *Satires and Epistles of Horace* (New York: American Book Co., 1939), p. 7. See also D. R. Shackleton Bailey, *Profile of Horace* (Cambridge, Mass.: Harvard University Press, 1982), p. ix; and *Vita Horati*, in *Suetonius*, trans. J. C. Rolfe (London: Heinemann, 1965); Jean Cousin, *Études sur la poésie latine: nature et mission du poète* (Paris: Boivin, 1945); Anne-Marie Guillemin, *Le Public et la vie littéraire à Rome* (Paris: Société d'édition: Les Belles Lettres, 1937); Balsdon, *Life and Leisure*; and Jasper Griffin, "Augustan Poetry and the Life of Luxury," *JRS* 66 (1976), 87–105. For a less sympathetic view of poets' otium by ordinary Romans of the first century CE, see Tacitus' *Dialogus de oratoribus*.

38 *Tristia* 3.2.9; cf. 4.10.40 and 105, and 1.1.41.

39 Propertius 2,10; Vergil, *Georgics [G]* 1.118ff., 2.173–6, and 4.558–65.

40 *Odes [Carm.]* 3.13.9–16; see Marie Desport, "L'Écho de la nature et la poésie dans les Églogues de Virgile," *REA* 43 (1941), 270–81; and Henry Bardon, "Un aspect méconnu de génie latin: le sens du mystère," *RCCM* 1 (1959), 7–14.

41 See Juvenal 6.1–13; 3.312–15; 13.38–57; and 14.156–72, among many others.

42 See, e.g., *Carm.* 2.3, 3.29; *Satirae [Sat.]* 2.7; and *Epodi* 1.10. For examples of Martial's Horatian echoes, see 1.15; 2.64; 1.39; 1.49; and 5.20. For a study of the religion of love as a form of contemplation in the elegists, see Luigi Alfonsi, "Otium e vita d'amore negli elegiaci augustei," *Studi in onore di Aristide Calderini e Roberto Paribeni* (Milano: Casa Ceschina editrice, 1956–7), III. 187–209.

43 See Peter White, "*Amicitia* and the Profession of Poetry in Early Imperial Rome," *JRS* 68 (1978), 74–92; M. L. Clarke, "Poets and Patrons at Rome," *Gr&R* 25 (1978), 46–54; Richard P. Saller, *Personal Patronage Under the Early Empire* (Cambridge: Cambridge University Press, 1982), esp. pp. 7–40, and "Martial on Patronage and Literature," *CQ* 33 (1983), 246–57; and Santirocco, *Unity and Design*, pp. 153–68.

44 Jean Lucas-Dubreton, *Daily Life in Florence at the Time of the Medici*, trans. A. L. Sells (New York: Macmillan, 1961), p. 66. See also E. Garin, *L'umanesimo italiano: filosofia e vita civile nel Rinascimento* (Bari: G. Laterza, 1958) 2nd edition, p. 104: in protecting literati, Lorenzo "transformed the existing culture into an elegant ornament of court, or into a desperate flight from the world."

45 Struever, *The Language of History*, p. 190; see also Ralph Roeder, *The Man of the Renaissance*; *Four Lawgivers: Machiavelli, Savonarola, Castiglione, Aretino* (New York: Meridian Books, 1958), p. 320. A case in point is the ill-fated Accademia degli Umidi, a group of Florentine intellectuals and wits in the sixteenth century given to oblique comment on local affairs reflected in the dialogues of Gelli. Within three years of

his coming to power, Duke Cosimo I had "upgraded" the Umidi to the "Florentine Academy." The political message of this allusion to the group of refined philosophers of Lorenzo's day must have been patent in the title. See Giovanni Battista Gelli, *Dialoghi*, ed. Roberto Tissoni (Bari: Laterza, 1967), p. xi; and M. Plaisance, "Culture et politique à Florence de 1542 à 1551," *Les Écrivains et le pouvoir en Italie à l'époque de la Renaissance* (Paris: Centre de Recherche sur la Renaissance Italienne, ser. 2 [1973–4]), pp. 149–242.

46 Emilio Bigi, *La cultura del Poliziano e altri studi umanistici* (Pisa: Nistri-Lischi, 1967), p. 87; E. Garin, "Poliziano e il suo ambiente," in *Ritratti di umanisti* (Florence: Sansoni, 1967), pp. 131–60; William Roscoe, *The Life of Lorenzo de' Medici, Called the Magnificent*, 2 vols. (Philadelphia: Carey and Hart, 1842; from the 6th London edn), I. 93f.; and E. Garin, *Giovanni Pico della Mirandola: Vita e Dottrina* (Florence: Le Monnier, 1937).

47 Werner Gundersheimer, *Ferrara: The Style of a Renaissance Despotism* (Princeton: Princeton University Press, 1973), p. 214; see also Gundersheimer, *Art and Life in The Court of Ercole I d'Este* (Geneva: Droz, 1972), pp. 234–62; Giacomo Grillo, *Poets at the Court of Ferrara: Ariosto, Tasso and Guarino, with a chapter on Michelangelo* (Boston: Excelsior Press, 1943); Edmund G. Gardner, *Dukes and Poets in Ferrara* (New York: Haskell House, 1968); and Rev. Henry Stebbing, *Lives of the Italian Poets*, 3 vols. (London: E. Bull, 1832).

48 Stebbing, *Lives of the Italian Poets*, I.336; see also *Renaissance Popes, Princes, and Prelates: The Vespasiano Memoirs*, trans. William George and E. Waters (New York: Harper, 1963), pp. 224–8 and *passim*.

49 Roscoe, *Lorenzo di Medici*, II.63. The crowning expression of this communality of culture is Poliziano's *Orfeo*. First produced at Mantua in 1471, it enshrines the Florentine belief in language as the cement of society, while at the same time locating the divinity of man in a Ficinian "absolute freedom of the creative moment" (Garin, "Poliziano e il suo ambiente," p. 158). See Cody, *Landscape of the Mind*, especially pp. 30–43; and *The Orpheus of Politian and the Aminta of Tasso*, trans. Louis E. Lord (Oxford: Oxford University Press, 1931), p. 64. In Landino's humanist dialogue, the *Disputationes Camaldulenses*, Alberti, speaking for the author, continually emphasizes the importance of a "humane mind" in a ruler: knowledge, and therefore virtue, must precede rule. See also Michael Baxandall, "A Dialogue on Art from the Court of Leonello d'Este," *JWCI* 26 (1963): 304–26, especially 304: "The humanist was typically a client and wrote to please, and when he spoke to please his master he spoke to a great extent for him; articulating his readers' tastes and assumptions was indeed his job." See also Charles Hope, "Artists, Patrons, and Advisors," in *Patronage in the*

Renaissance, ed. Guy F. Lytle and Stephen Orgel (Princeton: Princeton University Press, 1981), pp. 293–343.

50 John L. Lievsay, *Stefano Guazzo and the English Renaissance, 1575–1675* (Chapel Hill: University of North Carolina Press, 1961). For the text, see *The Civile Conversation of M. Steeven Guazzo*, trans. G. Pettie and B. Young, 2 vols., ed. Sir Edward Sullivan (London: Constable, 1925). On Ariosto, see Grillo, *Poets at the Court of Ferrara*, pp. 18f., and Arturo di Vita, ed., *Le Satire [d'Ariosto]* (Torino: G. B. Paravia and Co., 1935), p. xxiv; and cf. Dominique Clouet, "Empirisme ou egotisme: la politique dans la *Cassaria* et les *Suppositi* de l'Arioste," *Les Écrivains*, ser. 1, p. 34:

> In the sixteenth century the writer did not know literary independence. He had to provide images of power. But he was permitted to elect, within the context of an imposed regime, the themes of his choice. In the criteria of such a choice, and not in refusing praise, inconceivable in a poet–courtier, is situated...the true focus of resistance to the sovereign.

Machiavelli's *Florentine History*, written during the crucial years of Cardinal Giuliano de' Medici's gradual surrender of republican fantasies (1520–4), served as the medium of the historian's covert commentary on the Cardinal's dereliction; see also M. Marietti, "Machiavel Historiographe des Médicis," *Les Écrivains*, ser. 2, pp. 81–148. Similarly, Machiavelli's friend Guicciardini's *History of Italy* (1537–40), in expressing his own bitter judgments on the secular power of the papacy under the Medici popes, Leo X and Clement VII, constitutes an independent assessment of the regime he had served loyally for fourteen years.

51 See above, pp. 15f. Rinuccini argues that since humanism is ideally fulfilled in the writer's *potestas agendi*, without this power it is the individual's duty to remain at least internally free, as Rinuccini himself had done, by fleeing to a life of solitude outside the city. See also Francesco Adorno, "La crisi dell'umanesimo civile fiorentino da Alamanno Rinuccini al Machiavelli," *RCSF* 7 (1952), 30; and E. Garin, *Italian Humanism*, trans. P. Munz (Westport, Conn.: Greenwood Press, 1975), pp. 80f. For Rinuccini's letters, see Vito R. Giustiniani, ed., *Alamanno Rinuccini: Lettere ed Orazioni* (Florence: Olschki, 1953). For a comparable example of humanist resistance to the rise of the Medici, Agnolo Pandolfini, see Vespasiano, *Renaissance Popes*, p. 256.

52 V. Rossi, *Il Quattrocento* 6 (Milan: P. Vallardi, 1956), p. 142; for a different view of Alberti's emphasis on family and domestic society, see Hans Baron, "The Historical Background of the Florentine Renaissance," *History*, n.s. 22 (1938), 324.

53 Edouardo Saccone, *Il soggetto del "Furioso" e altri studi* (Naples:

Liguori, 1974) pp. 63f. On the Italian Renaissance epic in this context, see Aldo Scaglione, "Chivalric and Idyllic Poetry in the Italian Renaissance," *Italica* 38 (1956), 253.

54 Pettie, *Civile Conversation* II.123ff.; see also Thomas F. Crane, *Italian Social Customs in the Sixteenth Century and their Influence on the Literatures of Europe* (New York: Russell & Russell, 1971), pp. 400–4.

55 Elizabeth's court has been described as "a cultured court presided over by a prince" and supported by a "nobility of service who oversaw a new generation of university-bred seekers after public careers": Joel Hurstfield, *Freedom, Corruption and Government in Elizabethan England* (Cambridge, Mass.: Harvard University Press, 1973), p. 223. For a first-hand witness, see *The Court of Queen Elizabeth: originally written by Sir Robert Naunton, under the title of "Fragmenta Regalia." With considerable biographical additions*, ed. James Caulfield (London: G. Smeeton, 1814). This paragraph also draws on A. L. Rowse, *The Elizabethan Renaissance: The Life of the Society* (London: Macmillan, 1972), esp. pp. 73, 97; G. R. E. Elton, "The Rule of Law in Sixteenth Century England," in *Tudor Men and Institutions*, ed. A. J. Slavin (Baton Rouge: Louisiana State University Press, 1972), pp. 266–94; Neville Williams, *All the Queen's Men* (New York: Macmillan, 1972); Anthony Esler, *The Aspiring Mind of the Elizabethan Younger Generation* (Durham, NC: Duke University Press, 1966); Lawrence Stone, *The Crisis of the Aristocracy, 1558–1641* (Oxford: Clarendon Press, 1966), pp. 702f.; and Alan Sinfield, *Literature in Protestant England, 1560–1660* (London: Croom Helm, 1983).

56 Williams, *All the Queen's Men*, pp. 161–3. On the question of *Mother Hubberd*, see below, p. 117. Perhaps the peak of the use of costly vehicles of persuasion was Leicester's abortive propaganda campaign during his governorship of the Low Countries in 1585–6; see Roy C. Strong and J. A. Van Dorsten, *Leicester's Triumph* (Leiden: The University Press, 1964).

57 For recent work on Elizabethan patronage, see Patricia Thomson, "The Literature of Patronage, 1580–1630," *EIC* 2 (1952), 267–84; Eleanor Rosenberg, *Leicester, Patron of Letters* (New York: Columbia University Press, 1955); Wallace T. MacCaffrey, "Place and Patronage in Elizabethan Politics," in *Elizabethan Government and Society*, ed. S. Bindoff *et al.* (London: The Athlone Press, 1961), pp. 95–126; Arthur Marotti, "'Love is not love': Elizabethan Sonnet Sequences and the Social Order," *ELH* 49 (1982), 396–428; and Lytle and Orgel, *Patronage*, especially pp. 47–64 and 191–206. On humanism and classicism in Renaissance courts, see Arnold Hauser, *The Social History of Art* (New York: Knopf, 1951), pp. 51f.; and Stephen Orgel, *The*

Illusion of Power: Political Theater in the English Renaissance (Berkeley: University of California Press, 1975).

58 See, for example, *The Curial made by maystere Alain Charretier*, trans. William Caxton, 1484; reprt. ed. F. J. Furnivall (London: EETS, 1888); Chartier, who lived from about 1386 to 1457, was a famous orator at the Court of Charles VI and VII. For the later period see Pauline M. Smith, *The Anti-Courtier Trend in Sixteenth-Century French Literature* (Geneva: Droz, 1966).

59 Besides Esler, *The Aspiring Mind*, see also Javitch, *Poetry and Courtliness*, and Ruth Kelso, *The Doctrine of the English Gentleman in the Sixteenth Century* (Urbana: University of Illinois Press, 1929).

60 Daniel Javitch, "Rival Arts of Conduct in Elizabethan England: Guazzo's *Civile Conversation* and Castiglione's *Courtier*," *YIS* 1 (1971), 178–98. See also Lievsay, *Stefano Guazzo*, pp. 97–9; and Caroline Ruutz-Rees, "Some Notes of Gabriel Harvey's in Hoby's Translation of Castiglione's *Courtier*," *PMLA* 25 (1910), 609–39.

61 Williams, *All the Queen's Men*, p. 33. See *The Letters and Epigrams of Sir John Harington*, ed. N. E. McClure (Philadephia: University of Pennsylvania Press, 1930).

62 See, for example, Epigram 1.17: "Of writing with a double meaning," McClure, *Letters and Epigrams*, p. 155; and *Nugae Antiquae [NA]* (London: Vernor and Hood, 1804), 1.180: "The Queene well knoweth how to humble the haughtie spirit; and the man's soule seemeth tossed to and fro, like the waves of a troubled sea." All subsequent citations are to volume 1 of this work.

63 Printed in McClure, *Letters and Epigrams*, pp. 323–78, with notes.

64 *The English Courtier, and the Cuntrey-gentleman* (imprinted at London, by Richard Jones, 1586).

65 Bryskett, *A Discourse of Civill Life* (London: Edward Blount, 1606; reprt. New York: Da Capo Press, 1971). See Mary Augusta Scott, *Elizabethan Translations from the Italian* (Boston: Houghton Mifflin, 1916), p. 477; and Deborah Jones, "Lodovico Bryskett and his Family," in *Thomas Lodge and Other Elizabethans*, ed. C. J. Sisson (Cambridge, Mass.: Harvard University Press, 1933), pp. 243–63.

66 *The Court and the Country; or, A Briefe Discourse betweene the Courtier and Country-Man of the Manner, Nature, and Condition of their Lives.* Written by N. B. Gent. Printed by G. Eld from John Wright (London, 1618).

67 Cf. CI^v:

hee that lives at quiet and will not be contented, may change for the worse and repent it when he cannot help it … It is better to sit fast, then to rise and fall … the meane is sure.

Breton evidently intends his dialogue to be even-handed. To redress any bias toward the country he (or his printer) appends an apparently straightforward catechism called "Necessary Notes for a Courtier," in the dogmatically pro-courtly vein of the courtier in the dialogue proper. One specimen may serve to give the flavor of Breton's "Notes":

> Q. What is the life of a Courtier?
> A. The labour of pleasure, the aspiring to greatness, the ease of nature, and the command of reason. (E3v)

68 Bacon, *Works*, VI.138 and II.146f.

69 F. M. Padelford, ed., *Select Translations from Scaliger's Poetics* (New York: Holt, 1905), p. 21.

70 Thomas G. Rosenmeyer, *The Green Cabinet: Theocritus and the English Pastoral Lyric* (Berkeley: University of California Press, 1969), p. 89.

71 For an early instance of death as a port or refuge, see Sophocles, *Antigone* 1284; on the Cynics' *hesychia*, Cicero, *Tusculanae Disputationes* 1.43.103f. On the *limen* motif, see Grilli, *Il problema della vita contemplativa*, p. 167.

72 Keith Hopkins, "Elite Mobility in the Roman Empire," *P&P* 32 (1965), 12–26.

73 Rosenmeyer, *The Green Cabinet*, p. 43.

74 This connection is made by Andrew D. Weiner, *Sir Philip Sidney and the Poetics of Protestantism: A Study of Contexts* (Minneapolis: University of Minnesota Press, 1978), pp. 63f. Weiner's conclusion, however, that contemplation's pleasures "are not for man" (p. 63) is too strong. Aristotle allows that the "divine" element in man can exercise *theoria*, just as Spenser and others see even erotic love, properly sublimated, as offering the divine pleasures of contemplation. (See chapter 6, below.)

75 *Commentarium in canticum canticorum, ad* 1.7, in *Origen: The Song of Songs, Commentary and Homilies*, trans. R. P. Lawsen (Westminister, Md.: The Newman Press, 1957), pp. 119–25.

76 *Boccaccio On Poetry*, ed. and trans. Charles G. Osgood (New York: Liberal Arts Press, 1956), pp. 55f.

77 Though it has been questioned both before and since, the Renaissance by and large held these lines to be authentically Vergilian. Though the lines were known quite early on, and are cited in the Donatan and Servian *Lives* of Vergil, there is no reason to believe them to be authentic. For a brief summary of the case, see W. A. Camps, *An Introduction to Virgil's Aeneid* (Oxford: Oxford University Press, 1979), pp. 121–3.

78 Brinton, *Mapheus Vegius*, p. 22.

79 Robin P. Schlunk, *The Homeric Scholia and the "Aeneid"* (Ann Arbor: University of Michigan Press, 1974); see also Hugo Rahner, SJ, *Greek Myths and Christian Mysteries*, trans. Brian Battershaw (New York:

Harper and Row, 1963). In *The Allegorical Epic* (Chicago: University of Chicago Press, 1980), pp. 34–9, Michael Murrin locates the presumed philosophical content of the *Aeneid* in the epistemological debate between Academics (skeptics) and Stoics, a debate in which the poem reflects an "Academic scepticism" about the reliability of the senses.

80 *Exposition of the Context of Virgil According to Moral Philosophy*, no. 1, in Leslie G. Whitbread, *Fulgentius the Mythographer* (Columbus: Ohio State University Press, 1971), p. 119. See Nicola Terzaghi, *L'Allegoria nelle Ecloghe di Virgilio* (Florence: Seeber, 1900), pp. 11ff. The Fulgentian method is still alive in Iodicus Badius Ascensius' Renaissance edition of Vergil. In his introduction Badius writes: "Prima [opera] est rusticus pecoris cura, deinde agrorum, quorum cultu indursti, tandem ad arma gerenda idonei censentur"; quoted in Terzaghi, p. 14. On Donatus and Servius see H. W. Prescott, *The Development of Virgil's Art* (Chicago: University of Chicago Press, 1926), pp. 112–17.

81 *Commentarium in Vergili Aeneidos* (= Cod. Bibl. S. Marc. Venet. class. 13 [Lat.]), n. 61, col. 3; quoted in Domenico Comparetti, *Virgil in the Middle Ages*, trans. E. F. M. Benecke (Hamden, Conn.: Archon Books, 1966), p. 117n. Comparetti cites the same passage in a Viennese manuscript of the fourteenth century.

82 Plut. *Mor.* frag. 200; in Loeb ed. by F. H. Sandbach (Cambridge: Harvard University Press, 1969), xv. 369–73; see also Rahner, *Greek Myths*, p. 328; David Thompson, "Dante and Bernardus Silvestris," *Viator* I (1970), 202–6; and Thompson, *Dante's Epic Journeys*. On the "epic duplex" see James Nohrnberg, *The Analogy of the "Faerie Queene"* (Princeton: Princeton University Press, 1976), pp. 60–3. In the sixteenth century Minturno assumed that Aristotle had omitted the pastoral from his *Poetics* because he considered it a species of epic, and in many ways – metre for example – it shares the genre's formal features (Rosenmeyer, *The Green Cabinet*, p. 286).

83 Prologue to *Disputationes Camaldulenses* 3, in Thomas H. Stahel, SJ, "Christoforo Landino's Allegorization of the *Aeneid*" (unpublished dissertation, Johns Hopkins University, 1968), pp. 40, 52.

84 Murrin, *The Allegorical Epic*, p. 220n. In regard to ethical doctrine Landino recognizes four kinds of interpretation, loosely derived from the four-fold medieval exegesis, or what Dante calls "the allegory of the theologians." These are History, Etymology, Analogy, and Allegory, the latter being "not merely what the words signify, but something else hidden under a figure" (*ibid.*); see also Augustine, *De doctrina christiana* 1.2., and Thomas Aquinas, *ST* 1.1.10. In his apologia to Federigo, Duke of Urbino, in Book 4 Landino answers the physical allegorists of Vergil by insisting that as the "power of nature" is for the sake of man and not vice versa, so the ultimate reference of Vergil's allegory must be

to ethical and spiritual truths of man. In support of this view Landino cites Servius, Macrobius ("the excellent Platonic philosopher"), Jerome, Augustine, and Dante. Dante especially follows the example of the *Aeneid*, says Landino, in "look[ing] to the *summum bonum* and not anything physical" (Stahel, "Christoforo Landino's Allegorization of the *Aeneid*," p. 163).

85 Whitbread, *Fulgentius*, p. 87; Kaske, "*Sapientia et Fortitudo*," 426, cites a parallel in Isidore: "Aeros, vir fortis et sapiens."

86 Earl G. Shreiber and Thomas E. Maresca, eds. and trans., *Commentary on the First Six Books of Virgil's Aeneid by Bernardus Silvestris* (Lincoln: University of Nebraska Press, 1974), p. xxxi.

87 Whitbread, *Fulgentius*, p. 110; cf. Thompson, *Dante's Epic Journeys*, especially pp. 21–8. Fulgentius' fable has behind it Macrobius' and Cicero's *Somnium Scipionis*, and of course will be turned to its greatest account when Dante integrates the same ghost into a new odyssey with Aeneas as a major precursor (*Inferno* 2).

88 Bernardus Silvestris, like Fulgentius, reads the first six books of the poem as man's spiritual progress toward contemplation and the last six as its recapitulation in action. He too sees Book 6 as crucial: under the "divine counsel" of the Sibyl, Aeneas contemplates the vices and pitfalls of life before returning unscathed to the battles with vice allegorically unfolded in Books 7–12. The most recent edition is Julian Ward Jones and Elizabeth Frances Jones, eds., *The Commentary on the First Six Books of The Aeneid Commonly Attributed to Bernardus Silvestris* (Lincoln: University of Nebraska Press, 1977). (For a modern translation see n. 86, above.) The editors doubt Bernardus' authorship and suggest that the author might be Bernard of Chartres rather than Bernardus Silvestris, who is from Tours (pp. ix–xi). See also J. W. Jones' article in Bernard, *Vergil at 2000*, pp. 107–32.

89 *Convito* 4.24; p. 219. See also Thompson, "Dante and Bernardus Silvestris," 203f.; Charles S. Singleton, *Journey to Beatrice* (Baltimore: Johns Hopkins University Press, 1977), pp. 15, 26–31; and Shreiber-Maresca, *Commentary on the First Six Books of Virgil's Aeneid by Bernardus Silvestris*, p. xxvii. Thompson (205) further suggests that Dante is following the *Aeneid* in prefacing the descent/ascent of the *Inferno* and *Purgatorio* to the return of the *Paradiso*; he sees Ulysses in *Inferno* 26 as an emblem of the *via non vera* of Boethius, re-enacted in his own philosophical quest in the *Convito*, which he rejects in favor of "the Augustinian journey into the self" in the *Commedia* (*Dante's Epic Journeys*, p. 72).

90 Don Cameron Allen, *Mysteriously Meant: The Rediscovery of Pagan Symbolism and Allegorical Interpretation in the Renaissance* (Baltimore: Johns Hopkins Press, 1970), p. 149. Allen also cites allegorical readings

of the *Aeneid* scattered through Petrarch's *Rerum memorandarum libri*. See also Elizabeth Nitchie, *Vergil and the English Poets* (New York: Columbia University Press, 1919), pp. 70–8. Fulgentius' *Expositio Virgilianae Continentiae* was rediscovered in 1589, and his *Mythologiae libri tres* was printed as early as 1498 (Allen, *Mysteriously Meant*, p. 137).

91 Panofsky, *Studies in Iconology*, pp. 137f. Panofsky notes that Pico for one ranks the moral virtues under the active life, or *iustitia*, typified by Leah and Martha; the theological virtues under the contemplative life, or *religio*, represented by Rachel and Mary Magdalene.

92 V. Giustiniani, "Il Filelfo, l'interpretazione allegoria di Virgilio, e la tripartizione platonica dell'anima," in *Umanesimo e Rinascimento* (Florence: Olschki, 1980), p. 34. Giustiniani reproduces the Latin texts of the two letters on pp. 37–42 and 42–4, respectively. It is significant as well that the earlier letter antedates Landino's famous exposition in the *Disputationes Camaldulenses* by nearly fifty years and that Landino may well have known the letter.

93 The latter is underscored by Filelfo's glossing "ratiocinari" with "consultare" (p. 44; in a note, Giustiniani cites *NE* 1139a5–14).

94 Composed in 1475, perhaps first published before 1480, and widely known by 1487, the work was appended as an *Allegoria Platonica* to the Basel *Aeneid* of 1577 (Stahel, "Christoforo Landino's Allegorization of the *Aeneid*," p. 2; Allen, *Mysteriously Meant*, p. 143). Citations refer to the Stahel translation of Books 3 and 4.

95 Landino's model in approaching the *Aeneid* is Dante, whose own realization of such an allegorical quest led Landino to read the *Aeneid* as an "antique *Divine Comedy*" (p. 15).

96 Shreiber-Maresca, *Commentary on the First Six Books of Virgil's Aeneid by Bernardus Silvestris*, p. xxx; I am indebted to the translators for pointing out these three significant changes, though the explanation of their significance is my own.

97 See Cody, *Landscape of the Mind*, p. 108; cf. also p. 73 and *passim*.

2 Colin's Début

1 The most engaging and thorough discussion of this début is Richard Helgerson, "The New Poet Presents Himself: Spenser and the Idea of a Literary Career," *PMLA* 93 (1978), 893–901.

2 Here and throughout the following chapters I cite the texts of Spenser's poems in *Poetical Works*, ed. Smith and de Selincourt. The shepherd's boy is Colin Clout, but cf. E. K. (p. 422): "Under which name this Poete

secretly shadoweth himself, as sometime did Virgil under the name of Tityrus." The qualifier in the last clause suggests E. K.'s familiarity with Servius.

3 See the Dedicatory Verses to Sidney, *ibid.*, p. 416.

4 This view questions that of a more monolithic, dominant political authority as defined, e.g., in Goldberg, *Endlesse Worke*, pp. 122–65.

5 See Calvin R. Edwards, "The Narcissus Myth in Spenser's Poetry," *SP* 74 (1977), 63–88.

6 See Harry Berger, "Mode and Diction in the *Shepheardes Calender*," *MP* 67 (1969), 140–9; and "Orpheus, Pan, and the Poetics of Misogyny: Spenser's Critique of Pastoral Love and Art," *ELH* 50 (1983), 27–60.

7 See Louis A. Montrose, "Interpreting Spenser's February Eclogue," 69; cf. "'The perfecte paterne of a Poete': The Poetics of Courtship in *The Shepheardes Calender*," *TSLL* 21 (1979), 34–67.

8 David R. Shore, *Spenser and the Poetics of Pastoral* (Kingston and Montreal: McGill–Queen's University Press, 1985), p. 51, reads the *Shepheardes Calender* as essentially affirming "the inadequacy of pastoral values as a sufficient moral guide to action within a temporal urban context."

9 Cody, *Landscape of the Mind*, p. 73 and *passim*.

10 Cf. Cooper, *Pastoral: Medieval into Renaissance*, p. 154.

11 This section, and part of the next, are based on my article, "'June' and the Structure of Spenser's *Shepheardes Calender*," *PQ* 60 (1981), 305–22.

12 Theocritus 7.10, in *The Greek Bucolic Poets*, trans. J. M. Edmonds (Cambridge, Mass. Harvard University Press, 1960), p. 92.

13 See Michael J. K. O'Loughlin, "'Woods Worthy of a Consul': Pastoral and the Sense of History," in *Literary Studies: Essays in Memory of Francis A. Drumm*, ed. John H. Dorenkamp (Worcester, Mass.: Holy Cross College Press, 1973), pp. 153–5.

14 The full description of the festival comes at the end of the poem, ll. 135–57. Gilbert Lawall, *Theocritus' Coan Pastorals* (Washington: Center for Hellenic Studies, 1967), pp. 104 and 117, reads the poem as an "allegory of poetic inspiration" and the harvest as a metaphor for the "conventional harvest of poetry."

15 Vergil, *Eclogues*, ed. Robert Coleman (Cambridge: Cambridge University Press, 1977), p. 68.

16 C. P. Segal, "*Tamen Cantabitis Arcades* – Exile and Arcadia in *Eclogues* One and Nine," *Arion* 4 (1965), 251.

17 B. F. Dick, "Ancient Pastoral and the Pathetic Fallacy," *CL* 20 (1968), 44, sees love's defeat of pastoral unreality in Eclogue 10 as confirming that the Eclogues are deliberately "antipastoral."

18 Bruno Snell, *The Discovery of the Mind*, trans. T. G. Rosenmeyer (Cambridge, Mass.: Harvard University Press, 1953), pp. 281–309.

19 For a thorough study of the humanist eclogue, see W. Leonard Grant, *Neo-Latin Literature and the Pastoral* (Chapel Hill: University of North Carolina Press, 1965). Patrick Cullen, in *Spenser, Marvell, and the Renaissance Pastoral* (Cambridge, Mass.: Harvard University Press, 1970), pp. 2–4 and *passim*, uses the term "Mantuanesque" to denote this tradition or features of it, and "Arcadian" for the older Vergilian strain.

20 See especially S. K. Heninger, Jr., "Form in *The Shepheardes Calender*," *SRen* 9 (1962), 309–21, and Isabel MacCaffrey, "Allegory and Pastoral in *The Shepheardes Calender*," *ELH* 36 (1969), 88–109.

21 Shore, *Spenser and the Poetics of the Pastoral*, p. 94, modifying his earlier judgment (see note 8), concedes that "an acknowledgement of the practical limitations of the [recreative pastoral] ideal is not a denial of its imaginative value." This statement is close to my own position in the present chapter.

22 According to "The generall argument of the whole booke" (*Poetical Works*, p. 419), the twelve eclogues are either "Plaintive, as the first, the sixth, the eleventh, and the twelfth, or recreative, such as al those be, which conceive matter of love, or commendation of special personages [presumably the third, fourth, and eighth], or Moral: which for the most part be mixed with some Satyrical bitternesse," i.e., the second, fifth, seventh, ninth, and tenth.

23 Leo Spitzer, *Classical and Christian Ideas of World Harmony* (Baltimore: Johns Hopkins Press, 1963), p. 5.

24 H. S. V. Jones, in the *Spenser Variorum* (Baltimore: Johns Hopkins Press, 1943), *ad* 7.1.309, notes the relation of "June" to Vergil's first Eclogue, with Hobbinoll—Tityrus as the "Horatian philosopher of the tried estate."

25 For the figure of Orpheus in Vergilian pastoral, see Marie Desport, *L'Incantation virgilienne* (Bordeaux: Le Monnier, 1952).

26 Cf. also the ending of Eclogue 9.

27 Paul Alpers, "The Eclogue Tradition and the Nature of Pastoral," *CE* 34 (1972), 353. Alpers follows John S. Coolidge, in "Great Things and Small: The Virgilian Progression," *CL* 17 (1965), 1–23, in reading Eclogue 10 as Vergil's "farewell to pastoral poetry" (361).

28 Vergil's most recent editor, Robert Coleman, echoes those who identify the speaker's, and the poet's, mood absolutely with Gallus' (*Eclogues*, pp. 294–7). It is worth noting that Coleman ignores "saturae" in his gloss on the closing lines of Eclogue 10.

29 In addition to the studies cited in note 20 above, see Cullen, *Spenser, Marvell and the Renaissance Pastoral*, especially p. 123.

30 Cf. Ecl. 2, ll. 69–73:

> "a, Corydon, Corydon, quae te dementia cepit?
> semiputata tibi frondosa vitis in ulmo est.
> quin tu aliquid saltem potius, quorum indiget usus,
> viminibus mollique paras detexere iunco?
> invenies alium, si te hic fastidit, Alexim."

> ("Ah, Corydon, Corydon, what is this lunacy you're possessed by?
> You've left your vines half-pruned, and the leafy elms they grow on.
> Why not, instead of moping, get down to something useful,
> Weaving from reeds and withies some article that you need?
> If you're brushed off by this Alexis, you'll find another.")

Translation by C. Day Lewis, *The Eclogues and Georgics of Virgil* (New York: Anchor Books, 1963), p. 17.

31 Berger, "Mode and Diction," 145.

32 My clumsy pun does want to point out a fundamental paradox of pastoral. Though in its more extreme philosophical premises pastoral would seem to annihilate the Other in all its manifestations – political institutions, human society, even phenomena – the pastoral mythos as it evolved insists on imaginatively refabricating the Other according to the desires of the mind. Hence the pastoral poet may figure himself as a solitary singer, but even in solo the consolations of song include a reconstructed fellowship of those who share the "right" attitude toward life.

33 On the Cratylean play of Spenser on his own name in the 1590 *Faerie Queene*, see Elizabeth J. Bellamy, "The Vocative and the Vocational: The Unreadability of Elizabeth in *The Faerie Queene*," *ELH* 54 (1987), 7f.

34 For the most thorough recent reading of the Moral eclogues, see Shore, *Spenser and the Poetics of Pastoral*, pp. 7–67.

35 Ronald Bond seems to me to be oversimplifying here, when he claims that Spenser identifies himself with the powerful elders; see "Supplantation in the Elizabethan Court; The Theme of Spenser's February Eclogue," *SSt* 2 (1981), 56.

36 Berger, "Mode and Diction," 147; cf. A. C. Hamilton, "The Argument of Spenser's *Shepheardes Calender*," *ELH* 23 (1956), 171–82; reprt. in *Spenser: A Collection of Critical Essays*, ed. Harry Berger, Jr. (Englewood Cliffs, NJ: Prentice-Hall, 1968), pp. 30–9. Shore, in *Spenser and the Poetics of Pastoral*, p. 66, concedes Hamilton's point (cited on p. 8) that each of the Moral eclogues "recognizes the limitations of the ideal in a fallen world," while insisting that "they recreatively assert its value." Hence, "the moral eclogues point beyond the pastoral but remain within it" (p. 67).

37 Desport, "L'Écho de la nature," 270. On the intrinsic properties of the sestina-form, as well as their realization by Sidney in "Ye Gote-heard Gods," see William Empson, *Seven Types of Ambiguity* (New York: New Directions, n.d.), pp. 34–8.

38 Willye does not, like Hobbinoll, literally have the last word though, unless it is in his Emblem, where he is said to be "vanquished but not subdued" (*Vinto non vitto*).

29 See below, pp. 120 and 175.

40 Cf. Montrose, "The Elizabethan Subject," pp. 322f.: "The cultural work of the subject/poet, his informing power, contributes to the legitimation and implementation of the social and political order within which he himself is subjected. By calling attention to its mediatory relationship to the traditions, conventions, and devices of poetic discourse, on the one hand, and to the social conditions of its own production, on the other, the song of Colin/Spenser works not simply as a royal enconium but as a contextualization from within (so to speak) of its own encomiastic project."

41 Ellen Zetzel Lambert, *Placing Sorrow: A Study of the Pastoral Elegy Convention from Theocritus to Milton* (Chapel Hill: University of North Carolina Press, 1976), pp. 126–37.

42 Helgerson, "The New Poet," 899.

43 "In Cuddie is set out the perfecte paterne of a Poete, whiche finding no maintenaunce of his state and studies, complayneth of the contempte of Poetrie, and the causes thereof…" (*Poetical Works*, p. 456).

44 It is notable that Spenser's last poem, the *Prothalamion*, also begins on this note. See below, chapter 6, pp. 183f.

45 "The New Poet."

3 *The Faerie Queene* (1590)

1 See "Three Proper and Wittie Familiar Letters," *Poetical Works*, pp. 612, 628. Helgerson, "The New Poet," 900, notes that Gabriel Harvey thought *The Faerie Queene* the "least promising" of Spenser's "projects" in 1579.

2 Spenser of course appropriates this "humility," even in the act of naming himself, in the Dedication: "TO/THE MOST HIGH, / MIGHTIE / And / MAGNIFICENT / EMPRESSE…/…ELIZABETH…/…HER MOST / HUMBLE SERVANT / EDMUND SPENSER / DOTH IN ALL HU-/MILITIE DEDI-/CATE…HIS LABOURS TO LIVE / WITH THE ETERN-/TIE OF HER / FAME" (p. 2). Bellamy, "The Vocative and the Vocational," 22, notes that in one of the 1590 editions Ponsonby abandons the familiar anchor-shaped dedication from which the above is quoted, hyphenating (or, as she has it, "dis-uniting") Elizabeth's name.

3 Still the most stimulating discussion of the relation of pastoral and heroic elements in *The Faerie Queene* is Paul J. Alpers, *The Poetry of the "Faerie Queene"* (Princeton: Princeton University Press, 1967), pp. 370–405. See esp. p. 376.

4 With a few scattered exceptions, mostly in the notes, I focus my remarks in this chapter on Books 1 and 3 because it is my view that they represent the poles of Spenser's approach to pastoral in the 1590 edition.

5 Despite important differences in "character" and function, Guyon displays a similarly naïve superiority to the courtly blandishments of Phaedria in 2.6. An almost instinctive sense of decorum, associated in Book 2 with the rationally imposed Aristotelian mean, governs these "clownish" heroes in their encounters with the excessive complexities of thought or behavior in others. In the case of Guyon, this pastoral simplicity nearly fails him in the ambience of Acrasia's sensuality and the polymorphous harmonious pleasure of the Bower of Bliss.

6 Among several notable departures from his model in *Orlando Furioso* 6 (Astolfo-Ruggiero-Alcina), Spenser has his errant hero discover the tree's true identity while in the process of making a "girlond" for the supposed Fidessa. Throughout *The Faerie Queene* this ostensibly simple pastoral motif ominously implies various forms of idolatry. See the discussions below of the satyrs with Una and Hellenore, in 1.6 and 3.10 respectively. It hardly needs saying that Spenser would have been aware of the ultimate model for Fradubio in Vergil's Polydorus in *Aeneid* 3.32–63, mediated to Ariosto by Dante (*Inf.* 8) and others.

7 "Refuse such fruitlesse toile" is also the dangerous message delivered by Phaedria in 2.6 (st. 17), first in the totalizing context of Biblical pastoral – "Consider the lilies of the field" (stt. 15f.), and later in the more Roman–Stoical sense, discussed earlier in connection with Seneca and Pliny, of a temporary refuge from excessive or unrelieved labor (st. 23). The latter motif will be discussed at greater length below, in chapter 6.

8 It could be argued that Sansjoy's name primarily reflects the essential solemnity of Redcrosse established in the opening stanzas of Book 1.

9 On the *locus amoenus* see Ernst Robert Curtius, *European Literature and the Latin Middle Ages*, trans. Willard Trask (New York: Harper and Row, 1953), pp. 183–202. On Spenser's use of the topos in general, see K. I. MacDonald, "Allegorical Lanscape in the *Faerie Queene* (Books I–III)," *DUJ* 63 (1970), 121–4.

10 For a controversial reading of the episode, see Alpers, *The Poetry of the "Faerie Queene,"* pp. 352–61.

11 On satyrs in Renaissance pastoral see Padelford, *Select Translations from Scaliger's Poetics*, p. 28, where the Servian identification of *satyrus* with *Tityrus* in the Eclogues is traced to the whistling (*tityri*) of the

shepherd's pipe. The source for this identification seems to be Aelian, *Varia Historia* 3.40, ed. Mervin R. Dilts (Leipzig: Teubner, 1974), p. 58. See also Claudius Aelianus, *A Registre of Hystories containing Martiall Exploites*, trans. Abraham Fleming (London: Thomas Woodcocke, 1576).

12   But when their bootlesse zeale she did restraine
      From her own worship, they her Asse would worship fayn.

                                         (st. 19).

Una's displacement of the Hamadryads *et al.* does register Spenser's conceit of a continuity between the orders of nature and grace; see A. S. P. Woodhouse, "Nature and Grace in the *Faerie Queene*," *ELH* 16 (1949), 194–228.

13 See Richard Bernheimer, *Wild Men in the Middle Ages* (New York: Octagon Books, 1970 [1952]), pp. 9f.

14 In Book 2, this is most blatantly signalled in the Braggadocchio–Belphoebe encounter in canto 3: the isolated pastoral virtues of the Diana-like queen and huntress, chaste and fair, are schematically understood to figure forth Elizabeth as a private person and somehow to divorce her public person, represented by Gloriana (Letter to Raleigh; cf. 3.Pr. 5), from the courtly vices embodied in Braggadocchio. As I will argue below (chapter 4), the same intention results in some of the confusions and contradictions of *Colin Clouts Come Home Againe*.

15 Joseph B. Collins, *Christian Mysticism in the Elizabethan Age* (Baltimore: Johns Hopkins University Press, 1940), p. 193. Other useful studies of Contemplation and the structure of canto 10 include V. K. Whitaker, "The Theological Structure of *The Faerie Queene*, Book 1," *ELH* 19 (1952), 151–64; John M. Steadman, "Felicity and End in Renaissance Epic and Ethics," *JHI* 23 (1962), 117–32; Judith H. Anderson, "The July Eclogue and the House of Holiness," *SEL* 10 (1970), 17–32; and Carol V. Kaske, "Spenser's Pluralistic Universe: The View from the Mount of Contemplation," in *Contemporary Thought on Edmund Spenser*, ed. Richard C. Frushell and Bernard J. Vondersmith (Carbondale: Southern Illinois University Press, 1975), pp. 121–49. See also John E. Hankins, "Spenser and Revelation," *PMLA* 60 (1945), 364–81; and Jerome Oetgen, OSB, "Spenser's Treatment of Monasticism in Book 1 of the *Faerie Queene*," *ABR* 22 (1971), 104–20.

16 For the *locus classicus* in Plato, see above, p. 194, note 6. The Cave-topos will be evoked in Book 6, on the threshold of Calidore's parallel initiation into the *vita contemplativa*. See below, p. 150.

17 This topos is especially commonplace in the Guy of Warwick tradition enjoying a revival in Spenser's time. In a ballad version of 1591/2, for

example, a noble page wins the hand of his lord's daughter through a series of heroic trials, only to leave her and do penance as a pilgrim. Later, in disguise, he begs food from his wife and is revealed to her only on his deathbed; see "Guy and Phillis," in *Reliques of Ancient English Poetry*, ed. Thomas Percy, DD (London: Swan, Sonnenschein, Lowrey & Co., 1887), III.109–13.

18 On the dynastic dimension of Redcrosse's quest in its European context, see Fichter, *Poets Historical*, pp. 156–206 and esp. pp. 181f. For an argument that the hero's odyssey constitutes a Spenserian critique of that tradition, see Elizabeth J. Bellamy, "Pagan Prophecy and Christian Revelation: A Reassessment of Virgilian Parody in *The Faerie Queene*, 1.5 (abstract)" *Spenser at Kalamazoo, 1984* (Clarion, Pa.: Clarion State College 1984), pp. 21f.

19 Louis L. Martz, *The Paradise Within* (New Haven: Yale University Press, 1964); see also Eric Laguardia, *Nature Redeemed* (The Hague: Mouton, 1966), p. 8 and *passim*. It is, of course, chiefly our understanding that this is not a condition literally capable of fulfillment in this world that distinguishes this Eden from Acrasia's "Paradise" in 2.12.

20 On this "romance" aura see Northrop Frye, *Anatomy of Criticism* (Princeton: Princeton University Press, 1957), esp. pp. 186–203.

21 The whole episode informs Milton's conception of Eden in *Paradise Lost*, which seems especially indebted to the "sage and serious Spenser" for its depiction of Satan in the Garden in Book 4.

22 See above, chapter 1.

23 For a more typical, negative example, see Verdaunt in 2.12.76–84.

24 On Renaissance music, see John Hollander, *The Untuning of the Sky: The Idea of Music in English Poetry, 1500–1700* (Princeton: Princeton University Press, 1961); on the philosophical underpinnings, see S. K. Heninger, *Touches of Sweet Harmony: Pythagorean Cosmology and Renaissance Poetics* (San Marino, Calif.: Huntington Library, 1974).

25 Clearly, this consummation of Redcrosse's heroics will be balanced against its negative image in the corresponding scene in the Bower of Bliss at the end of Book 2. Likewise, if "melt in pleasures" anticipates Acrasia (and Pyrochles), "exceeding merth" evokes Phaedria (and Cymochles). With stt. 40–1, cf. 1.47, where Archimago makes Redcrosse "dreame of loves and lustfull play, / That nigh his manly hart did melt away, / Bathed in wanton blis and wicked joy." I owe this parallel to an observation by Robert Gregory.

26 See Jerome S. Dees, "The Ship Conceit in the *Faerie Queene*: 'Conspicuous Allusion' and Poetic Structure," *SP* 72 (1975), 208–25.

27 Naturally, one cannot simply identify the narrator of *The Faerie Queene* with Edmund Spenser; yet one can, I think, trust the former to state the

latter's feelings, however "clownishly." The ship-figure for Una's return, with its echo if the *limen* motif alluded to earlier (p. 38), is echoed in 2.1.2.

28 Sessions, "Spenser's Georgics."

29 For the identification of georgic with the life of pleasure, see above, p. 41.

30 On pastoral as a mode expressed in various genres, see William J. Kennedy, *Rhetorical Norms in Renaissance Literature* (New Haven: Yale University Press, 1978), p. 3.

31 The confusion about temperance and continence goes back to the discussion of *akrasia* and *sophrosyne* in *NE* 7. See *Variorum*, II.414–26, esp. p. 418 (Winstanley). Spenser's Acrasia in canto 12 and elsewhere is, or should be, Aristotle's incontinence, as 6.1 clearly implies.

32 A possible exception is the Phaedria episode in canto 6; see William V. Nestrick, "Notable Prosopopoeias: Phaedria and Cymochles," *Spenser at Kalamazoo, 1983* (Clarion, Pa.: Clarion State College, 1983), pp. 57–72.

33 For an analysis of the latter, see Alpers, *The Poetry of the "Faerie Queene,"* pp. 397–405; cf. the discussions by Thomas P. Roche, *The Kindly Flame* (Princeton: Princeton University Press, 1964), pp. 62–88; and Harry Berger, "Busirane and the War Between the Sexes," *ELR* I (1971), 99–121.

34 I prefer this term to Renato Poggioli's "pastoral of love," *The Oaten Flute*, pp. 42–63. Pastoral can exhibit a range of attitudes toward the erotic, from favoring extreme chastity in, say, Marvell to a fairly casual homosexual bawdry in Theocritus. I locate the present cantos in the free-love tradition of the Italian pastoral drama and Shakespeare's pastoral comedies.

35 Roche, *The Kindly Flame*, p. 55, has, it seems to me, inverted cause and effect when he views Britomart's chastity as the source of her political destiny. On the search for a determining *discordia concors*, usually in the relations among Britomart and the minor heroines, see Lila Geller, "Venus and the Three Graces," *JEGP* 75 (1976), 59–60; and Dwight J. Sims, "The Syncretic Myth of Venus in Spenser's Legend of Chastity," *SP* 71 (1974), 427–50. For the specific reading of Britomart as "infolding" the whole complex of qualities "unfolded" by the other heroines, see A. C. Hamilton, *The Structure of Allegory in the "Faerie Queene"* (Oxford: Clarendon Press, 1961), pp. 140–7. Harry Berger, Jr., adapts the Neoplatonic scheme to his own Hegelian system in the notion that the minor heroines are "boundary figures"; see "The Discarding of Malbecco," *SP* 66 (1969), 149. A critique of this approach may be found in Hamilton, "Spenser's Pastoral," *ELH* 33 (1966), 527.

36 Isabel MacCaffrey, *Spenser's Allegory* (Princeton: Princeton University Press, 1976), p. 267.

37 This would imply that Britomart is intended not only to outgo her prototype Bradamante in *Orlando Furioso*, but also to synthesize in one personage the private and public aspects of Elizabeth assigned by Spenser in the Letter to Raleigh respectively to Belphoebe and Gloriana. Earlier in the Letter Spenser alludes to the tradition of allegorical epic, from Homer to Tasso, in which similar *male* virtues are alternatively "dissevered" between distinct characters (Homer, Tasso) or "comprised" in a single one (Vergil, Ariosto).

38 See Fichter, *Poets Historical*, pp. 173–81.

39 See Roy A. Strong, "The Popular Celebration of the Accession Day of Queen Elizabeth I," *JWCI* 21 (1958), 86–103. Most readers, following Spenser's cue in the Letter to Raleigh, detect in Spenser's depiction of Belphoebe an effort by the poet to portray Elizabeth's steadfast determination not to marry, an aspect of her beneficent public policy.

40 Of the many excellent and perplexing discussions of the Garden(s) of Adonis, see especially those by Edwin Greenlaw, Josephine Waters Bennett, and Brent Stirling in *Variorum*, III.343–52; Berger, "Spenser's Gardens of Adonis," *UTO* 30 (1961), 128–49; Humphrey Tonkin, "Spenser's Garden of Adonis and Britomart's Quest," *PMLA* 88 (1973), 408–17; and Richard Neuse, "The Garden of Adonis: The Death – And Rebirth – Of the Author," an unpublished paper read at a session of the Nineteenth International Congress on Medieval Studies, Western Michigan University (Kalamazoo), 10–13 May, 1984.

41 The quoted phrase is C. S. Lewis', in *English Literature in the Sixteenth Century Excluding Drama* (Oxford: Clarendon Press, 1962), p. 381.

42 The association of satyrs with the pastoral is a long and complex one, the outstanding Renaissance example, in this connection, being Tasso's *Aminta*, where (as normally) the satyr is a symbol of unbridled eroticism. The satyrs who worship Una in *FQ* 1.6. are disarmed by the miraculous power of her beauty (see above, p. 85); but the one who rapes Satyrane's mother, Thyamis, (6.22) has the usual attributes. Satyrs make their pastoral début in Theocritus 4.62. Associated since Hesiod with Pan and his nymphs, they seem "almost a bestial parody of the *voluptates* of the pastoral myth" (Coleman, *Eclogues*, Commentary *ad Ecl.* 5.73 *satyros*, p. 169). See note 11, above.

43 Like a hind pursued by a "ravenous beast," Florimell

> flyes away of her owne feet affeard,
> And every leafe, that shaketh with the least,
> Murmure of winde, her terror hath encreast.

When she has been "rescued" by Proteus, she is merely "chaung'd from one to other feare" (8.33).

44 It is notable that Spenser's corresponding treatment of the psychology of eros in Book 2 lacks the resonance of such passages as this, and of the House of Busyrane episode, in Book 3. The reason may lie in Spenser's superficial adherence to Aristotelian categories of ethical analysis in Book 2, in the centrality of female consciousness, or in both. In the Aristotelian framework all weakness is "womanish" (since women lack the rational faculties of the soul), and conversely female characters can only embody *threats* to rational control of the passions.

45 The Squire of Dames at first seems a male counterpart to Florimell, her escape from the Hyena being immediately mirrored in his entrance in the clutches of Argante. Nevertheless, it is he who initiates the series of implicit comments on courtly love; while even Satyrane, whose binding of the Hyena implies a control of the erotic impulses lacking in the Squire (and by implication in Columbell), is captured by Argante, needs help from the chaste female knight Palladine to escape, and markedly shares the cynical courtly outlook on ladies of the Squire of Dames and later of Paridell (7.57f).

46 On the protean nature of love in canto 8, cf. Jove as lover in 11.30–5.

47 The discussion of Spenser's narrative strategy in the following pages draws freely on my article, "Pastoral and Comedy in Book III of *The Faerie Queene*," *SEL* 23 (1983), 5–20.

48 H. C. Gilde has characterized Ovid's normal tone as "seemingly heartless, actually ironic, sympathetic but detached." See "Spenser's Hellenore and Some Ovidian Associations," *CL* 23 (1971), 234.

49 On the origin and possible significance of such passages as this in pastoral poetry, see Phillip Damon, "Modes of Analogy in Ancient and Medieval Verse," *California Publications in Classical Philology*, 15.6 (1961), 291–8. See also Alpers, *Singer of the Eclogues*, pp. 152–4.

50 For some views of Malbecco's metamorphosis, see Berger, "Discarding of Malbecco," esp. 148f.; Humphrey Tonkin, *Spenser's Courteous Pastoral* (Oxford: Clarendon Press, 1972), p. 412; Fletcher, *Prophetic Moment*, pp. 49f.; and Michael Murrin, "The Varieties of Criticism," *MP* 70 (1973), 348f.

51 Spenser evidently perceived the problem inherent in Ariosto's Brada-mante, as opposed to his Marfisa, and tried to fuse the two characters' virtues in a single figure of heroic chastity. Marfisa's totally sexless knightly prowess appears to fill the gap left by Bradamante's increasingly feminine and vulnerable need for Ruggiero. Britomart manifests her susceptibilities chiefly in the Malecasta episode in canto 1; after Merlin's revelations, however, she exhibits a Marfisa-like invulnerability that is "perfected" in her liberation of Amoret from Busyrane. On Ariosto's

female characters, see Margaret Tomalin, "Bradamante and Marfisa: An Analysis of the 'Guerriere' of the *Orlando Furioso*," *MLR* 71 (1976), 540–52; Pamela Benson, "A Defense of Bradamante," *Quaderni d'italianistica* 4 (1983), 135–53; and Peter de Sa Wiggins, *Figures in Ariosto's Tapestry* (Baltimore: Johns Hopkins University Press, 1986), pp. 161–204.

4 Colin Clout

1 See Frederic Ives Carpenter, *A Reference Guide to Edmund Spenser* (Chicago: University of Chicago Press, 1923); Alexander C. Judson, *The Life of Edmund Spenser* (Baltimore: Johns Hopkins University Press, 1945); the brief early biographies of Winstanley (1687), Church and Upton (1758), Craik (1845), and Higginson (1912); and the groundbreaking article by John W. D. Draper, "Spenserian Biography," in *The Colonnade* 14 (1919–22; Andiron Club of New York City, 1922), 35–46. On Spenser in Ireland, in addition to these see Philo M. Buck, "New Facts Concerning the Life of Spenser," *MLN* 19 (1904), 237–8; C. Litton Falkiner, "Spenser in Ireland," *Edinburgh Review* 201 (1905), 164–88; Carpenter, "Spenser in Ireland," *MP* 19 (1922), 405–19; Raymond Jenkins, "Spenser with Lord Grey in Ireland," *PMLA* 52 (1937), 338–53, and "Spenser: The Uncertain Years: 1584–1589," *PMLA* 53 (1938), 350–62; and Pauline Henley, *Spenser in Ireland* (Cork: Cork University Press, 1928).

2 Stephen J. Greenblatt, *Sir Walter Raleigh: The Renaissance Man and his Roles* (New Haven: Yale University Press, 1973), pp. 60–2.

3 For another view of "retrospection" in Spenser's works, see Harry Berger, Jr., "Two Spenserian Retrospects," *TSLL* 10 (1968), 5–25, and "The Mutability Cantos: Archaism and Evolution in Retrospect," in *Spenser: A Collection of Critical Essays*, pp. 146–76.

4 On the dating of these works see esp. H. S. V. Jones, *A Spenser Handbook* (New York: Appleton-Century-Crofts, 1930), p. 76.

5 See my discussion of the theories of Louis A. Montrose, above, pp. 2–5.

6 On the structural principles of the collections of Theocritus and Vergil, see Lawall, *Theocritus' Coan Pastorals*, pp. 5–13; Brooks Otis, *Virgil: A Study in Civilized Poetry* (Oxford: Clarendon Press, 1963), pp. 128–34; and Alpers, *Singer of the Eclogues*, pp. 102–13.

7 The Shepherd of the Ocean disappears even sooner, less than half-way into the poem.

8 Greenblatt, *Sir Water Raleigh*, p. 60; Williams, *All the Queen's Men*, p. 187.

9 For a radically different view of the Shepherd of the Ocean, as the "Right poet" of Sidney's *Apology*, who corrects Colin's misreading of

his own role, see A. Leigh DeNeef, *Spenser and the Motives of Metaphor* (Durham, NC: Duke University Press, 1982), pp. 53f. DeNeef's reading of *Colin Clout* is grounded on the a priori assumption that Spenser is "a humanist poet concerned primarily with reforming society" (p. 182, n. 15).

10 See *Variorum*, VII.ii, 281–3.

11 George L. C. Craik, *Spenser and His Poetry*, 3 vols., (London: C. Knight & Co., 1845), I.186.

12 Abbreviations of the titles of Spenser's poems in *Complaints* are those employed in the forthcoming *Spenser Encyclopedia*, ed. A. C. Hamilton *et al.* (Toronto: University of Toronto Press).

13 Jones, *Spenser Handbook*, pp. 81f.

14 Israel Gollancz, "Spenseriana," *Proc. Brit. Acad.* 3 (1907–8), 105, claims that only *Mother Hubberds Tale* was "called in" after the publication of *Complaints* in 1591. For a discussion of this question, and an affirmation that the whole volume was recalled, see Jones, *Spenser Handbook*, pp. 74f. The key phrase is from an epigram by John Weever published in 1599 (Jones, p. 74).

15 Cf. Hugh Maclean, "'Restlesse anguish and unquiet paine': Spenser and the Complaint, 1579–90," in *The Practical Vision*, ed. Jane Campbell and James Doyle (Waterloo, Ont.: Wilfrid Laurier University Press, 1978), p. 38. For a contrary view see Carl J. Rasmussen, "'How Weak Be the Passions of Woefulness': Spenser's *Ruines of Time*," *SSt* 2 (1981), 159–81.

16 In his *Black Book*, 1604; see Jones, *Spenser Handbook*, p. 74.

17 On Spenser's relative wealth and security by 1590, see Henley, *Spenser in Ireland*, pp. 45–58 and *passim*.

18 For a good recent discussion of *Mother Hubberd*, including some reflections on the "additions" of 1590, see Kent T. Van Den Berg. "'The Counterfeit in Personation': Spenser's *Prosopopoeia, or Mother Hubberds Tale*," in *The Author in His Work*, ed. Louis Martz (New Haven: Yale University Press, 1978), pp. 83–102. For the present argument, the questions whether or not *Mother Hubberd* refers to the projected Alençon marriage, and to whom among the principals the Fox and the Ape correspond, are irrelevant. On this point see Dennis Moore, *The Politics of Spenser's Complaints and Sidney's Philisides Poems* (Salzburg: University of Salzburg Press, 1982), p. 61.

19 See Edwin Greenlaw, "Spenser and the Earl of Leicester," *PMLA* 25 (1910), 535–61; and, for a critique, Jones, *Spenser Handbook*, pp. 95ff. While Greenlaw's specific thesis is unfounded, it is hard to resist his general conclusion, *pace* Moore, *Politics of Spenser's Complaints*, p. 49.

20 The sonnet, like the acknowledgment that the poem is dedicated to

the deceased Leicester, clearly argues for a deliberate revelation of the circumstances of the poem's earlier composition. Leicester died on 4 February 1588. See Harold Stein, *Studies in Spenser's Complaints* (New York: Oxford University Press, 1934), p. 77; and Moore, *Politics of Spenser's Complaints*, pp. 48f.

21 This may be the implication of the Ovidian trees and flowers of ll. 193–224, which, like a similar passage in *FQ* 1.1.8–9, alert the reader to the moral dimension added by literature and the literary tradition to the conduct of life; see Fletcher, *The Prophetic Moment*, p. 25.

22 Robert Brinkley, "Spenser's *Muiopotmos* and the Politics of Metamorphosis, "*ELH* 48 (1981), 668–76. I am indebted to this stimulating essay in the paragraphs that follow.

23 Neuse, "The Garden of Adonis," reads the Garden as a garden of words; see above, chapter 3, note 40.

24 The lines echo the argument of Ottaviano Fregoso in Castiglione's *Courtier*, 4.10. See John D. Bernard, "Castiglione's Gentle Art of Persuasion in Book IV of the *Courtier*," *RenP 1983* (Southeastern Renaissance Conference, 1984), pp. 1–15.

25 See George M. Logan, *The Meaning of More's "Utopia"* (Princeton: Princeton University Press, 1983), p. 265.

26 See Stein, *Studies in Spenser's Complaints*, p. 42 and note; and Jones, *Spenser Handbook*, pp. 86ff.

27 See *Variorum*, VII.i.484–6.

28 See Lambert, *Placing Sorrow*, chapter 6, esp. p. 143 and note 11 (p. 221).

29 The name recalls Ovid's Alcyone in the *Metamorphoses*; but of course its irenic connotations, deriving from both ancient pagan and Christian myth, align it with pastoral otium or *hesychia*.

30 As Rosenmeyer's title acknowledges, Spenser seems to associate "Cabinet" with the pastoral; cf. "December," l. 17.

31 The excessive numerological consciousness that dictates the $7 \times 7 \times 7$ formula imparts a heavy archaizing aura to the work. For the argument that Spenser intends his poem to be read as a warning against excessive grief, see William A. Oram, "*Daphnaïda* and Spenser's Later Poetry," *SSt* 2 (1981), 141–58.

32 The latter's status may be hinted at in the speaker's referring to him as a shepherd's "swain" rather than a shepherd; cf. *FQ* 6.9.1 for a similar "class" distinction, and see below, p. 150.

33 The flexible Elizabethan orthography permits a possible pun on *poured/ powered*. On this passage and the corresponding apology in *FQ* 6.10.28, see Thomas H. Cain, *Praise in the "Faerie Queene"* (Lincoln: University of Nebraska Press, 1978), pp. 58–61.

34 Neither Douglas Howard nor Gorges was evidently as close to Spenser

as was Sir Philip Sidney, whose intimacy with Spenser has also been widely questioned. We may infer, I believe, that the relative degrees of personal involvement in the two poems indicate Spenser's attitude toward the respective speakers, his avatars in the poems, and their relations to those they honor as well as to the community of readers as a whole.

35 The most fruitful modern discussions of the poem are Thomas R. Edwards, *Imagination and Power: A Study of Poetry on Public Themes* (New York: Oxford University Press, 1971), pp. 48–63; Nancy Jo Hoffman, *Spenser's Pastorals: "The Shepheardes Calender" and "Colin Clout"* (Baltimore: Johns Hopkins University Press, 1977), pp. 119–42; David R. Shore, "Spenser's *Colin Clouts Come Home Againe*: The Problem of Poetry," *ESC* 8 (1982), 262–81; and Shore, *Spenser and the Poetics of Pastoral*.

36 The phrase is Fletcher's, *Prophetic Moment*, p. 115n. With its image of a moving temple, Fletcher sees the sea-voyage as a type of the Argo/ark which conveys imperialism as prophetic ordering in Elizabethan travel literature, symbolizing the "extension of heroic control" over the entire ocean. Fletcher relates the passage to Spenser's common trope of *The Faerie Queene* as a ship and Faeryland as an undiscovered country. But part of my argument is that in the final third of *Colin Clout* Spenser dissociates himself from Raleigh and the imperialist pastoral and identifies his own power with a more platonic contemplative-erotic pastoral.

37 With stories like that of Arthur Gorges' marriage to Douglas Howard, not to mention Raleigh's own to Elizabeth Throckmorton, in the air to give specificity to this allegory of Elizabethan parental tyranny, we may well believe Spenser that this fable is "auncient truth confirm'd with credence old" (l. 103).

38 Although Spenser does allow his narrator the Chaucerian aside of l.129: "For love will not be drawne, but must be ledde."

39 Cf. Edwards' rather different construction of the political motive in this fable, *Imagination and Power*, p. 57.

40 On Elizabethan flattery, see Javitch, *Poetry and Courtliness*, p. 116; Javitch does not make the following point about the poet's derived power or the Platonic justification of royal hyperbole. Instead, he goes on (pp. 134f.) to endorse Spenser's continuing "faith in the amending powers of Elizabeth" in *Colin Clout*. See also G. K. Hunter, *John Lyly: The Humanist as Courtier* (Cambridge, Mass.: Harvard University Press, 1962), esp. chapters 1 and 3.

41 On the Elizabethan personal mythology, see Frances Yates, *Astraea: The Imperial Theme in the Sixteenth Century* (London: Routlege and Kegan Paul, 1975).

42 Cf. Montrose, "The Elizabethan Subject," p. 308: "As the focal point of [a] hierarchical and homological system within which her subjects' social positions and interrelationships were constituted, the Queen was represented as not only requiring the collective subjection of her subjects, but also guaranteeing their particular subjectivities."

43 Unlike Vergil's in the second eclogue, Spenser's Thestylis is apparently male.

44 The standard treatment of Spenser's Platonism remains Robert Ellrodt, *Neoplatonism in the Poetry of Spenser* (Geneva: Droz, 1960). See also M. Bhattacherye, *Platonic Ideas in Spenser* (London: Longman, Green and Co., 1935; reprt. 1970).

45 For recent discussions of the question of authority, see John D. Guillory, *Poetic Authority: Spenser, Milton, and Literary History* (New York: Columbia University Press, 1983), esp. chapter 2; and Jonathan Goldberg, *Voice Terminal Echo* (New York: Methuen, 1986).

46 Of course, distinctions of class may always be implied in lines such as these. But comparable passages from Book 6 (e.g. 10.9 or 10.37), it seems to me, are more explicit about the social basis of their discriminations.

47 *The Eclogues and Georgics of Virgil*, with trans. by C. Day Lewis (Garden City, NY: Doubleday and Co., 1964), p. 157.

48 Cf. Shore, *Spenser and the Poetics of Pastoral*, p. 115: the essential action of *Colin Clout* is that "at the very centre of the courtly world, face to face with the fairest reflection of heavenly beauty the earth contains, Colin discovers that his proper function is to celebrate his devotion in the timeless music of the pastoral pleasance."

5 Exit Colin Clout

1 Such, at least, is the implication of *Amor.* 80: see below, pp. 172f., and cf. Kate Warren in *Variorum*, VI.320f.

2 On the question of Spenser's pension, procured during his otherwise unsuccessful visit to London in 1589–91, see *The Lives of the Most Famous English Poets (1687) by William Winstanley*, ed. William Riley Parker (Gainesville, Fla.: Scholars' Facsimile Reprints, 1963), p. 91; Craik, *Spenser and His Poetry*, I.186; an anonymous review article, "Edmund Spenser," *Westminster Review* 87 (1867), 143; and many later editions of Spenser's works which repeat the same essential story with different inferences. One such version of the story dates from shortly after the poet's death: "When hir Majestie had given order that Spenser should have a reward for his poems, but Spenser could have nothing, he presented hir with these verses:

It pleased your Grace upon a tyme
To graunt me reason for my ryme,
But from that tyme untill this season
I heard of neither ryme nor reason.

(*Diary of John Manningham... 1602–1603* [Westminster: Camden Society, 1868], p. 43).

3 See especially Richard Neuse, "Book VI as Conclusion to the *Faerie Queene*," *ELH* 35 (1968), 329–53; reprt. in *Essential Articles for the Study of Edmund Spenser*, ed. A. C. Hamilton (Hamden, Conn.: Archon Books, 1972), pp. 366–88.

4 The contrast in this respect with her prototype, Bradamante, tends to foreground the waning emphasis on *The Faerie Queene* as the dynastic epic.

5 For a reading of the concluding cantos of Book 5 with reference to Spenser's relations with Elizabeth and James VI of Scotland, see Goldberg, *James I*, pp. 1–17.

6 On the wedding of the rivers, see Fichter, *Poets Historical*, p. 198; and David Quint, *Origin and Originality in Renaissance Literature: Versions of the Source* (New Haven: Yale University Press, 1983), pp. 149–66. The darkest reading of Book 4 is that of Goldberg in *Endlesse Worke*.

7 Beginning with *Variorum* VI.300, 320–1, and most recently by Tonkin, *Spenser's Courteous Pastoral*, pp. 300–1.

8 A few of the more important modern discussions of these issues are: Dorothy F. Atkinson, "The Pastorella Episode in *The Faerie Queene*," *PMLA* 59 (1944), 361–72; J. C. Maxwell, "The Truancy of Calidore," in *That Soveraine Light*, ed. William R. Mueller and D. C. Allen (Baltimore: Johns Hopkins University Press, 1952), pp. 63–9; Harry Berger, Jr., "A Secret Discipline," in *Form and Convention in the Poetry of Edmund Spenser*, ed. William Nelson (New York: Columbia University Press, 1961), pp. 35–75; William V. Nestrick, "The Virtuous and Gentle Discipline of Gentlemen and Poets," in *ELH* 29 (1962), 357–71, reprt. in *Spenser*, ed. Berger, pp. 132–45; Neuse, "Book VI as Conclusion"; and David L. Miller, "Abandoning the Quest," *ELH* 46 (1979), 173–92.

9 Cf., for example, *FQ* 4.2.; on Spenser's version of Orpheus, see Thomas H. Cain, "Spenser and the Renaissance Orpheus," *UTQ* 41 (1971), 24–47; reflecting on the tension in the *FQ* between Hercules and Orpheus as the types of the hero and artist respectively, Cain sees Orpheus dominant in Book 4; Hercules in 5 till the very end; and Calidore, a humanist composite figure, in 6.

10 Scudamour will encounter Artegall again as the Salvage Knight in 4.6.2.

11 Aemylia's lover, Amyas, likewise encounters the Carle's opposite number, Corflambo, in lieu of the assigned tryst (8.50–1).

12 The question of the source or origin of virtue is a lively issue in the Renaissance, deriving from Plato's *Meno* and other dialogues by way of Plutarch. See, e.g., Castiglione's *Courtier*, 4.8–13, and my remarks in "Castiglione's Gentle Art of Persuasion," pp. 9f.

13 He even appeals to a Queen whose heart is said to have been softened by Cupid against her own "awfull Majestie," to "hearke to love, and reade [his] lesson often" (Pr.5). On the ghost of Burghley haunting 4.Pr. 1 see Richard Helgerson, *The Elizabethan Prodigals* (Berkeley: University of California Press, 1976), p. 31. Helgerson reads the stanza as acknowledging that the 1590 *FQ*, like all poetry, "might be expected to violate the patriarchal and humanistic values that Burghley represented."

14 Although I do not always agree with his conclusions, I am indebted throughout my discussion to Tonkin's treatment of courtesy; see especially pp. 11, 19, and 123.

15   Since brass, nor stone, nor earth, nor boundless sea,
       But sad mortality o'ersways their power,
       How with this rage shall beauty hold a plea,
       Whose action is no stronger than a flower?

16 The trick is as transparent as the similar attempt in *Colin Clout* to have the Queen and her court somehow simultaneously image both a golden world of perfect virtue and the iron one it is conjured to redeem. See above, pp. 129–31.

17 Miller, "Abandoning the Quest," 180.

18 The broader ambiguity is epitomized in the opening stanzas of canto 2, where Spenser replays the debate about *grazia* in Book 1 of Castigliano's *Cortegiano*, first affirming that courtesy is a gift of "dame Nature" (2.1.), then allowing the merit of "good thewes [habits], enforst with paine" (2.9), and finally endowing Calidore with the benefit of both versions through an equivocal "that": "That well in courteous *Calidore* appeares" (3.1).

19 See *Variorum*, VI.317–48; and Kathleen Williams, *Spenser's World of Glass: A Reading of the "Faerie Queene"* (Berkeley: University of California Press, 1966), p. 196.

20 On the names of Calidore, Calepine, and Turpine, see John W. Draper, "Classical Coinage in the *Faerie Queene*," *PMLA* 47 (1932), 97–108; and Donald Cheney, *Spenser's Image of Nature: Man and Shepherd in "The Faerie Queene"* (New Haven: Yale University Press, 1966), pp. 204–6. My own hunch is that Calidore (= "beautiful gift") embodies courtesy as the intuitive gift of nature, whereas Calepine (= "beautiful

labor" or "good by effort") exemplifies the exigencies of the acquired virtue. It has been suggested that as a perfect exemplar of courtesy Arthur duplicates Calidore's role; see P. C. Bayley, "Order, Grace and Courtesy in Spenser's World," in *Patterns of Love and Courtesy*, ed. John Lawlor (Evanston, Illinois: Northwestern University Press, 1966), p. 188.

21 This is an episode that seems to divide readers in their judgment of Calidore: see, e.g., Neuse, "Book VI as Conclusion," 353. But *pace* Calidore's calumniators, it is not the knight's defective courtesy that causes his embarrassing intrusion; this is purely fortuitous, and the hero handles it as best he can. That the knight's or anyone else's resources are inadequate to protect one's reputation in a darkened social milieu is, of course, the whole point of the Blatant Beast.

22 For a study of the Serena story and its conclusion in the light of its supposed sources, see Walter F. Staton, Jr., "Italian Pastorals and the Conclusion of the Serena Story," *SEL* 6 (1966), 35–42.

23 On the historical context of Spenser's Hermit, see above, pp. 19f. and 197 n. 23.

24 This example fits the type of Hermit–Counseller; see Clay, *Hermits and Anchorites*, pp. 148–56.

25 Nohrnberg, *The Analogy of the "Faerie Queene*," p. 724.

26 I owe this observation to Donald Cheney in a private correspondence made in his capacity as an editor of the *Spenser Encyclopedia*.

27 C. S. Lewis, *The Allegory of Love* (Oxford: Oxford University Press, 1959), p. 350. On Calidore's "truancy," in addition to sources cited in note 8 above, see William Nelson, *The Poetry of Edmund Spenser* (New York: Columbia University Press, 1965),. p. 293; M. F. N. Dixon, "Fairy Tale, Fortune, and Boethian Wonder: Rhetorical Structure in Book VI of the *Faerie Queene*," *UTQ* 44 (1974), 156f.; Lila Geller, "Spenser's Theory of Nobility in Book VI of the *Faerie Queene*," *ELR* 5 (1975), 49–57; and Harry Rusche, "The Lesson of Calidore's Truancy," *SP* 76 (1979), 149–61. An earlier version of this section appears under the title "Calidore, Acidale, and Spenserian Narration," in *Spenser at Kalamazoo 1983*, ed. Francis G. Greco (Clarion, Pa.: Clarion State College, 1984), pp. 1–13.

28 Dixon, "Fairy Tale, Fortune, and Boethian Wonder," 156.

29 Berger, "A Secret Discipline," p. 66, sees a temporary merging of Spenser's present epic voice with his former pastoral one, "the man momentarily transformed into the pure poetic voice, the recreative voice [of poetry as pure play] re-created" in the present moment.

30 Cf. Patricia A. Parker, *Inescapable Romance* (Princeton: Princeton University Press, 1979), pp. 62f. Elsewhere (p. 43 and n.), Parker speculates that the motif of *errores* in Renaissance romantic epic may

derive from Servius' reading of the *arma virumque* as modified by Minturno and others, who assimilated the wanderings of the *Odyssey* to the narrative pattern of romance.

31 On the kind of symbolic landscape in *The Faerie Queene* in general, see Fletcher, *The Prophetic Moment*.

32 Oddly enough, the same narrative trope appeared in the last stanza (3.12.[47]) of the 1590 *Faerie Queene*:

> But now my teme begins to faint and fayle,
> All woxen weary of their journall toyle:
> Therefore I will their sweatie yokes assoyle
> At this same furrowes end, till a new day:
> And ye faire Swayns, after your long turmoyle,
> Now cease your worke, and at your pleasure play,
> Now cease your worke; to morrow is an holy day.

Both figures contrast with the pastoral–bucolic one of the poet as courtly–chivalric hero, "wandering by the way" in a temporary and restorative sojourn through a landscape imaging the *vita contemplativa*.

33 Berger, "A Secret Discipline," pp. 49f.

34 In one sense this formula is a passive counterpart to the "georgic" formula, *ab aspera ad astra*.

35 See, e.g., Berger, "A Secret Discipline," p. 61; and, for a corrective, Tonkin, *Spenser's Courteous Pastoral*, pp. 115–21. On the possible sources of Melibee see Michael Murrin, *The Veil of Allegory* (Chicago: University of Chicago Press, 1969), p. 119.

36 See above, pp. 99–103.

37 On Spenser's erroneous association of the battle of the Lapiths and centaurs with Theseus and Ariadne, see *Variorum*, VI.251, and Tonkin, *Spenser's Courteous Pastoral*, p. 129.

38 Neuse, "Book VI as Conclusion," 353; cf. Ronald Bond, "'The Triall of True Curtesie': Calidore on Acidale," in *Spenser at Kalamazoo 1983*, pp. 14–20. See also Kenneth Gross, *Spenserian Poetics: Idolatry, Iconoclasm, and Magic* (Ithaca: Cornell University Press, 1985), p. 213: Calidore, an "alienated voyeur, ... is divided from himself by that self-wounding form of seeing which is *invidia*." In the pages that follow (pp. 213–24), Gross discusses the Acidale episode as a species of self-reflexive pre-emptive idolatry, by which Spenser attempts (and fails) to protect his poetic practice.

39 Bond, "'The Triall of True Curtesie'," pp. 17f.

40　　　　　They teach us, how to each degree and kynde
　　　　　We should our selves demeane, to low, to hie;
　　　　To friends, to foes, which skill men call Civility.　　(10.23)
Cf. the similar language applied to Calidore's conduct in 12.2.

41 Bellamy, "The Vocative and the Vocational," 16, presents no evidence for her belief that "the 'Damzell' is ... a vision of Elizabeth."

42 Of course this rhetorical ruse is also politically expedient. Spenser is free to disclaim any dereliction on *his* part, as opposed to Colin's; and the reader may even disclaim Colin's disclaimer – as Bellamy does (see preceding note) – and identify the Fourth Grace with the Queen.

43 I cannot agree with Neuse's comment on this stanza ("Book VI as Conclusion," 349) that Calidore "sees in [Colin's exposition of this vision] no relevance to himself as he strives to ingratiate himself with the rival piper."

44 E.g., by Cain, "Spenser and the Renaissance Orpheus," 40–2.

45 Wind, *Pagan Mysteries*, pp. 128–40. The ultimate source of the two Venuses for the Renaissance is of course Plato, *Symposium* 189d–2a.

46 See Desport, "L'Écho de la nature," 270, and *L'Incantation virgilienne*, pp. 254f.; cf. Damon, "Modes of Analogy," 281–90.

47 For similar readings see Nestrick "Virtuous and Gentle Discipline"; Kathleen Williams, *Spenser's World of Glass*, pp. 189–23; and Tonkin, *Spenser's Courteous Pastoral*, passim.

6 The pastoral of the self

1 S. K. Heninger, "The Renaissance Perversion of Pastoral," *JHI* 22 (1961), 254–61.

2 See, among others, Neuse, "Book VI as Conclusion," 353; Helgerson, "The New Poet," 906; and Miller, "Abandoning the Quest," 189.

3 Neither Raleigh nor Harington, among Spenser's contemporaries, had much luck: on Raleigh's see Greenblatt, *Sir Walter Raleigh*, pp. 132–5; on Harington, see above, p. 34. Regarding Spenser's own troubles with the then King James VI of Scotland, see Goldberg, *James I*, pp. 16f.

4 The 1609 Folio printed by Matthew Lownes, in which the Cantos first appeared, tells us that they "both for Forme and Matter, appeare to be parcell of some following Booke of the *Faerie Queene*, Under the Legend of Constancie" (*Poetical Works*, p. 394). For a review of the critical reception of this claim see Jones, *Spenser Handbook*, pp. 301f.

5 Cheney, *Spenser's Image of Nature*, p. 247, and Harry Berger, Jr., "*The Mutabilitie Cantos*: Archaism and Retrospect," in *Spenser: A Collection of Critical Essays*, p. 148.

6 *Purgatorio* 18.32; cf. Francis Fergusson, *Dante's Drama of the Mind: A Modern Reading of the "Purgatorio"* (Princeton: Princeton University Press, 1953), pp. 88–93 and *passim*.

7 Mutability makes speeches to Cynthia and Mercury (indirectly narrated in 6.11 and 18 respectively) and to Jove (6.26–7), while her powerful defense to Nature (7.14–27, 47, and 49–56) is interrupted only by the procession of seasons, months, and hours summoned as witnesses to the validity of her claim to universal sway. Mercury's speech to Mutability (6.18) is reported in indirect discourse; Jove's to the assembled gods (6.20–1) and to Mutability herself, and Nature's (7.58–9) to the ensemble, round out the "action."

8 Structurally speaking, a similar digression occurs in canto 7 in the long description (stt. 27–46) of the procession of Mutability's witnesses. This passage again constitutes fully a third of its canto, and its gratuitousness is underscored by the fact that these witnesses remain mute and that Mutability's resumed defense proceeds to enumerate qualities of the planets, without summoning their presences, clearly more to the point of her argument than the more ceremonial–emblematic features in the narrator's account of the seasons, months, and hours.

9 On Spenser's "unexceptional" use of "dilate" here and in *FQ* 6.10.21, see Nohrnberg, *The Analogy of the "Faerie Queene"*, p. 729. Parker, *Inescapable Romance*, pp. 54–113, discusses Spenser's "dilation" in the *Faerie Queene* in terms of Derridean deferral/*différance*.

10 For a similar conclusion, though from a radically different point of approach, see Quinones, *The Renaissance Discovery of Time*, pp. 247–88, esp. pp. 262f.

11 For the traditional view of Spenser's relationship with Elizabeth Boyle and its connection with these two works, see "Edmund Spenser," *Westminster Review* 87 (1867), 144f.; and Henley, *Spenser in Ireland*, p. 80; cf. the earlier view of C. G. Halpine, "Colin Clout and the Faery Queen" in *Reprints and Excerpts from the Atlantic Monthly* (n.p., 1858), pp. 674–88. The question is again raised by P. W. Long, in "Spenser and Lady Carey," *MLR* 3 (1908), 257–67. The arguments on both sides are reviewed by Jones, *Spenser Handbook*, pp. 336f. For the later history of Elizabeth Boyle, see *The Lismore Papers*, ed. A. B. Grosart (London, 1886–88), 1st ser., I.205–12, II.94.

12 Recent criticism of the *Amoretti* has played down the biographical element in the sequence and focused instead on its autonomous structure. See especially Robert Kellogg, "Thought's Astonishment and the Dark Conceits of Spenser's *Amoretti*" (1965), reprt. in *Prince of Poets*, ed. John R. Elliott, Jr. (New York: New York University Press, 1968), pp. 139–51; Peter M. Cummings, "Spenser's *Amoretti* as an Allegory of Love," *TSLL*, 12 (1970), 163–79; and the articles cited in note 20 below. Kellogg's is an especially sensitive argument for taking the work as an "allegory of the poet" in which personal allusions are

transmuted into myth. Yet even he concedes that there is some relation between the fictional plot of the sequence and the events of Spenser's life in 1594.

13 I omit, here and in the following discussion, the anacreontics that conclude the work in all editions. The present discussion of the *Amoretti* appeared in an earlier form as "Spenserian Pastoral and the *Amoretti*," *ELH* 47 (1980), 419–32.

14 This phrase, as well as that in my chapter title, are borrowed from Poggioli, *The Oaten Flute*, especially chapters 2 and 8.

15 For a different conclusion regarding sonnet 72 see Cummings, "Spenser's *Amoretti*," 170.

16 A summary of the differences between the love doctrines of the *Amoretti* and Petrarch's *Canzoniere* can be found in O. B. Hardison, Jr., "*Amoretti* and the *Dolce Stil Nuovo*," *ELR* 2 (1972), 215–16.

17 On this motif in the service of the "theme of heroic love" in Spenser's work, see J. C. Gray, "Bondage and Deliverance in the 'Faerie Queene': Varieties of a Moral Imperative," *MLR* 70 (1975), 1–12. Gray notes the relevance of his argument to sonnets 65 and 67–8 but is not centrally concerned with the *Amoretti* as a whole. We have seen this idea already in *The Faerie Queene*, Book 3, where the major thrust of the multiple plots involving Britomart, Amoret, and Florimell is just such a purgation under the aegis of Merlin's dynastic prophecies and the innocent fertility of the Garden of Adonis. See above, chapter 3, section II.

18 See, for example, Arthur to Redcrosse, *FQ* 1.8.44f.

19 For a recent conjecture as to the source of this sonnet, see Anne Lake Prescott, "The Thirsty Deer and the Lord of Life: Some Contexts for *Amoretti* 67–70," *SSt* 6 (1985), 33–76.

20 The present argument complements, I believe, rather than contradicts the findings of the calendar school of *Amoretti* criticism. I am personally less than convinced by the detailed analogies between individual sonnets and liturgical readings for each day in the Lenten season found by William C. Johnson in "Spenser's *Amoretti* and the Art of the Liturgy," *SEL* 14 (1974), 47–61. But with Johnson's general argument that the structure of the sequence identifies – or, as I would prefer to say, analogizes – human love with the "Christian's love for Christ" (p. 50), I wholly concur. Johnson's article expands upon an earlier one by Alexander Dunlop, "The Unity of Spenser's *Amoretti*," in *Silent Poetry*, ed. Alastair Fowler (London: Routledge, 1970), pp. 153–69, which in turn reflects the work done by Fowler himself and by A. Kent Hieatt on numerological symbolism and the structure of *The Faerie Queene* and *Epithalamion* respectively.

21 *The Greek Bucolic Poets*, ed. J. M. Edmonds (Cambridge, Mass.: Harvard University Press, 1960), pp. 10–13. On the ecphrasis in Greek

literature down to Theocritus and its significance as stylized allusion, see
Rosenmeyer, *The Green Cabinet*, pp. 191–4.

22 See, for example, Seneca, *Ep.* 84.3, which probably derives from
Isocrates, "To Demonicus" 52; cf. also Lucr. 3.11–12.

23 Richard Neuse, "The Triumph Over Hasty Accidents: A Note on the
Symbolic Mode of the *Epithalamion*," *MLR* 61 (1966), 163–74.

24 On the sources of Ovid's *maiestas* (*Fasti* 5.11–54), see P. Ovidius Naso,
Die Fasten, ed. Franz Bomer (Heidelberg: Carl Winter, 1958), II.291f.;
and Brooks Otis, *Ovid as an Epic Poet* (Cambridge: Cambridge
University Press, 1970), p. 123.

25 For the ultimate Plotinian prototype of this construct, see above,
chapter 1, p. 18.

26 For the essential data regarding the publication of the *Hymnes*, see
Jones, *Spenser Handbook*, pp. 357f.; and *Variorum*, VII.i.657–62. The
scholarly consensus remains against taking at face value Spenser's
claims, in his Dedication to the Countesses of Cumberland and Warwick
(*Poetical Works*, p. 586), to have tried in vain to "call in" the two
"earthly" hymns (*Hymne of Love* and *Hymne of Beautie*) and then
written the "heavenly" ones.

27 This action of poetry would seem to parallel that of "the Gods" alluded
to in *The Faerie Queene* Book 6 (Pr.3.5–6). For a recent account of
Spenser's platonic poetics in relation to Sidney's "Idea" and "fore-
conceit," see DeNeef, *Spenser and the Motives of Metaphor*, especially
pp. 3–14.

28 A recent discussion of the breakdown of the Renaissance "incarnational
theology" as reflected in the depiction of carnality in religious art is Leo
Steinberg, *The Sexuality of Christ in Renaissance Art and Modern
Oblivion* (New York: Pantheon Books, 1984). In his shift from incarnational or immanent beauty in the early hymns to a transcendental
view in the later ones, Spenser may be recapitulating this collapse of the
High Renaissance paradigm.

29 For a discussion of "speculation" and "contemplation" in this passage,
in the Platonic ambience of Spenser's England, see Gordon W. O'Brien,
Renaissance Poetics and the Problem of Power (Chicago: Institute of
Elizabethan Studies, 1956), pp. 9–40.

30 Hankins, "Spenser and Revelation," 379.

31 On the relation of Sapience to the *vita contemplativa*, see above, p.
23.

32 Harry Berger, Jr., "Spenser's *Prothalamion*: An Interpretation," in
Hamilton, *Essential Articles*, p. 510. Berger sees the poem as effecting the
"mastery of fact by imagination" and as celebrating poetry's triumph
over time and the impulse to escape. See also M. L. Wine, "Spenser's
'Sweet Themmes': Of Time and the River," *SEL* 2 (1962), 111–17.

33 A similar point is made by John Hughes, *The Works of Mr. Edmund Spenser* (London: Jacob Tonson, 1715): "The Allegory breaks before the Reader is prepar'd for it." Quoted by Wine, "Spenser's 'Sweet Themmes,'" 113.

34 The failure of the *Prothalamion* has been interestingly challenged by Patrick Cheney in an unpublished paper, "*Prothalamion* and *The Faerie Queene*: Spenser's Spousal Verse as a Defense of Allegorical Love Poetry." Cheney reads the tripartite structure of the poem as "Withdrawal from 'Princes Court'" (st. 1), "Espial of the Flower Ceremony" (stt. 2–7), and "Return to 'Mery London'" (stt. 8–10). He labels these three "stages" respectively "Withdrawal from Reality," "The Creation of Allegory," and "The Moral Effect of Allegory," explaining the different poetic modes of the three parts as "Images of Career Complaint," "Images of Artistic Creation," and "Images of History and Politics." Hence the structure of the *Prothalamion* is intended to mirror and "defend the moral and national unity of allegorical love poetry in *The Faerie Queene*." For another appreciation of the poem and meditation on its influence on later poets, see John Hollander, "Spenser's Undersong," in *Cannibals, Witches, and Divorce: Estranging the Renaissance*, ed. Marjorie Garber (Baltimore: Johns Hopkins University Press, 1987), pp. 1–20. Hollander locates the poem's refrain in the Theocritean tradition and connects it to the *Stimmung* that underlies European pastoral. For Spenser, running water is "an almost natural trope of poetic discourse" and signifies "the everlasting universe of things running through the mind" (pp. 18f.).

Index

233

Index

Index

Index

Index

Index

Malecasta, 97, 138, 218 n.51
Manningham, John, 224 n.2
Mantuan (Battista Spagnuol), 45, 51, 53; *see also* pastoral, humanist
Marietti, M., 202 n.50
Marinell, 97, 135, 136
Marot, Clement, 49, 51, 112
Marotti, Arthur, 203 n.57
Martial, 25, 26f.
Martz, Louis L., 215 n.19
Marvell, Andrew, 53, 216 n.34
Maxwell, J. C., 224 n.8
media via motif (pastoral), 51–4, 62
Medici family, 21, 29, 202 n.51
   Duke Cosimo I, 201 n.45
   Lorenzo de' ("il Magnifico"), 22, 28f., 31, 42, 47
Melibee, 146, 147, 151f.
Meliboeus, 53, 60, 61, 67, 109f., 124
Menander, 38
Mercury, 178, 229 n.7
Merlin, 93, 94, 218 n.51, 230 n.17
Middleton, Thomas, 115
Miles, Gary, 192 n.20
Miller, David L., 224 n.8, 225 n.17, 228 n.2
Milton, John, 80, 101, 215 n.21
Minturno, Antonio Sebastiano, 206 n.82, 226 n.30
Mitchell, Charles, 191 n.8
Moeris, 52, 54
Mole, 110, 128, 169
Montrose, Louis A., 2, 4f., 6f., 11, 50, 188, 190 nn. 2, 5, 191 nn. 11, 12, 15, 193 n.31, 212 n.40, 219 n.5, 223 n.42
Moore, Dennis, 220 nn.18, 19, 221 n.20
More, Sir Thomas, 4, 5, 23, 192 n.22
Mulla, 127f., 131, 169
Murrin, Michael, 206 nn.79, 84, 218 n.50, 227 n.35
Mutability, 166–70; *see also* Spenser, Mutability Cantos

narrator (in *FQ*), 90f., 99, 101–3, 141f., 147f., 152f., 153–9, 165–8, 170, 171
Nature, 96, 166–9
Naunton, Sir Robert, 203 n.55

negotium, 16, 19, 25, 189
Nelson, William, 226 n.27
Neoplatonism, 15, 17, 19, 20, 22, 39, 42, 45, 157
Nestrick, William V., 216 n.32, 224 n.8, 228 n.48
Neuse, Richard, 176, 217 n.40, 221 n.23, 224 nn.3, 8, 226 n.21, 227 n.38, 228 nn.43, 2, 231 n.23
Nietzsche, Friedrich, 197 n.21
Nitchie, Elizabeth, 208 n.90
Nohrnberg, James, 206 n.82, 226 n.25, 229 n.9

O'Brien, Gordon W., 231 n.29
O'Connell, Michael, 193 n.26
O'Connell, Robert J., 197 n.24
Oetgen, Jerome, OSB, 214 n.15
O'Loughlin, Michael J. K., 209 n.13
Oram, William, 221 n.31
Orfeo (Poliziano), 201 n.49
Orgel, Stephen, 190 n.2, 204 n.57
Orgoglio, 81, 83, 84
Origen, 39f.
Orpheus, 177, 224 n.9
Orphic attributes, 26, 56, 108, 138, 140, 160
Otis, Brooks, 219 n.6, 231 n.24
otium (otium), 10, 16f., 19, 22–7, 34, 35f., 37–9, 51, 81, 83, 96, 117, 171–3, 178, 179, 186, 189, 221 n.29
Ovid, 25, 49, 50, 101, 118f., 120f., 178, 221 nn.21, 29

paideia, 10, 186
Palinode, 66
Pallas, 118–20
Pan, 52, 63, 70f., 217 n.42
Panaetius, 15, 196 n.14
Panofsky, Erwin, 199 n.32, 208 n.91
Paridell, 98f.
Parker, Patricia A., 226 n.30, 229 n.9
Parmenides, 12
pastoral, Christian, 39, 82
   erotic, 71, 89f., 93, 97–103, 105, 153, 171, 173, 176
   humanist ("Mantuanesque"), 5, 53, 61, 66, 117

Index

Index

Index

Index